DIVINE RASCAL

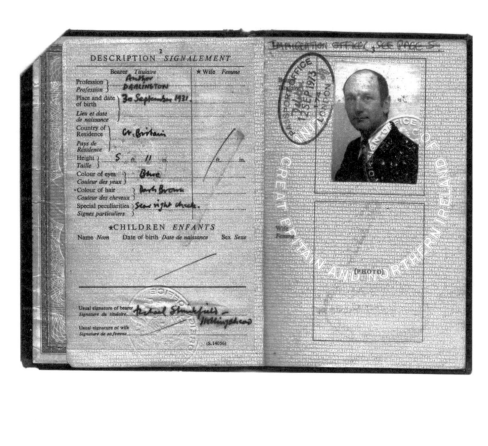

DESCRIPTION *SIGNALEMENT*

2

	Bearer *Titulaire*	★Wife *Femme*
Profession } *Profession*	Author DARLINGTON	
Place and date of birth } *Lieu et date de naissance*	30 September 1931.	
Country of Residence } *Pays de Résidence*	Gr. Britain	
Height } *Taille*	5 ft. 11 in.	ft. in.
Colour of eyes } *Couleur des yeux*	Blue	
•Colour of hair } *Couleur des cheveux*	Dark Brown	
Special peculiarities } *Signes particuliers*	Scar right cheek.	

★CHILDREN *ENFANTS*

Name *Nom*	Date of birth *Date de naissance*	Sex *Sexe*

Usual signature of bearer *Signature du titulaire*	Arthur Stanley Darlington
Usual signature of wife *Signature de sa femme*	

(S.14056)

(PHOTO)

DIVINE

On the Trail of LSD's Cosmic Courier, Michael Hollingshead

RASCAL

Andy Roberts

Divine Rascal by Andy Roberts
First published by Strange Attractor Press 2019
ISBN: 9781907222788

Strange Attractor Press
BM SAP, London,
WC1N 3XX, UK
www.strangeattractor.co.uk

Distributed by The MIT Press, Cambridge, Massachusetts.
And London, England
Printed and bound in the UK by TJ International

Contents

List of Illustrations

Acknowledgements

Many people have been of assistance with my research into the mystery that is Michael Hollingshead. They are listed below and my apologies if I have missed anyone. My greatest thanks are to Michael's eldest daughter, Vanessa Hollingshead. Despite being only too aware of her father's foibles Vanessa has been unstinting in her support for *Divine Rascal* and an invaluable source of information, documents and photographs and this book could not have been written without her encouragement and assistance.

Steve Abrams, Brian Barritt, Bear, Peter Beren, John Barth Beresford, Rosemary Beresford, Jo Berke, Steve Bissette, Anthony Blond, Bodil Birke, Virginia Blyth, Janette Boggon, Tim Booth, Bob Campbell, Chris Case, Tony Cook, Mike Crowley, Age Delbanco, Paul Devereux, Jeff Dexter, Liz Elliot, Jenny Fabian, William Patrick Forbes, Robert Forte, Michael Froehlich, Caroline Frusciante, Oli Genn-Bash, Christopher Gibbs, Kristof Glinka, Nigel Gordon, Judy Hargreaves, Tim Hargreaves, Lee Harris, Graeme & Nicky Hartley-Martin, Kevin Hebrides, Gregg Hermetech, Roger Hermiston, Ev Hesketh, Philip Hesleton, Albert Hofmann, Hoppy, Jean Houston, Martin Izat, Kami Kanetsuka, Paul Krassner, Susan Kruglinski, Martin Lee, Joe Mellen, Ralph Metzner, Patricia McCann, Joe Mellen, Modafanil, Karen O'Brien, Mark Pilkington, Auriol Roberts, Ciaran Shaman, Paul Sieveking, Alan Shinkfield, Timothy Shinkfield, Pat Smith, Jamie Sutcliffe, Mandy Roberts, Ben Sessa, Gunther Weil, Timothy Wylie

Introduction

This they tell, and whether it happened so or not I do not know; but if you think about it, you can see that it's true.[1]

I've always known who Michael Hollingshead was. Or I thought I did. He was the guy with the mayonnaise jar full of LSD-infused sugar paste who acted as midwife to Timothy Leary's first LSD trip in 1961 and helped give birth to the psychedelic revolution of the 1960s. He was famous, wasn't he? Yet when I was carrying out research for *Albion Dreaming*, my social history of LSD in Britain, other than a few references in Leary's books and histories of psychedelic culture I found hardly any information about this enigmatic character. For someone who played such a crucial role in the early days of LSD culture, Hollingshead's role was minimised, even written out of popular histories and memoirs of the era. Even his appearance was mysterious. The handful of poor-quality photographs available on the internet showing a stern, conservatively-dressed man of indeterminate age were at odds with the joyful, colourful culture he was central to. The circumstances of his arrival on the psychedelic scene in 1961 and his role within it exuded an air of mystery, amplified by the fact that Michael Hollingshead wasn't even his real name. So, who was Michael Hollingshead?

This lack of information, and the mystery which accompanied it, piqued my curiosity about his life before and after his fateful meeting with Tim Leary. As I dug deeper into the arcane reaches of psychedelic history, I found references to Hollingshead everywhere, Zelig-like, stalking the landscapes of western psychedelic culture's most iconic events. Look back to 1961 and there he is in Boston, Massachusetts, an enthusiastic catalyst for Leary's lysergic initiation and ascension to fame and guru-status. In 1962 you'll find him assisting with the legendary Harvard-Concord prison and Marsh Chapel psilocybin experiments, and in 1963 heavily involved with the little known but highly influential Agora Scientific Trust. In 1964, Hollingshead is trying to stage an LSD exhibition at the World's Fair in New York while simultaneously debating the founding of Sigma with beat poet and author Alex Trocchi, before collaborating with Leary again in LSD fuelled mischief at the infamous Millbrook mansion.

In 1965 Hollingshead returned to Britain, roaming swinging London like a sinister Austin Powers; making everything psychedelic baby by turning on the hip, the rich and the famous, whether they wanted it or not. If you were in prison during the 1966 and '67 Summers of Love, you might have heard Hollingshead tell how he gave LSD to a Russian spy or how trepanation was the new method of consciousness change. In 1968 you'd find Hollingshead hanging out with the fabled Brotherhood of Eternal Love in the mountains and beaches of California, before flying to Kathmandu in 1969 to cause ripples on the hippie trail and start a psychedelic poetry magazine. Fast forward eighteen months and he's back in Britain, founding a hippie commune on a Scottish island with the aid of Franciscan monks before in 1972 creating the world's first multi-media predictive art installation in Edinburgh. Hollingshead later enjoyed daring psychedelic escapades in Tonga, Scandinavia and Europe before dying in mysterious circumstances in Bolivia.

These discoveries, and the intriguing information I unearthed about his life before he met Tim Leary, led me to realise I didn't really know Michael Hollingshead at all. Nor, it seemed, did anyone else. Many people thought they knew him, and to an extent they did, but with the exception of his daughter Vanessa, they only knew the Michael Hollingshead he wanted them to know. The real Michael Hollingshead was a highly intelligent, articulate and astute man with a powerful personality and the charismatic ability to influence and manipulate people and situations for his own ends. In whatever social scene he was involved, LSD related or not, Hollingshead made a significant impact, negative or positive, sometimes both, on almost everyone he met. He elicited strong reactions and emotions in people and was loved, admired and respected by some but feared and mistrusted by others. If you encountered Hollingshead's dark side you were in danger of losing your money, your mind or possibly both.

The information I discovered about Hollingshead has cast new light on many aspects of the worldwide psychedelic revolution. I decided to write his biography, not only to add his story to the growing body of literature on the social history of LSD, but to place him amongst the pantheon of British expatriates – Gerald Heard, Aldous Huxley and Alan Watts – who were seminal to the development of psychedelic culture.

I have been as comprehensive as possible in my use of the source material which underpins this book. Hollingshead is dead and thus could not be interviewed, although I have quoted from the few he gave during his life. Biographies often rely on the subject's relatives for background information, but at the time of writing Hollingshead has only two surviving close family members, his sister Janette and his daughter Vanessa. Because of the impact Hollingshead's exploits have had on his family Janette, perhaps understandably, was unwilling to discuss her brother's life beyond offering some very basic details. By way of contrast Vanessa, who has forged a career as a stand-up comedian and actress in

America, was encouraging, wanting her father's story to be told warts and all, and contributed information and insight without which this book could not have been written. The long and tangled relationship between Vanessa and her father provides a unique personal perspective on his life and a valuable counterpoint to the views of people who knew him for a short time and thought they understood him.

I have also drawn on information provided by several of Hollingshead's ex-partners, and numerous friends and acquaintances, in the form of interviews, letters and contemporary recollections. Material from official and legal documents, books, newspapers and other media sources have added veracity and the background hum of authenticity to my research. Although Hollingshead lived in the pre-internet, email and mobile phone era he was a skilled communicator, and fully understood the importance of making and sustaining contacts with people he considered useful or influential. When not communicating in person, he was a prolific letter writer, maintaining lengthy correspondence with many friends and acquaintances. Fortunately, some of these letters have been saved by individuals or conserved in libraries and archives. Most of Hollingshead's letters were hand written and several pages long, their deciphering further complicated by his frequently convoluted language, 'in jokes' and habit of writing when obviously under the influence of LSD or other drugs.

Hollingshead's 1973 autobiography, *The Man Who Turned On The World,* is a mine of information, replete with his thoughts and opinions. But it is a far from comprehensive or trustworthy account. The memoir, which covers only nine years of his life, is often self-serving and is peppered with omissions, errors and extravagant claims for which there is no evidence. Hollingshead lived a peripatetic life, rarely living in the same place longer than 18 months and sometimes for only a few weeks. At a time when air travel was expensive, he travelled extensively, between Britain and America, in Europe and Scandinavia, and to Nepal and the South Pacific islands. He held at least three passports and the portions of the two I obtained were vital in tracking his movements and triangulating destinations, arrival and departure dates against other documentation. Even with the wealth of biographical and historical information available it has not always been possible to date with certainty some of the events I describe. This is due either to a lack of accurate documentation, or because people's recollections differ as to the month or year an event took place in. Adding to this jigsaw puzzle of shifting facts and fictions, Hollingshead and his contemporaries were using copious amounts of LSD and other drugs, so the problems of accuracy and veracity are multiplied. Despite these issues, every event described, and every quote used in this book, is referenced to a checkable source. Where there are time disparities or contradictory recollections, I have used the most probable date or version as true, while noting alternate possibilities.

Besides the problems inherent in interpreting the source material there is an 'elephant in the room' of any book dealing with the history of LSD. Until recently, few people have questioned the orthodoxy of LSD's discovery and the motivations of the personalities who steered the drug to become the driving force behind the psychedelic cultural explosion of the 1960s and beyond. However, since the early years of the 21st century a growing number of researchers have been carefully examining the accepted history of LSD, querying previously held certainties.

At a simplistic level this historical revisionism is being carried out by conspiracy buffs linking disparate facts and events in a join-the-dots fashion to create a picture which supports and reinforces their existing beliefs, but doesn't bear close analysis. But LSD's history is also being challenged by knowledgeable researchers many of whom, including Robert Forte and Mark Stahlman in America and Alan Piper in Britain, have themselves been involved in psychedelic culture for decades. Their research has revealed puzzling anomalies in previously held beliefs and certainties about LSD's history and diffusion through society. These anomalies strongly suggest that secret intelligence services, initially in America and Britain and latterly in former Iron Curtain countries, may have played a subtle but carefully-planned role in LSD's discovery and penetration of western culture. It is suggested these agencies introduced LSD into certain demographics for reasons ranging from observing how psychedelic drugs affect individuals to the intentional creation of the hippie counter culture with the aim of undermining and disrupting organised political opposition and radical social change.

Some commentators have shoehorned Hollingshead into this brave new world of heterodox psychedelic history, claiming he was an asset of the British secret intelligence services and a police and FBI informer. No evidence other than the anecdotal has yet been produced in support of these claims, but I have unearthed information suggesting there is at least a degree of truth to some of them. However, it is extremely difficult to prove unequivocally that someone was a police informant or worked for the intelligence services, and almost impossible to prove that they weren't.

Hollingshead's involvement with LSD and the culture it spawned is the central pillar of his life, notably between the years 1961 and 1984. But this book is about Hollingshead's life and times, not about the pharmacology or legality of LSD, although those subjects are touched on when necessary. There are a plethora of theories as to what LSD does to the mind but any attempt to define its effects and qualities is doomed to failure. For the purposes of this book, and to help readers unfamiliar with the drug to understand the psychedelic experiences described by Hollingshead and others, I suggest using Stanislav Grof's definition that "the best way of understanding LSD is to see it as an unspecific amplifier of psychological processes".[2] As regards the legal position, LSD is not and never has been illegal. It is, however, a controlled drug and human actions relating to it, including its manufacture, distribution and possession, are against the law and punishable by severe penalties.

Join me now on the trail of Michael Hollingshead, one of the most influential and enigmatic figures in the history of psychedelic drugs. It's a convoluted trail through an era during which millions of people believed they could improve themselves, society and the world around them by taking LSD and living by the experiences and insights it granted them. One dose of LSD changed Michael Hollingshead forever, but behind his psychedelic experiences and philosophising, was a complex, complicated human being trying to make sense of himself and the world around him. This is the story he left behind.

Notes

1   Neihardt, J.G, *Black Elk Speaks*, University of Nebraska Press, 2014, p.3

2   www.psychedeliclibrary-library.org/grofpref.htm

Sorrow and Dreams

I know what you did, I know what was wrong. Nobody else here does.
And so, the great experiment begins. [1]

The town of Darlington, County Durham, in the north east of England, has its origins as an Anglo-Saxon settlement but remained relatively unknown until the 19th century. Daniel Defoe, author of *Robinson Crusoe*, visited Darlington in the 18th century and was unimpressed, dismissing the place as having "nothing remarkable but dirt and a high stone bridge over little or no water".[2] But the industrial revolution, which began shortly after Defoe's visit, was to change Darlington dramatically. Coal, which had been mined in the area for centuries, was suddenly in huge demand to fuel the furnaces needed for ship building and heavy industry, and large collieries sprang up across the region. By the mid-19th century Darlington was an important centre for mining, engineering and railway manufacturing, leading to an increased population and, by the 1930s, it was a thriving and prosperous town which attracted tradespeople of all kinds from across Britain.

It was this growing prosperity which led Michael Shinkfield's great grandfather, William Shinkfield, and his wife Anne, to leave Blakeney in Norfolk in the mid-1860s to move north, settling in Jarrow. The youngest of their six children, Robert, completed his apprenticeship as a grocer in Jarrow and, with his wife Mary, moved to Darlington. Robert and Mary had nine children, seven sons and two daughters and it is their second youngest son, William Ewart Gladstone Shinkfield (WEGS), born in 1898, who is of interest.

WEGS, a Colliery Clerk with the National Coal Board, was a devoted family man who enjoyed playing football but was, like so many men in the industrial north east of England, a heavy drinker. He met Edith Ridehaugh, from Harrogate, and on 14 March 1931 they married, possibly in haste, as their first child, Michael John Shinkfield was born just over six months later, on 30 September. When Michael was very young, the Shinkfields lived at 6 Hillside Road but by 1937, following the birth of two more children, they had moved to a three-storey, mid-Victorian house at 23 South End Road in Darlington. Michael attended Beaumont Street school before passing the 11-plus exam and moving on to Darlington Grammar School. No school or family records exist from his childhood and even Michael's younger sister Janette remembers little about the boy destined to become the 'black sheep' of the Shinkfield family.

Had it not been for an incident which took place when he was fourteen years old, Michael Shinkfield might never have left Darlington, become an advocate for psychedelic drugs or achieve the notoriety that he did. Exactly what this incident was is unknown, but it was such an embarrassment to Michael's parents that they rarely spoke of it. Those who knew what happened, Shinkfield's parents, aunts and uncles, are now dead, and it was kept secret from his sister Janette, but Shinkfield family legend, passed down to cousins and to his daughter Vanessa, offers some clues.

According to his cousin Beth Shinkfield, Michael was a rebellious teenager. That's not unusual as most children go through an unruly phase in their teens. The mystery is exactly what behaviour this rebellion, an urge invariably driven by hormonal development, brought about in Michael. In his 1973 autobiography, Shinkfield (by then writing as Hollingshead) didn't mention his childhood at all, choosing instead to begin his story in 1960. Was the omission of the first twenty nine years of his life because he was trying to hide information which might have cast him in a poor light? It's extremely possible, likely even; being evasive and lying to serve his own ends were core elements of Shinkfield's future personality.

At various times until his death in 1984, Shinkfield occasionally shared selected childhood memories with his daughter Vanessa. He told her that his relationship with his father, a heavy drinker who frequently indulged in domestic violence against Shinkfield's mother, was a difficult one. One of the more disturbing stories was of the day he came home to find his father assaulting his mother. Shinkfield immediately intervened to defend her, but she became angry at what she saw as his interference and told him to stop. This reaction is not uncommon in domestic violence cases and was widespread in the past, when women were less able to extricate themselves from abusive relationships and unwilling to report domestic violence to the police, or friends, for fear of being judged or punished.

The fourteen-year-old Shinkfield couldn't understand his mother's reaction to his attempt at protecting her and the incident (there may have been more than one) had a profound effect on his psyche at a pivotal time in his emotional development. Many years later he told Vanessa, "When my mother did that, I locked the door and threw away the key",[3] metaphorically disowning parents who were unable to display the affection toward him and between themselves that he expected. It was around this time that Shinkfield's own behaviour changed dramatically, and the unknown incident which resulted in his forced exile to Red Hill School in East Sutton, Kent, almost 300 miles from Darlington, took place.

In lieu of the details, speculation about the incident which led to Shinkfield being sent to Red Hill School is redundant, but it must have been a serious one. Unless a child, especially one from a respectable and aspiring working class family, had committed a serious crime it was unusual for them to be removed from their home and almost unheard of to be sent to somewhere like Red Hill. In that era of educational conformity, when schools were bound by strict rules and codes of conduct governing every aspect of school life, Red Hill School was an anomaly. When it opened in 1934 founder Otto Shaw described Red Hill as "a private boarding school for a limited number of difficult children",[4] Shaw's ethos being "the strong belief that to understand is to cure".[5] Following the 1944 Education Act, when the school was officially recognised by the Ministry of Education, its description changed to "a grammar school for the education and psychological treatment of maladjusted boys of very high intelligence".[6] In a school prospectus from the 1940s, Shaw claimed that Red Hill had "a reputation for success with sexual cases, asthma, nervous afflictions, stealing, untruthfulness, aggressiveness, bedwetting, night terrors, apathy to school work, backwardness at school and speech difficulties."[7]

'Maladjusted' might have been the term used to categorise children sent to Red Hill in the 1940s, but in the 21st century such children would be described as having undergone Adverse Childhood Experiences (ACE). That term was coined in 1985 to describe traumatic experiences occurring before the age of 18 which leave deep and lasting impressions and negatively affect future behaviours. One study suggests, "children who experience stressful and poor-quality childhoods are more likely to develop health-harming and anti-social behaviours, more likely to perform poorly in school, more likely to be involved in crime and ultimately less likely to be a productive member of society."[8] Of course, not all children who suffer ACE develop these behaviours, but the fact that Shinkfield clearly suffered several ACE should be borne in mind and set against his personality and behaviours described in this book.

ACE don't excuse negative behaviour patterns, but they do offer a reason for them.

Selection of pupils for Red Hill School was initially via referral from a local education authority, in Shinkfield's case the Darlington Educational Authority. Red Hill School was funded solely by local education authorities, and considering there were hundreds of thousands of children between the ages of 14-18 in 1945, that Shinkfield met Red Hill's criteria speaks volumes about the gravity of the transgression that caused him to be sent there. Red Hill had a capacity of fifty five pupils with an annual turnover of twelve. Up to a thousand referrals were received each year and only the most appropriate referrals were admitted. The school's over-arching principle was that of a therapeutic community. Otto Shaw was influenced by Freudian insights into so-called maladjusted behaviour and how these insights could be transferred into practice. For ideas Shaw looked to people like the radical educator A.S. Neil, founder of Summerhill School, who provided an anti-authoritarian, therapeutic environment which encouraged the emotional as well as the academic development of children. As Red Hill was independent of local authority control, Shaw was free to experiment with educational and behavioural techniques that state schools would never consider.

Before accepting a potential pupil Shaw had to be certain they met specific criteria, which were assessed by the referral paperwork rather than in an interview. The first criterion was that the applicant must be agreeable to psychoanalysis. The second criterion was that the applicant must be intelligent. Red Hill School would not accept pupils who had an IQ of below 130, and the average IQ of a 14-year-old (Shinkfield's age on admission) in the general school population of the 1940s was between 90-110. Another criterion was that the School did not take anyone who had been diagnosed as, or was exhibiting, schizophrenic, psychotic or psychopathic behaviours. From this we can deduce that Hollingshead was intelligent, with an IQ of at least 130, and that the issues which led to his referral to Red Hill were rooted in behavioural or personality problems, not any form of diagnosed mental illness.

Approximately half of all Red Hill pupils underwent psychoanalysis during their stay. The remainder were treated by careful guidance, advice, friendship and constructive criticism. All the school's pupil records were destroyed except for a handful to which access is restricted for a hundred years from date of their creation. Shinkfield family oral tradition suggests he did undergo psychoanalysis and he told his daughter Vanessa that he often had sessions but was able to deceive and outwit the therapist. Whether it's true, or an early example of Shinkfield's self-aggrandisement, his claim reveals his attitude to the psychoanalysis carried out at Red Hill. Rather than accept it, Shinkfield seems to have actively worked against it and tried to understand its techniques so he could use them on others. Shinkfield even told some people that he had received psychoanalysis from Sigmund Freud's daughter, Anna, who at the time was working in London and had connections with the school.

Although records of individual pupils are unavailable, some traces of Shinkfield's years at Red Hill have survived; a photograph taken in November 1946 shows him in the back row of a group of pupils, looking confident, his right arm firmly gripping a younger boy in front of him. According to pupils who remembered him Shinkfield was outgoing, self-confident and able to mix easily with children of any age or sex. Tony Cook, who shared a dormitory with him, recalled he was secretary of the school's social committee for a while and instigated the annual Red Hill School Halloween party. He was also very active in school theatre productions, playing the key Shakespearean role of Henry VIII to Cook's Catherine of Aragon. Cook remembered an occasion when Shinkfield combined his imagination with his mimicry and acting skills: "There was a polio scare and four of us were isolated in a sickroom, where we spent our time pretending to be escaped Russian salt miners, cod accents and all!"[9]

Shinkfield could be mischievous at times and took part in the usual schoolboy shenanigans such as tuck shop raids and night time sorties to steal fruit from nearby orchards. Sometimes there could be an 'edge' to him in his interactions with other people; a talent for calculated confrontation when he pushed people too far, with occasionally painful results. For example he used his vocal mimicry skills to imitate staff member Paul Pollock's central European accent, goading him until

Pollock lost control and knocked out one of Shinkfield's teeth. These behaviours, including the desire to organise, the ability to act and mimic, a penchant for deception and the ability to provoke people to extremes, became embedded in Shinkfield's personality and would be frequently used throughout his life.

Red Hill gave Shinkfield the opportunity to develop his literary and artistic side, skills which he excelled at and enjoyed immensely, and it was there that his first writings were published. Pupils were encouraged to write their own newspapers and magazines as part of the creative, therapeutic process, and in 1948, Shinkfield contributed four pieces – more than any other pupil – to the 44-page *The Christmas Review*. 'Fire Burn and Cauldron Bubble', 'The Weather for December', 'Dr Margaret Phoebe's Column', and *Steiner*[10] were short items, the first two being about exaggerated antics at the school and a spoof weather forecast, while the latter two pieces survive in name only. Short and slight these early writings might have been, but they demonstrated Shinkfield's ability to translate his powerful imagination into words. He also had a talent for visual art, dabbling in a variety of media.

Art was very much encouraged by Otto Shaw, who saw it as a vital form of therapeutic expression: "Is not the artist better for releasing some of that pent and distorted emotional energy on paper?"[11] Shaw was very proud of the art his pupils created and went to great lengths to enable the public to view and purchase it. Between 1946–52 he arranged three 'Magic Eye' exhibitions at the prestigious Cooling Galleries in London's New Bond Street. The 1948 exhibition, which ran between 26 January and 6 February, was billed as "A Second Exhibition of Imaginative Paintings and Drawings made by children at Red Hill School, east Sutton, near Maidstone, Kent", and featured two pieces by Shinkfield,[12] a painting called *Dream* and a charcoal sketch called *Sorrow*. The originals are lost but their titles hint at themes which haunted him throughout his life; his dream of being famous, influential, loved and valued, and his sorrow at how these dreams were constantly thwarted and frustrated, invariably by his own behaviours. The drive to write and create art was strong and until his death Shinkfield was a writer, poet, journalist and chronicler, and produced all kinds of art to accompany and enhance the psychedelic experience.

Although a boarding school, Red Hill was unable to provide accommodation all year round and it was an expectation that during at least some of the holidays pupils would make other arrangements. Where they believed it safe to do so the school encouraged pupils to visit parents during holiday periods and Shinkfield returned to Darlington on several occasions. One photograph of him, taken in his parents' garden in June 1948, shows him looking happy and relaxed, standing next to his younger siblings Janette and David.

Overall, Red Hill seemed to have a positive effect on the young Michael, but school days don't last forever and in 1949 he had to leave. For a young man in the late 1940s there was little choice of occupation and he was conscripted into the armed forces courtesy of the National Service Act (1948), which was compulsory for all men under the age of 21 unless they were conscientious objectors or in an occupation deemed an essential service. Shinkfield was conscripted into the Royal Air Force (RAF) at RAF West Kirby no. 5 on the Wirral, where he did his 8-week period of basic training, before being posted elsewhere. Shinkfield's National Service records have not been retained by The National Archives at Kew in London, but his sister Janette believes he was stationed for a while at RAF Dalcross in Scotland after leaving West Kirby. RAF West Kirby veteran's society have no information about Shinkfield other than a faded black and white photograph taken in 1949 showing him uniformed and armed, standing to attention outside a Nissan hut.

After being de-mobbed from the RAF in the early 1950s Shinkfield moved to London, family legend suggesting he worked for Thomas Cook Travel Agents, although there is no substantive evidence for that claim. He did, however, follow up his school acting debut by becoming involved in a small London theatre company, where he befriended John Beresford, who would become key in Shinkfield's transition from the straight to the psychedelic world. Beresford, then training to be a doctor at London Hospital Medical College, was the previous boyfriend of one of Shinkfield's girlfriends and remembered Shinkfield as having a talent for mimicry, "he could take off someone with a different accent than his own, with a remarkable memory for the nuances of that accent",[13] the same talent that earned him a punch in the face at Red Hill! Beresford believed Shinkfield was attempting to break into the theatre world, but nothing came of that ambition. Beresford, Shinkfield and three girls shared a flat in Hampstead. Years later, Shinkfield remembered the newly qualified Beresford as being, "the most unusual doctor I'd ever met".[14]

In September 1951 Shinkfield obtained his first passport and moved, for reasons unknown, to Denmark. The move suggests he learnt Danish and Norwegian during his National Service because only French was taught at Red Hill, and Danish and Norwegian were not on the English school curriculum in the 1940s. In Denmark he was soon able to secure paid employment at the University of Copenhagen, teaching English to Danish students. It was at the University he met Ebba Riis-Peterson, with whom he fell in love and married in 1952.

Vanessa Hollingshead remembers her father boasting of the adventures he and Ebba had on their honeymoon, driving across Europe, staying at the best hotels and negotiating free or reduced accommodation because Shinkfield claimed he was writing travel brochures. It's easy to imagine how the tall, well spoken Hollingshead could pull off such a deception, moving on quickly, often across borders, before his ruse came to light. Honeymoon adventures aside, the Shinkfields' marriage soon began to disintegrate. Shinkfield was a heavy drinker and when friends visited, he would often play mind games, frequently bragging about non-existent achievements and over exaggerating past exploits. He and Ebba often argued; trivial disputes about tidiness, for instance, escalating to household items being thrown from windows, before the inevitable reconciliation and the love-hate cycle beginning again.

Whether through love, financial necessity or a combination of the two, Ebba and Michael remained married and together for most of the 1950s and a son they named Timothy was born on 11 December 1953. A passport entry for 1 June 1952 suggests Shinkfield was working for Scandinavian Student Travel Services at that time. Other passport entries for the 1950s show he was coming and going from Denmark on a regular basis, to the Netherlands, Germany, Finland, Belgium, Norway and France. Shinkfield made several visits to England in the 1950s, accompanied by Ebba on at least five occasions and for up to several weeks at a time, visiting friends and relatives in and around Darlington. He was always popular with his young cousins on home visits and was given the nickname 'Uncle Muncle'.

At some point in the late 1950s Shinkfield and Ebba visited his old Red Hill schoolfriend Tony Cook, telling him he was now working in broadcasting. This suggests his frequent visits to England were to carry out paid research for some of the radio shows he presented or co-presented on Danish radio between 1956 and 1958. These were either documentaries such as *Exploring Soho, The Changing Face of Oxford Street* and *London Street Music* or English classes for students of varying abilities, such as *Advanced English: by Radio/University Professor Ingeborg Nixon, assisted by Michael Shinkfield*. He even ran a series about British literary greats, including *An Introduction to the Writings of W. Somerset Maugham*.

His other travels in the second half of the fifties revolved around two major writing projects, his first since the amateur scribblings of the Red Hill days. The 62-page A *Student's Guide to Copenhagen* was published in 1957 by Danmarks Internationale Studenterkomite (DIS). The 118-page *A Student's Travel Guide to the Netherlands*, was published by the Netherlands Office for Foreign Student Relations in 1958. Shinkfield's writing, teaching and broadcasting jobs were well paid and consistent, but time consuming and he was often away from home for days or weeks. Ebba couldn't always go with him and these absences added to their already fraught relationship; they finally separated in 1958. Almost immediately, Shinkfield left Denmark and his teaching and broadcasting jobs and flew to London, taking up residence at 14 Cliveden Place in Belgravia, a three-minute walk from Pont Street where he would later create the LSD-drenched World Psychedelic Centre.

Shinkfield might not yet have heard of LSD when he returned to London, but it was there he became involved with three men – Alex Trocchi, Brian Barritt and Desmond O'Brien – who were all involved in the drug world, who would become significant influences on his future trajectory. Trocchi was well-known, infamous even, in the early 1950s, having edited the Paris based magazine *Merlin*, which published Henry Miller and Samuel Beckett among other literary and beat luminaries. Trocchi would become famous in his own right as the author of several books, many erotic and pornographic in nature, as well as conventional novels like *Young Adam*. He was a heavy drinker and a heroin addict, a habit picked up in Paris, and in London he became a well-known heroin dealer to support his habit. Hollingshead, already a big drinker, discovered he had a taste for heroin and began to buy from Trocchi.

It was at Trocchi's flat that Shinkfield first met Brian Barritt, who recalled, "My first meeting with Michael Hollingshead... was in pre-acid days, round at Trocchi's place while we were both waiting to score".[15] Around the same time, Shinkfield met Desmond O'Brien, the disowned ex-Etonian black sheep of a wealthy Cheshire family, who had fallen into crime, hard drinking and drug taking. O'Brien and Shinkfield became good friends and spent time carousing together in London's nightlife. Shinkfield later told his partner Auriol Roberts stories of him, O'Brien and Trocchi visiting clubs and drinking establishments frequented by wealthy young debutantes with the intention of exploiting them for sex and money. Shinkfield told Roberts he didn't consider himself an addict at that time though he was regularly using both heroin and cocaine, often together; one tale involved him and Trocchi injecting a mixture of cocaine and heroin in the toilets of a Mayfair hotel during a society ball. With his University of Copenhagen employment over, his writing and broadcasting left behind in Denmark and his drug and drink addiction worsening in London, Shinkfield needed another job and a new start. In August 1958 he applied to the American Embassy in London for a non-immigrant visa and in December flew into New York City where he met Dr John Beresford who had moved there in 1952 and was now an Instructor in Paediatrics at the prestigious New York Medical College. After a brief stay with Beresford, Shinkfield returned to London for several months before making the decision to permanently move to America. On 8 September 1959, he boarded the Greek Line passenger ship 'New York' at Southampton, the passenger manifest listing his occupation as lecturer, and his marital status as single. The first statement was dubious, the second a lie because in 1959 Shinkfield was still legally married to Ebba Shinkfield.

Shinkfield was twenty-seven-years old when he arrived in New York. The choices he had made, the lies he'd told, and the opportunities he'd seized all conspired to bring him to America. Here he thought he could carve out a new life, re-invent himself, erase his past and be anyone he chose. He had no idea that within a couple of years, Michael Shinkfield would morph into another version of himself, with a different name, and become a key player in the biggest consciousness-changing movement in the history of the world.

Notes

1   *Everybody's Weekly*. School Without Fear. 26/1/52

2   Defoe, D. *A Tour Through the Whole Island of Great Britain*. Penguin Classics, 1978 p.533

3   Hollingshead, V. *LSD Mafia*. Unpublished MS. 2012 p.4

4   http://www.pettrust.org.uk/index.php?option=com_ content&view=article&id=604:up-rhs-overview-understanding-up-rhs-red-hill-school-collection&catid=199&Itemid=406

5   Shaw, O. *Maladjusted Boys*. Allen & Unwin, 1965 p.14

6   Ibid. p.5

7   http://www.pettrust.org.uk/index.php?option=com_ content&view=article&id=604:up-rhs-overview-understanding-up-rhs-red-hill-school-collection&catid=199&Itemid=406

8   http://www.wales.nhs.uk/sitesplus/888/page/88524

9   Cook, T. Email 3/12/13

10   *The Christmas Review*. Red Hill School. 1948

11   *The Magic Eye*. The Cooling Galleries. 1948

12   Ibid, p.9

13   Beresford, J. In *Magic Grams*. Stafford, Peter. Privately published. 1988 p.69

14   Hollingshead, M. ibid. p.155

15   Barritt, B. *The Road of Excess*. PSI, 1998 p. 248

An Englishman in New York

It was a very strange first trip indeed.[1]

In 1959 the 'British invasion' of America, bringing new ideas in culture, fashion and music, was still some years distant but, ahead of the pack, Michael Shinkfield maximised the role of ex-patriate Englishman for fun and profit. His native Geordie accent and dialect were gone, replaced with an upper-class southern English pronunciation which, coupled with his tall, striking appearance, intelligence and quick wit assisted his integration into New York life. He rented a flat above Jim Paul Eilers' Showplace, a recently-opened nightclub on West 4th Street, just off Washington Square in hip Greenwich Village, and began to look for work.

Within weeks of arriving in New York Shinkfield visited the Oxford University Press offices and met Sophie Naimon, a twenty-nine-year-old secretary and honours graduate of Brooklyn College of Music. Their mutual attraction turned into a whirlwind romance, Sophie becoming pregnant soon after their first meeting. In early March 1960 Shinkfield received the decree absolute for his divorce from Ebba Shinkfield, enabling him to marry Sophie a few weeks later in Manhattan and spare their child the stigma of illegitimacy. He renewed his friendship with Dr John Beresford, who was now Director of the Paediatric Teaching Programme for Second Year students at the Medical College. At work Beresford was conscientious and highly respected, the epitome of a straight employee. Out of work, he had developed an interest in psychedelic drugs after reading Aldous Huxley's mescaline experiences in *The Doors of Perception*. He decided to try mescaline and had no difficulty ordering a supply from Hoffmann La Roche pharmaceuticals who delivered it by same-day courier. Beresford enjoyed the mescaline and, looking for similar experiences, became involved with a small coterie of New York drug users who were also fond of the psychedelic experience.

Beresford's friend Tony Cox, who later married Yoko Ono, introduced him to Chuck Bick who operated a mail order drug service and kept a wide selection in his basement on the Lower East Side. Cox also introduced Beresford to Eric Loeb, owner of what was arguably the world's first psychedelic shop, situated on East 9th Street in Greenwich Village, which opened four days a week to sell unregulated substances including mescaline, peyote, harmaline and ibogaine. Beresford was in his element and was soon taking mescaline and other drugs practically every weekend. Besides buying drugs from Bick and Loeb, Beresford obtained psychoactive substances from pharmaceutical companies like Hoffmann La Roche and Light & Co. Although he enjoyed their effects, Beresford wasn't convinced that pleasure alone was reason enough for taking psychoactive drugs. As he became familiar with the dosage and effects of the various drugs he began to feel as if he were being guided, or impelled, to use them, developing "a vague sense that something important was taking place".[2] This is reminiscent of the "peculiar pre-sentiment"[3] Albert Hofmann experienced in his early experiments with LSD; the sense of an unknown purpose behind the revelations evoked by the drug. Beresford told Shinkfield of his mescaline experiences and this piqued his interest as to what psychedelic drugs might have to offer. Meanwhile, Shinkfield had begun work as the Executive Secretary of the Institute for British-American Cultural Exchange (IBACE), "This grandiose title meant I was in the service of a semi-official British propaganda agency in the field of international cultural relations."[4] IBACE, about which little is known, was constituted in New York as a not-for-profit organisation on 2 November 1959. Its board of directors boasted several well-known people such as poet W.H. Auden, literary critic Lionel Trilling, and millionaire New York patron of the arts Huntington Hartford. John Beresford became involved with IBACE, albeit briefly, as Secretary and Treasurer. He found IBACE to be innocuous, remembering little about the organisation other than attending parties at Huntington Hartford's luxurious flat, where Auden read poetry while Shinkfield schmoozed with journalists and decimated the expensive wine cellar.

Some conspiracy theorists and revisionists of psychedelic history believe IBACE could have been a front for an intelligence service such as MI6 or the CIA, but no evidence other than the anecdotal has been offered to substantiate this. The lack of information about IBACE and Shinkfield's unqualified description of the company as being a "propaganda agency" appear to have been the genesis for this rumour. Shinkfield's IBACE office was in the plush Huntington Hartford building in New York where his work was varied, including selecting American students for scholarship programmes at British universities and placing British students in American universities. Using his English charm Shinkfield was a successful fund raiser for IBACE, meeting representatives from wealthy institutions like the Rockefeller Institute and the Carnegie Foundation. Besides benefitting IBACE, Shinkfield's fund-raising activities opened doors into New York's elite and wealthy society circles where he forged many useful connections.

Shinkfield and Beresford were having regular discussions about the possibilities other psychedelic drugs might offer and decided it was time to try LSD, which had been receiving increasing media coverage. It's at this point that Shinkfield's life goes, as they say in the psychedelic subculture, down the rabbit hole, his experiences and memories often diverging from those of his contemporaries and making any absolute 'truth' about what happened a shimmering lysergic mirage. Shinkfield and Beresford are dead and neither left a contemporaneous record explaining how or why they obtained what has become known as the 'Magic Gram', their initial supply of LSD, or how Shinkfield contacted Tim Leary.

The accepted historical narrative of the acquisition and distribution of the Magic Gram has been based on the first written accounts by those involved, Leary's 1978 book *High Priest* and Shinkfield's 1973 autobiography *The Man Who Turned On The World*. Both narratives have since been endlessly repeated, embellished and intertwined, but have never been questioned to any degree. John Beresford rarely spoke about the Magic Gram and never published his version of events, which is quite different to that of Shinkfield's or Leary's. By analysing the earliest references, including John Beresford's recently-unearthed comments, fresh light can be shed on this Ur-moment of psychedelic history.

Shinkfield's account of how he came to obtain the Magic Gram begins with his claim to have telephoned Aldous Huxley for advice about where to obtain mescaline. Considering Beresford already had a source, the account Shinkfield gives in his autobiography seems dubious. Years later Shinkfield changed his story, stating he contacted Huxley in his capacity as Secretary of IBACE to invite him to become a Director, an offer Huxley declined. In his original account Shinkfield claims the conversation about mescaline turned to psychedelic drugs and LSD, which Huxley recommended with some caveats: "It is much more potent than mescaline, though Gerald (Heard) and I have used it with some quite astonishing results, really."[5] Suitably enthused,

Shinkfield claims he then discussed buying LSD with Beresford who allowed him to order a gram of LSD from Sandoz Pharmaceuticals in Switzerland, using hospital letterheaded paper, claiming he needed it for bone marrow research. The receipt for the Magic Gram of LSD no longer exists so when it was ordered is unknown; Shinkfield gives various dates, placing its acquisition between 1959-60. In his autobiography he claims it was seventeen years after Albert Hofmann's 1943 discovery of LSD's effects, "New York City, seventeen years later...a small package from Switzerland arrived..."[6] Elsewhere he remembers a similar date "It arrived in 1960 – at the end of '59"[7] and in a 1975 interview he says he obtained the drug "In 1960, Aldous Huxley told me he had achieved amazing results with LSD..."[8] Based on those dates the Magic Gram arrived in early 1960, but Hollingshead had only just arrived and settled in New York at that time, which argues against that date. And if this approximate date is correct it's a puzzle why he chose to wait at least eighteen months before approaching Leary. In *Magic Grams*, Peter Stafford's unpublished collection of interviews with psychedelic celebrities, Shinkfield adds to the mystery when he says he ordered it six months before he introduced the drug to Leary, which suggest they obtained it in the late spring of 1961. This makes much more sense than them obtaining it in the late '59, early '60 period, and it is just possible he and Beresford became confused about the dates over the years.

Beresford's recollections differ slightly, but meaningfully, to Shinkfield's. In *Magic Grams* he doesn't mention Shinkfield's involvement at all, merely stating that the acquisition of the LSD was part of his belief that he was being guided to investigate psychedelics and ordered it because, "If I don't do it, it probably won't get done."[9] Beresford's family believe Shinkfield had little or nothing to do with the acquisition of the Magic Gram and that he effectively stole both the drug, and the credit for obtaining it, from Beresford. There is enough doubt and contradictory evidence in Shinkfield's narratives to believe that they are not totally accurate and that Beresford did indeed play a far more significant role than has been previously acknowledged.

According to Shinkfield, the gram of LSD arrived from Sandoz in Switzerland (Beresford later said Sandoz in New Jersey, no one is certain), well packaged, and with a bill for $285 (Beresford said $269). Labelled 'Lot Number H-00047', Shinkfield describes the LSD as being a malted-milk like powder in a small dark glass jar. Shinkfield and Beresford had no idea about dosage or even how to divide the LSD powder into manageable and consistent doses. After some discussion they reasoned that a gram could be broken down into 5000 individual doses of 200 micrograms each, so Shinkfield mixed a stiff paste of icing sugar (confectioner's sugar in the US) into which he stirred the LSD powder, dissolved in distilled water. The psychedelic goo was then laboriously transferred into a sixteen-ounce mayonnaise jar which, according to Shinkfield, measured exactly 5000 teaspoonfuls. This method of division and storage gave rise to the Myth of the Mayonnaise jar and is worthy of comment and query.

Did the fabled mayonnaise jar even exist? The answer is yes. Writing in 2018 Ralph Metzner, one of the first people to see the jar, confirmed "Yes, I saw the jar; I and TL were into carefully planned and measured usage of drugs, we couldn't relate to his [Shinkfield's] attitude to the jar."[10] Shinkfield makes it very clear that he used a 16 ounce jar, into which he stirred the entire Magic Gram, resulting in a container holding exactly 5000 teaspoonfuls of the LSD paste, a claim he repeated often. But his account of the Magic Gram's division and storage falters when his method is tested. A simple kitchen experiment reveals a 16 ounce jar will take a maximum of 100 teaspoonfuls of a paste made from icing sugar. So what did Shinkfield do with the remaining paste, the other 4900 spoonfulls? He makes no mention of storing the remainder in other jars, or elsewhere, and to do so he would have needed an extra forty nine jars! If, as Beresford claims, Shinkfield only had half of the Magic Gram he would have had one jar containing 100 spoonfulls and enough paste remaining to fill twenty four jars. Was this story another of Hollingshead's manipulations of reality at the expense of people who couldn't be bothered to check the facts? The most likely explanation is that Shinkfield mixed *some* of the gram he shared with Beresford into the sugar paste and retained the rest in liquid form, possibly topping up the magic mayonnaise jar as the paste was used. This theory is given some credence by Richard Alpert who later recalled, "It was the Englishman Michael Hollingshead who came up from New York, with a huge supply of LSD in liquid form."[11]

Returning to Shinkfield's account, during the dilution process, and ignorant of the drug's potency, he occasionally licked his fingers, later estimating he probably ingested over 1000 micrograms of pure LSD. Alone and sensing that something powerful was going to happen he managed to get to the roof terrace of his Greenwich Village flat before the full force of the LSD hit, changing the course of his life forever. As the drug suffused his brain, Shinkfield was catapulted from everyday consciousness into the realms of the primordial, becoming lost in a kaleidoscopic whirl of sensation. His descriptions of this first experience, as those who have taken a significant dose of pure LSD know, are inadequate to convey the drug's potency, and his written recollections offer only fragmentary glimpses of an experience in which he "stepped forth out of the shell of my body, into some other land of unlikeliness, which can only be grasped in terms of astonishment and mystery, as an *etat de l'absurde*, ecstatic nirvana".[12] In Shinkfield's case he became a god, taking the form of legendary heroes such as King Arthur and Lancelot, and bestrode the sky as the doors of heaven swung open for him to witness the dawn of humankind. Shinkfield's post-trip hyperbole still couldn't meaningfully capture the continuous shifting of perception and rise and fall of imagery he experienced during his first LSD experience. He estimated that the trip lasted almost fifteen hours, during which, freed of his body and of normal perceptions of space and time, his mind roamed the psychedelic multiverse, the perceiving 'I' he knew to be 'Michael Shinkfield' clinging on, unable to direct or moderate the drug's effects but experiencing every second as inestimable periods of time.

"It was a very strange trip indeed",[13] he remarked later, with not a little understatement. As the effects of the drug faded, Shinkfield tried to make sense of the experience, attempting to rationalise the irrational and searching for logic in the illogical. At first he thought LSD was a bundle of solutions looking for a problem, that problem being the limiting factor of modern man's sceptical intelligence. He reflected that humans had become so concerned with the world of external appearances they were strangers to themselves and their internal processes. LSD promised Shinkfield "a vision of some ideal existence in which there was only the sense of wonder, and all fear gone; of a certain state of being that was there not to be judged, but simply to be".[14] The psychedelic koan offered by LSD was deceptively simple; how to use the mind to overcome its natural resistance to the effects of LSD so they could be understood and integrated into the psyche. In his musings, Shinkfield had the prescient insight that psychedelic experiences could be "the impetus that makes a few travellers in each generation set off in search of the grail, the genii in the bottle, the magic ring..."[15] By which he meant the existential awe and glimpses of other realities LSD bestowed would lead people to pursue altered states of all kinds, whether by psychedelics, religion, occultism, body work, yoga, diet or permutations of all those and more. Which is exactly what happened as the psychedelic sixties unfolded.

Prior to taking LSD Shinkfield had been reading Carl Jung's essay, *The Spirit Mercurius*, and now felt the symbolism of the trip conferred on him the magical essence of alchemical quicksilver, a belief he would hold for many years, until he visited Nepal in 1969. Even thus exalted he had no idea what to do with the remaining LSD, but after discussing the problem with John Beresford they decided they should share the experience with others. Before they did this Shinkfield claims he went to Texas to take LSD in an environment isolated from other people. Of course, he could have easily found a similar location much nearer New York and his real reason for choosing Texas is a mystery. On his return he phoned Huxley for advice about the meaning of his LSD revelations and was advised to contact Dr Timothy Leary at Harvard University who was researching visionary mental states induced by psilocybin. "If there is any one single investigator in America worth seeing", Huxley told Hollingshead, "it is Dr Leary".[16]

John Beresford's memory is that it was *he* who suggested Shinkfield get in touch with Leary, thinking "maybe he would like to try his hand with him, because there didn't seem to be much he could do in New York. Michael went up, and I gave him some LSD to take up…"[17] Beresford's claim that he gave Shinkfield LSD for Leary adds weight to the Magic Gram having been obtained by Beresford, not Shinkfield, then divided equally between them. In a document Beresford provided to Peter Stafford, he writes the LSD, "appeared in two half-gram ampoules labelled 'Lot Number H-00047', one ampoule was opened immediately, the second half-gram wasn't tried out until 1964."[18] Beresford's description of how the LSD was packaged differs also considerably from Shinkfield's and was omitted from the final version of Stafford's book, but suggests that Shinkfield only took half of the Magic Gram with him – 2500 doses and not the 5000 he always claimed. Further doubt is cast on Shinkfield's version of events by Beresford's claim that some of his portion of the Magic Gram was used in LSD sessions at the Agora Trust, which wasn't operational until 1963. This is supported by an entry in Beresford's Sandoz 1963 diary for 14 January 1963 (congruent with the Agora Scientific Trust) where he writes, among unrelated comments, "50 ??? H-00047", a clear reference to the lot number of the Magic Gram which Shinkfield claims he completely dissolved in sugar paste and took with him when he parted company with Beresford.

Shinkfield and Beresford's friendship was beginning to fracture and it's easy to see why. As young men in the early 1950s they were good friends, but by the time they reacquainted in the late 1950s their personalities and values were very different. Rosemarie Beresford saw Shinkfield as assertive, colourful and good in social settings, whereas Beresford was the opposite. Shinkfield began to overshadow Beresford's personality, bizarrely believing he had a huge ego which needed "stepping on" when the reverse was true, Beresford practising "absolute non-interference, that is he let Shinkfield be Shinkfield, even if it meant being overshadowed in the process".[19] Beresford's passiveness and non-interference are the main reasons he chose not to publish his version of events, allowing Shinkfield to later distort the real history of the acquisition and distribution of the Magic Gram. Beresford saw the potential inherent in LSD though, and after taking it a few times he concluded it to be "the most critical event in human history… Take it once and you know that all you've known about consciousness is wrong."[20]

In the spring of 1960, artist Claus Oldenburg staged a series of 'Happenings' in New York at the Judson Memorial Church on Washington Square. These multi-media, audio-visual, participatory events foreshadowed the more ambitious psychedelic public events staged in the late '60s. Shinkfield attended one of these in May 1960, where he met John Beresford's wife to be, Rosemarie, who thought him, "charming, very personable, sophisticated and an Englishman."[21] He invited Rosemarie to a party he and Sophie were hosting the following weekend at which she met John Beresford. Rosemarie watched Shinkfield closely during his first couple of years in New York noting he was, "actively observing, observing Americans and making connections", and finding him to be "ambitious, bordering on audacious"; she also saw he had an attractiveness which "lay in that there was an air of expectation, an energy, momentum about him".[22] These qualities, learnt and developed in his childhood and at Red Hill School, on National Service and during his time teaching and broadcasting in Scandinavia, would come to the fore as he began to mix with New York's intelligentsia and the emerging psychedelic movement.

When Shinkfield wasn't taking LSD, his and Sophie's social life was a whirl of drinks parties and entertaining. Through his connections in the drug world and IBACE, the couple became quite well known in New York, and in the late Spring of 1960 they appeared on Johnny Carson's *Who Do You Trust?* TV game show in which married couples were asked a series of questions, the husband deciding whether he or his wife answered them. They did well and won over $500, a considerable sum of money in 1960. Always extravagant, Shinkfield spent a portion of his winnings on a monkey named Bobo, remembered mainly for throwing banana skins and excrement out of its cage. On the surface at least, Shinkfield's life in New York was satisfying and productive: he was the head of a loving family, enjoying a vibrant social life and had a job which offered opportunity for progression. But being comfortable and prosperous was a dangerous position for him to be in. Throughout his life, when things were running smoothly Shinkfield invariably became self-destructive, bringing on personal transformations which often harmed those around him as much as they changed him.

Sophie gave birth to a girl on 16 August 1960. This event should have helped cement her and Shinkfield's relationship but instead it heralded a rift. Against Sophie's wishes Shinkfield insisted on calling the child Vanessa, a name Sophie loathed so much she often deliberately mispronounced or misspelled it as 'Varnessa'. Echoing the problems which contributed to the disintegration of his first marriage, Shinkfield began to spend longer periods away from home working and socialising. These behaviours, along with his drinking, drug use and arguments about how to raise Vanessa caused the rift between him and Sophie to widen. One example of the many problems was their different approach to parenting skills when Vanessa, as most babies do, cried unconsolably for hours. Shinkfield's response was to leave her to cry herself to sleep whereas Sophie wanted to offer physical affection to soothe the child.

The writing was on the wall for the Hollingsheads within a year of them meeting and marrying.

Shinkfield didn't legally change his surname to Michael Hollingshead until 1962 but was using the new name as early as January 1961, evidenced by a telegram addressed to 'Michael Hollingshead' sent by Republican Congressman Jacob Javits. He never revealed the real reason for the name change nor why he chose Hollingshead. He told his daughter Vanessa it was because 'Hollingshead' sounded ancient and freighted with gravitas, redolent of a traditional English name such as the English chronicler Raphael Holinshed. He led his friend Brian Barritt to believe the name Hollingshead was related to trepanation, a practice Hollingshead became interested in years later. Others have suggested the name change was to prevent him being found by the police, a plausible theory on the face of it but one which fails because his passports and other official documents recorded his name as 'Michael Shinkfield-Hollingshead'. The most likely reason is that it was a continuation of the personal reinvention started when he arrived in America, choosing a serious, traditionally British-sounding name he hoped would stand out above the ordinary. His sombre passport photograph from the period adds to this speculation. Dressed in a dark suit, white shirt and plain tie, Hollingshead affects an academic, almost monastic expression which, coupled with his doubled barrelled name, would no doubt help speed his passage through customs without too much interest being shown in what he was carrying.

Hollingshead continued his personal experiments with the Magic Gram and slowly began to understand how to navigate the "incessant barrage of sense-eclipsing distractions, pleasant and unpleasant, delightful and horrible, which acid induces."[23] With each successive trip he began to experience a profound metamorphosis. He felt cut off from his roots, drifting, with no destination in sight. The everyday reality he tried so carefully to control was slipping away and leaving nothing concrete in its wake. Hollingshead described his reality being dissolved into *Maya*; the phenomenal world which was once full of certainty and consistency was now an ever-changing illusion. This experience is common in people who take high doses of LSD and years later books abounded with advice about how to navigate and understand this often-terrifying state. But in the early sixties there were no such guides, and what information there was on dealing with the psychedelic experience was embedded in the context of cultures that employed psychoactive plants or fungi in ritual settings.

The psychological tensions created by Hollingshead's LSD use left him enervated and depressed. Although he didn't know it, Shinkfield was in Chapel Perilous, Robert Anton Wilson's term for the metaphorical (but no less real) state in which a person is exposed to, and confounded by, information at odds with their perception of reality. The experience of Chapel Perilous is different for each person and can be psychological, spiritual, social, physical or a combination of those qualities. Wilson wrote:

> *Chapel Perilous, like the mysterious entity called "I," cannot be located in the space-time continuum; it is weightless, odourless, tasteless and undetectable by ordinary instruments. Indeed, like the Ego, it is even possible to deny that it is there. And yet, even more like the Ego, once you are inside it, there doesn't seem to be any way to ever get out again, until you suddenly discover that it has been brought into existence by thought and does not exist outside thought. Everything you fear is waiting with slavering jaws in Chapel Perilous...*[24]

Trapped in an-LSD induced Chapel Perilous, with his relationship foundering, it was inevitable that Hollingshead's work at IBACE would suffer. Ostensibly he was working hard, but in his own words, "Most of the time I spent smoking grass; and, towards the end, getting stoned on acid".[25] Being permanently high took its toll on Hollingshead's ability to work; his timekeeping became erratic and he was either late or absent altogether from the office. He fell behind with his responsibilities, messing up the dates of the various programmes, forgetting to book accommodation, failing to answer correspondence and no longer able to fundraise for IBACE. When he was in the office he was often stoned and incoherent, declaiming anti-British rants and verbally attacking the Queen and British culture. The aftermath of his LSD experiences had overwhelmed him, his interest in IBACE now overshadowed by visions, such as a "'Golden Dawning' of consciousness in man which would enable us to get things whole, to see life's magic miracles, to know that indeed all is in everything from blade of grass to man and woman."[26] Something had to give and Hollingshead jumped before he was pushed, resigning from IBACE in the early summer of 1961 and leaving behind a trail of administrative and financial devastation.

Hollingshead and Sophie separated, and he moved out of their apartment not long after he quit IBACE. Though he was now without a partner or a source of income, he certainly wasn't short of money. On 27 June he flew from New York to the Mediterranean island of Majorca for a two-week holiday with his recently divorced Danish wife Ebba and their son Timothy, now six and a half years old. Edith, Hollingshead's mother, and his younger brother David, also holidayed with them. Photographs show Hollingshead smartly dressed, smiling and enjoying himself in a restaurant, gazing at Timothy with a mixture of admiration and pride. The purpose of this family reunion is unknown, as is whether his newly-estranged wife, Sophie, was aware her husband was taking a holiday with his former wife.

On his return from Majorca and free from the temporal strictures of work, if not the need for an income, Hollingshead turned his attention to spreading the word about LSD. In September 1961, following up the advice he claimed Aldous Huxley gave him, Hollingshead phoned Tim Leary's office, hopeful of arranging a meeting to discuss his LSD experiences. Accounts of their initial contact, subsequent meetings and how Hollingshead came to be invited to live with Leary differ, more in emphasis and nuance than fact, depending on the narrator. Anyone looking for ulterior, possibly sinister, motives in Hollingshead's determination and purpose in meeting Leary will find anomalies and contradictions aplenty in his narrative.

In *High Priest*, Leary gives a detailed account of their first contact, remembering an autumn morning in late October 1961 when his secretary put a telephone call through to him from Oxford, England. This is something of a puzzle because according to his passport

Hollingshead was in New York in October 1961, not England. Leary took the call and Hollingshead introduced himself in his upper-class English accent, immediately trying to impress him by claiming he been working with Professor G.E. Moore at Oxford, adding that Leary would be interested in what Hollingshead had to tell him about this work. Hollingshead's own account of this conversation with Leary, perhaps conveniently as we will see, omits mention of using Moore's name by way of introduction and notes only that Leary was cautious and apprehensive during the call.

Hollingshead said enough to Leary for him to agree to a lunch time meeting the following Tuesday at the Faculty Club off Harvard Square. Leary clearly didn't give much thought to Hollingshead's claim of mutual friendship with G.E. Moore because, had he done so, he would have discovered that the eminent British philosopher had died on 24 October 1958, thirteen months before IBACE was incorporated as a company and three years before Hollingshead's call to Leary. Considering that Hollingshead had spent the majority of the 1950s in the RAF or working and travelling in Scandinavia and Europe, it is highly unlikely he knew Moore in any context. Hollingshead even got Moore's university wrong; he was a professor at Cambridge, not Oxford. Years later Hollingshead corrected this error in a letter to Leary, but if he had really known or worked with Moore why did he make those fundamental errors in his first call to Leary? Conversely, if Hollingshead *was* working for an intelligence service and seeking to gain Leary's confidence for purposes unknown then his introductory credentials would surely have been watertight to ensure authenticity.

The planned lunch took place, but Leary was bored, noting that Hollingshead had little to say about Professor Moore and was evasive as to the reason for wanting the meeting. He eventually revealed he was a writer and regaled Leary with details of his unfinished novel about a bank clerk who learnt to levitate using yoga and meditation. This caused

Leary to be late for a faculty meeting, so Hollingshead walked with him and finally began to talk about his LSD experiences. Leary was interested but in a rush so he bade Hollingshead goodbye and agreed they should meet again soon to continue the conversation, recalling that Hollingshead said he would phone to arrange the date and time.

Hollingshead's version of the meeting is a bright and breezy account of how Leary seemed distracted throughout and claimed it was Leary, not he, who broached the subject of psychedelic drugs. In his autobiography, Hollingshead states by the time he met Leary he had been taking LSD about once a week for six months and was more confused than illuminated as a result. This suggests, based on his claim to have obtained the LSD about six months prior to meeting Leary, he had taken approximately 26 LSD trips, probably more than anyone else in history at that time. Although from both Leary and Hollingshead's accounts of their first meeting it was clear Hollingshead had been deeply affected by his LSD experiences there was nothing in his demeanour to suggest he was anything other than sound in mind and body.

Leary claims he forgot about his meeting with Hollingshead until the following Thursday when he received a letter from him describing his and Beresford's LSD experiments. Hollingshead confessed how overwhelmed they had left him and begged for Leary's help, saying he was so desperate to get to know Leary he had now moved to a boarding house on Brattle Street in Cambridge, a few miles from Leary's home. Hollingshead closed the plaintive letter with a stark ultimatum; if Leary didn't contact him by 5 p.m. that day, Hollingshead was going to kill himself. Leary read the letter to his research assistant, George Litwin, and while Litwin's account differs slightly from Leary's, they both decided they had no choice but to help a fellow psychonaut who was going through a difficult time. Litwin remembers Leary saying, with typical beneficence, "This man seems to have experimented in the area we are working in and has come to some difficulty. I just do not feel we can leave him in some lonely apartment in Cambridge. As researchers in this field it is up to us to look into cases like this where circumstances have caused a certain effect, as well as to conduct experimental studies."[27]

Hollingshead rarely acted without a very good reason and the carefully structured contents of his letter to Leary, in view of the deceptions in his initial phone call, could have been a clever *fait accompli* formulated to force a meeting at short notice, and on Hollingshead's terms. In his autobiography, Hollingshead plays down the content of the letter. There is no mention of his suicide ultimatum, just the brief observation, contrasting his cheery description of the lunch meeting, that "By the end of my third day in Cambridge I was feeling suicidal…I had already mailed him a short note the night before, alerting him to my inability to cope with my life situation due to the disruptive influence of acid."[28] It is possible Hollingshead *was* being completely honest, but it should be borne in mind there is no evidence, even in the depths of his subsequent drug and alcohol addictions or other personal problems, that Hollingshead ever again contemplated suicide.

Leary was thrown into a quandary. He was due to leave for the airport for a flight to New York but in view of Hollingshead's threat couldn't just abandon him. Thinking quickly, he sent George Litwin to get Hollingshead and they listened to his tale of woe on the way to the airport. Hollingshead explained he was penniless, out of work and separated from his wife and child. Not something worth killing yourself over, thought Leary, who immediately suggested Hollingshead borrow his car, pick up Sophie and Vanessa from New York and move into the third floor of Leary's house that same day. Other than a shared interest in LSD, Leary and Hollingshead had little in common and it says a great deal about Leary's character and compassion that he decided to help Hollingshead to such a degree. It also says something about Hollingshead's powers of persuasion, if not manipulation, that he had managed to position himself exactly where he wanted to be just over a week after his first meeting with Leary.

At the airport Hollingshead followed Leary to the Eastern Airlines departure lounge door and just as Leary was about to say goodbye, Hollingshead took him to one side and nervously made a startling confession. He told Leary that for the past six months he had been working for a well-known New York multimillionaire by the name of Winston London. Leary nodded. He knew London to be a man of integrity who was constantly financially exploited by people who took advantage of his good will. Hollingshead revealed that he and London parted company on very bad terms, not specifying why but cleverly manipulating Leary's perception of the situation. Hollingshead was concerned that if Leary contacted London he would try to blacken Hollingshead's character with all kinds of spurious claims, claims which Leary should ignore as they said much more about London's personality than Hollingshead's.

Hollingshead's predicament was still puzzling Leary when he landed in New York and he wanted to know more about his problems with Winston London. Leary visited Max Fox (almost certainly a pseudonym for Van Wolf), a Hollywood publicity agent of his acquaintance, and asked him his opinion. Fox telephoned an ex-bodyguard of London's to ask him what he knew. With the phone on loudspeaker Leary heard the vitriolic response, referring to Hollingshead as a con man and advising Fox that neither he nor Leary should have anything to do with him. The tirade continued as the bodyguard told Fox Hollingshead had caused more trouble for London than any other con man and warned Leary to stay away from him. No trace of the unlikely-sounding Winston London has been found and it's possible the name was a pseudonym for Huntingdon Hartford, or one of the other wealthy directors or patrons of IBACE, who Hollingshead had let down without notice or apology, possibly having also ripped them off financially.

Perhaps Leary should have heeded this warning but instead he phoned George Litwin in Cambridge to ask his opinion of Hollingshead. Having had time to speak with Hollingshead on his own, Litwin was full of praise for him noting to Leary that although he seemed somewhat mixed up, Hollingshead was interesting and imaginative and his experiences with LSD could teach the Harvard crowd a great deal. Litwin and Leary debated the pros and cons of inviting Hollingshead into Leary's home and social circle, reasoning they had nothing to lose and much to gain from Hollingshead and his LSD experiences.

Neither Hollingshead nor Litwin record anything about the drive to the airport, Leary's flight to New York or of the discussions about Winston London and the possibility that Hollingshead was a con man. Their recollections are that after reading the letter, Leary phoned Hollingshead, arranging for Litwin to bring him first from Brattle Street to Leary's office and then to Leary's Newton Center house.

Whichever recollection is correct, that night Michael Hollingshead moved in to Tim Leary's home in Cambridge, Massachusetts, a decision that would have a massive and far reaching effect on the lives of both men.

Notes

1   Hollingshead, M. *The Man Who Turned On The World*. Blond & Briggs 1973 p.9
2   Beresford. J. *Magic Grams*. Privately published 1985 p.63
3   Hofmann, A. *LSD – My Problem Child*. McGraw-Hill 1980 p.11
4   Hollingshead op. cit. p.13
5   Ibid p.7
6   Ibid p.7
7   Ibid p.14
8   Beresford 1985 op cit p.156
9   Ibid p. 62
10   Metzner, R. Email 24/11/18
11   Dass, R. & Metzner, R. *Birth of a Psychedelic Culture*. Synergetic Press 2010 p.25
12   Hollingshead 1973 op cit p.9
13   Ibid p.9
14   Ibid p.10
15   Ibid p.10

16   Ibid p.11
17   Beresford 1985 op cit p.71
18   Beresford, J. Account given to Peter Stafford during compilation of *Magic Grams*
19   Beresford, R. Email 11/2/14
20   Hunter, R. *The Storming of the Mind*. McClelland and Stewart 1971 p.92
21   Beresford, R. Email 11/2/14
22   Beresford, R. Email 11/2/14
23   Hollingshead 1973 op cit p.9
24   Wilson, R. A. *Cosmic Trigger*. New Falcon 2013 p.6
25   Hollingshead 1973, op cit p.14
26   Ibid p.14
27   Dass, R. & Metzner, R. *Birth of a Psychedelic Culture*. Synergetic Press 2010 p.30
28   Hollingshead 1973 op cit p.18

Meetings With Remarkable Men

LSD is a winner, because generation after generation will take it.[1]

Hollingshead borrowed Leary's car and drove the 430-mile round trip to New York, returning with Sophie and Vanessa. They moved into Leary's spacious third floor attic room, but this arrangement was not destined to last. Each morning Hollingshead left the house telling Leary and Sophie he was looking for work, but Leary suspected he was spending his days drinking in bars or high on LSD in the Boston Museum. Before Leary could confront him Sophie announced she was leaving. Leary was right, Hollingshead hadn't been looking for work but had been pressurising Sophie to obtain money by persuading her father to cash in his saving bonds. Tears trickled down Hollingshead's cheeks as he said his farewells as the taxi taking Sophie and Vanessa disappeared into the night. Leary watched their parting closely and for a moment doubt crossed his mind. Was Hollingshead's display of belated affection and loss genuine or artifice? If the latter, Leary was impressed with Hollingshead's ability to deceive even his closest family members. There were other reasons for Sophie's decision to leave; besides being coerced into obtaining money she felt frozen out of her husband's affections and sexually neglected, writing later, "...if the little lady doesn't get her sex attentions she gets pouty, and yet when I came up to Newton Center...I was totally ignored, not to say banished to the attic."[2] Though they would remain in contact for Vanessa's sake, Michael and Sophie's marriage was over.

With Sophie and Vanessa gone, and still with no source of income, Hollingshead took a job at the Harvard Square Bookstore. Working in a book shop had many advantages for the well-read Hollingshead, including the opportunity to chat to strangers and meet women. Leary remembers he often brought home strange, thin, long haired girls, eventually forming a longer term relationship with a woman he refers to only as Karen (who Ralph Metzner remembers as being called Britta, Hollingshead's on-off girlfriend until 1965). Besides Leary and Hollingshead, the other occupants of Leary's Grant Avenue house were his children Jack and Susan aged 12 and 15, who Hollingshead liked, often playing baseball with them in the nearby Little League Baseball ground. As Hollingshead and Leary got to know each other, Richard Alpert noted that Hollingshead began to act as an "*amanuensis*", helping Leary with his paperwork and general office duties, a role which Leary was happy for Hollingshead to take on.

Leary had heard of LSD long before he met Hollingshead and, though he had not taken it, other psychedelic compounds had made a big impression on him. On holiday in Mexico in August 1960 Leary had eaten seven *Psilocybin cubensis* mushrooms, called by the Aztecs *teonanacatl*, the flesh of the gods. The mushrooms launched him into a universe he was hitherto unaware of, the three-hour trip showing him many other ways of experiencing the world. On psilocybin Leary experienced the world quiver and shimmer with rich colours and saw vividly-hued exotic landscapes, ancient cultures, jewels and serpents and watched as human life returned to the primordial slime. It was a very different experience to that offered by alcohol and he later remarked to his colleague Richard Alpert that he'd learnt more in a few hours under the influence of mushrooms than he had in all his years of psychiatric training.

The psychedelic mushroom experience was pivotal for Leary and on his return to Harvard with Frank Barron he founded the Harvard Psychedelic Project (HPP) to pursue research with psilocybin. This research was fully sanctioned by the Harvard authorities but instead of using the raw fungi Leary procured the drug in pill form from Sandoz Laboratories, where it had been recently synthesised by Albert Hofmann. Sandoz were keen to sponsor Leary's research and sent him the psilocybin free of charge with the proviso that he submit a report of his results. Between taking his first dose of psychedelic mushrooms in August 1960 and meeting Hollingshead in September 1961 Leary expanded and developed the HPP with sessions taking place on a regular basis, turning on many people who would become influential, including Allen Ginsberg, Huston Smith, Arthur Koestler and Jack Kerouac, as well as Harvard colleagues Richard Alpert and Ralph Metzner. In March 1961 Leary began work on the Concord Prison Project, an initiative which involved Leary and other psychedelic drug practitioners taking psilocybin with prisoners, guiding them through the trip in the hope that the experience would emancipate them from their underlying addictions and personality issues. Leary was thrilled with the effects of the drug but completely unaware that psilocybin was an aperitif compared to the potency of Hollingshead's LSD-infused sugar paste.

The details of Leary's first LSD trip, administered and guided by Michael Hollingshead, have been repeated in many histories of psychedelic culture and are rarely questioned. However, an unpublished interview with Tim Leary has cast a minor doubt on the accepted version of events. In an interview with Peter Stafford, author of *The Psychedelics Encyclopedia*, Leary makes the startling claim, "The first

time I took LSD was not with Michael Hollingshead. It was with Alan
Watts on Easter Sunday of 1961."[3] Other than that one interview with
Stafford none of Leary's autobiographies, biographies, or letters allude
to anyone other than Hollingshead giving him his first dose of LSD. Nor
does Watts ever claim he was responsible for Leary's first trip. In a letter
to Leary, written on 27 February 1961, Watts discusses a proposed visit
to Leary in March of that year, "We'll probably drive east this time,
leaving here about March 16th. Expect to be with you the 31st and for
the weekend...I'll probably call you as soon as we hit NYC (about the
27th) and make last minute arrangements".[4] Easter Sunday in 1961 fell
on 26 March, by which time Watts wouldn't have even left New York.
Intriguing and paradoxical as that singular claim of Leary's is, there is
no actual or anecdotal evidence to support it.

Having now inveigled himself into his house, and his confidence,
Hollingshead was keen for Leary to sample LSD from the legendary
mayonnaise jar. Leary, however, was less enthusiastic about this new
drug, having read reports linking LSD to chemical warfare and psychosis.
He believed the mushrooms which had blown his mind in 1960 were
safe in comparison and felt comfortable using them. Moreover, they
were underpinned by centuries old traditions of structured ritual usage,
whereas in 1961 recreational LSD had no culture attached to it. But
Hollingshead was persistent and, one evening in early winter, he invited
Leary to his bedroom and showed him the mayonnaise jar, challenging
him to take it and telling him it contained the secret to understanding
the mysteries of existence. Leary demurred, claiming the effects of
psilocybin mushrooms were enough for him but agreeing he would take
LSD in the near future.

Leary wasn't ready for LSD, but he was happy to share his psilocybin
with Hollingshead, who didn't need much persuading. Because Leary
and colleagues were taking two 20mg psilocybin pills per session
Hollingshead upped the ante and took three, finding the experience
mild and of short duration compared to LSD. He liked how the drug

deepened colours and turned the house into a Persian miniature of exquisite beauty concluding, "The effect was excellent, though not as powerful as LSD...But I enjoyed it and used to take it pretty regularly after that."[5] But even when he took 5 20mg pills, he thought the effect of psilocybin was still nowhere as potent as that of LSD. By his adherence to psilocybin and his refusal to try LSD Hollingshead thought Leary was displaying chemical cowardice and an inability to conceptualise the magnitude of what he was missing. He sarcastically taunted Leary about his use of psilocybin, referring to it as child's toy when compared to the potency LSD. It was only a matter of time before Leary's curiosity would overcome his fears.

That time came in early December 1961 when jazz trumpeter Maynard Ferguson and his wife Flo visited Leary for the weekend, a gig in Boston giving the Fergusons the perfect opportunity to meet their close friend and jazz aficionado. Hollingshead hadn't previously met the Fergusons but found them great company; young and hip with a liking for marijuana he was happy to indulge them in. Fearing arrest and reputational damage for him and Harvard, Leary forbade marijuana smoking in his house, so Hollingshead had to take the Fergusons out for a drive while they got high. Late on the Sunday afternoon as they sat in the glow of the open fire Hollingshead regaled them with hilarious tales of his LSD adventures, noticing the Fergusons' reactions which suggested to him they hadn't tried it. His hunch proved correct – they thought it was a high on a par with marijuana – and when they discovered Hollingshead had some LSD they asked if they could try some.

Hollingshead needed no further encouragement and rushed upstairs, returning with the mayonnaise jar from which he and the Fergusons each ate a teaspoonful of the sugar paste. Leary, who was listening to music and marking university students' coursework, declined. He was too busy, but more than happy for Hollingshead to turn Maynard and Flo on to the drug he was studiously avoiding. While waiting for the

LSD to work its magic Hollingshead flitted about the room, carefully preparing the setting by lighting candles and incense. After thirty minutes Maynard and Flo fell silent as they felt the first sensory tingles, closing their eyes and laying back as the LSD's effects pulsed through them. Leary looked up from his paperwork, noticing the Fergusons had entered a wordless, motionless, trance. Suddenly, Flo sat up, opened her eyes, waved her arms at Leary, grinned and said, "You gotta try this, Tim, baby. It's f-a-n-t-a-s-t-i-c!". Maynard confirmed his wife's experience, "Yeah, really, Tim. It really gets you there – wow – it's really happening, man..."[6] Leary thought Flo's descriptions of what she was experiencing sounded like pure Hindu philosophy but coming from someone who had flunked high school and who had never read a philosophy book in her life. Having seen the Fergusons, now high as a kite, raving about how good LSD was, Leary caved in and asked Hollingshead for a spoonful. Leary's assistant George Litwin was about to leave for home, but when he saw what was happening he also asked for a spoonful. Hollingshead unscrewed the jar and gave them both a spoonful, knowing exactly what was going to happen.

Though only Hollingshead and Leary have ever written at length about Leary's first trip there is a minor anomaly with the date of December 1961, worth noting in view of Leary's odd claim that Alan Watts first gave him LSD. In *Flashbacks*, Leary's 1983 autobiography, he dates his first trip with Hollingshead as 'Spring 1962', which when taken in context with other, verified dates for Leary's movements and activities, is demonstrably wrong.

Leary's first LSD experience took him deep inside himself, deep inside human evolution and back down the world tree of mythology to a central point where he came to rest and merged with the light at the centre of everything. This was no ordinary light, it was a permanent, pulsating flame encompassing all things. From within this all-consuming light he observed the timeless cosmic drama of the multiverse at play, everything that ever existed or would exist emanating from the eye of God he found himself in. Time had no meaning for Leary as his awareness ranged across aeons of cosmic spectacle in which he saw all physical and mental phenomena as an illusion, his life but a theatre performance. He knew whatever he wrote about the experience afterwards wouldn't even come close to describing it. After what seemed like centuries but were just hours, Leary glanced across at Hollingshead who was sitting on the floor, head between his knees. Leary now saw him not as a mortal man but as a sorcerer, a trickster figure responsible for initiating the revelatory experience he was undergoing. As he studied the face of this mysterious arrival in his life Leary knew Hollingshead was in the grip of a higher power, compelled to turn him on to LSD. Leary's lysergic vision of what he saw as Hollingshead's compulsive behaviour was astute. Although he had only known Hollingshead for a few months he had glimpsed a key part of his personality. He had to turn people on, it was his self-conferred mission.

By dawn the LSD's effects were beginning to fade but Leary was still higher than he'd ever been, and sleep was out of the question. He checked on the Fergusons who were still in front of the fire in a post psychedelic daze, finding difficulty coming to terms with being reborn as corporeal beings when just hours earlier they were soaring with the angels. Leary too was feeling bereft, unable to rationalise or reconcile his abrupt return from paradise. Until he realised he was overthinking the experience and the solution was simple; stop trying to force his tired old world view and constricting mental games on the ineffable mystery of being and just go with the flow. The effects and aftermath of that first LSD trip with Michael Hollingshead echoed through the rest of Leary's life. His previous ontological paradigm, already fractured and made shaky by psilocybin, had been completely shattered by the realisation that everything he perceived and had previously thought 'real' was a construct of his own mind.

Leary's behaviour in the days after his first trip gave his colleagues cause for concern. The paradigm shattering experience had left Leary with a fresh regard for Hollingshead. Leary previously thought Hollingshead fascinating and enigmatic, if slightly deviant, but now he was in awe, seeing him as a messenger from God and finding it apt his emissary came in the form of a strange and irascible Englishman. He was, thought Leary, "a raffish sad clown of a god but unmistakably divine."[7] Others who observed Leary and Hollingshead in the wake of the trip noticed Leary was literally following him around like one of Konrad Lorenz's hand-reared goslings which imprinted on him as though he were their mother. Hollingshead also thought Leary became fixated on him, "After the session with Tim where he immediately called me, 'Oh, curandero', which was Mexican for guru, it took me two days to dislodge him, in the sense that he was fixated on that idea." Leary estimated it was seven days before his vision of Hollingshead as a superior being diminished.

Leary claimed he never again took himself seriously after that first trip with Hollingshead and subsequently interpreted all his perceptions as creations of his own consciousness. This idea became one of Leary's central themes; that whether humans realise it or not, they create their own social reality, a metaphor best expressed as 'game theory'. Leary believed psychedelic drugs gave an awareness of these 'games', described by Ralph Metzner as:

> *The game is a sequence of interpersonal social behaviour that has certain rules and rituals and structures and understandings and roles, clearly defined roles by agreement. And then they're subject to change and playing new roles, and it's helpful to be very clear about what games you play. It's the idea of bringing more consciousness to your interpersonal relationships.*[8]

Metzner believed that Leary admired Hollingshead's understanding of this psychedelic game theory, and it's something that his new trickster-guru would develop extensively, though perhaps with less integrity than Leary would have envisioned.

Following this psychedelic initiation, taking LSD became the norm at the Newton Center house, Hollingshead encouraging everyone who visited to turn on. During this time Leary devised a tongue-in-cheek scale of moral reprehension ranging from rascal, to rogue, scoundrel and beyond, and often playfully teased Hollingshead about his place on the scale, bestowing on him the sobriquet 'Divine Rascal', which Hollingshead accepted.

Hollingshead's attitude to taking LSD seemed very different to that of others in Leary's circle. Leary was working toward a structured, almost ritual, approach towards the psychedelic experience, involving the careful calibration of set and setting, whereas Hollingshead was experimental and unstructured. For instance, Hollingshead would take a large daily dose of LSD from the Magic Gram mayonnaise jar, pour himself a glass of whiskey and settle down in front of the TV. This ostensibly 'straight' behaviour puzzled many, including Ralph Metzner. Hollingshead didn't seem to be interested in self-insight or personal growth through LSD and nor did Metzner see any evidence of him using the drug for spiritual experience or development. Quite the reverse; Metzner's observations of Hollingshead suggested he used LSD, "just to freak out, to go as far as possible to the outermost edge of the hitherto experience and beyond and yet stay cool and in control, keep up the game".

This wouldn't be the last time fellow psychonauts commented on Hollingshead's strange LSD behaviour. Metzner again:

I always found Michael's descriptions of his psychedelic experiences baffling. I could not relate to what he was describing. He completely shattered all our assumptions and premises. Instead of following our code of openness, trust, sharing and sincerity, Michael made use of the awesome suggestibility of the LSD state to confuse, bewilder, astound and manipulate awareness and perception.[9]

Hollingshead's techniques and success in manipulating others when on LSD was balanced with his ability to defuse or deflect any negative or unintended consequences of his behaviours. When confronted "he would deny it stoutly and protest his innocence in such a guileless, humorous, friendly manner that it was impossible not to like the man." This too was another manipulation technique: confuse and disorientate people, and if challenged pull the perceptual rug from under them by shrugging it off as a joke, which made those in a psychedelic state feel uncertain, and thus malleable and open to suggestion.

Manipulation is one word for Hollingshead's attempt at controlling people when under the influence of LSD, "mind fucking" was Ralph Metzner's term. "I kept vacillating between being charmed by him, laughing at his outrageous stories and quirky comments, and being spooked by stuff he did."[10] Once, as Metzner was describing a holiday in a tiny Swiss village, Hollingshead insisted he knew the place well. Metzner was incredulous and annoyed at Hollingshead's certainty but Hollingshead wouldn't back down, maintaining he knew the village. When both men had later taken LSD Hollingshead returned to the subject, describing the village in great detail and such was his conviction that Metzner started to doubt himself, and to believe Hollingshead. Suddenly, the stress of this psychedelic battering became too much to bear and Metzner "flipped out", partially losing consciousness. "When I 'came to', he was just sitting there, grinning like the Cheshire Cat. It was like a kind of mental ju-jitsu manoeuvre. But was the point of that?"[11] What indeed? That was Hollingshead's idea of fun; a game he played simply because he could, to demonstrate superiority over Metzner in their heightened psychedelic state. Whether Hollingshead had been to the village or not was immaterial: by being able to convince Metzner that he did actually believe Hollingshead, and so making him doubt his own mind, Hollingshead had 'won' the transaction.

Richard Alpert's opinion of Hollingshead was that he was not a clever man, and from an academic perspective he was correct – Hollingshead hadn't attended university and had no known qualifications. But academics and intellectuals can be easy to fool; their education confers knowledge and certainty, but it can also constrain them into rigid modes of thinking and behaviour that leave them susceptible to more agile, and perhaps less ethical, minds. With his wit, cunning and charm – all underpinned by his ability to function on high doses of LSD – Hollingshead could easily gain many people's trust and confidence, allowing him to exploit loopholes or weaknesses in their personalities.

Alpert, who had not yet taken LSD, thought Hollingshead was a sociopath, believing his influence on Leary's move from psilocybin to LSD was happening too rapidly and would prevent their ambitions to win Nobel Prizes and professorships at Harvard. Metzner took a more benevolent, but no less critical view of Hollingshead, believing him to have had a "tricksterish element, which seems completely amoral" while at the same time displaying, "...insight, fantastic verbal skill, and cleverness".[12] There is a school of thought that believes people who display the qualities and behaviours Hollingshead did were 'crazy wisdom teachers', unconventional individuals who exhibited outrageous, spontaneous and unpredictable behaviour. When it came to Hollingshead, Metzner thought there was "more emphasis on the crazy than on the wisdom".[13]

In early 1962 Leary returned to lecturing, employing Hollingshead on a formal basis, helping him help run sessions at the Concord State Prison. For this and other services Leary paid him $400 a month from January to the end of May, which Hollingshead referred to as his "pocket money", as well as giving him $200 toward his proposed return flight to Britain. Hollingshead was satisfied with this arrangement and gave Leary $200 a month for rent and food at Newton Center. The work wasn't too onerous and there was still plenty time for turning people on to LSD, including heiress Peggy Hitchcock who had a great time, finding Hollingshead very funny and laughing hysterically at him throughout the session. She thought he was a "a truly unique and bizarre human being" and sensed what many others subsequently thought, that "Michael had set himself up as a guru, dispensing LSD to the world. I found him to be ridiculous".[14] Hitchcock didn't believe Hollingshead was malicious, but couldn't trust his judgement because she believed he lacked common sense.

Not everyone felt negative about Hollingshead, however. Al Hubbard visited Leary and Hollingshead at Harvard early in 1962 to discuss their mutual LSD research. Reputed to have introduced over 6000 people to the drug, earning him the nickname The Johnny Appleseed of LSD, Hubbard was a wealthy maverick who, like Leary, believed LSD was a sacrament that could alter the course of humanity. He became heavily involved with the movers and shakers of the early years of recreational LSD use and, like Hollingshead, was also suspected of working for the CIA and other US government agencies. Hubbard was initially impressed with both men, writing to his colleague Myron Stolaroff, "Myron, we've got to have Leary and Hollingshead on our advisory board."[15] Stolaroff demurred, unwilling to sign anyone up to their International Foundation for Advanced Study, without having first met him.[16] When Stolaroff did meet Leary and Hollingshead in the spring of 1962 he had no qualms about inviting Leary to join the group, but refused Hollingshead, writing that he "...never found anything to encourage me to put Hollingshead on."[17]

Hollingshead enjoyed working with Leary at the Concord prison and assisted him with the 'Behaviour Change Program' in which psilocybin was administered to prisoners. Leary hoped the program would prevent or reduce recidivism which in 1962 was running at 70% in Massachusetts prisons. The inmates loved Hollingshead for his mellow insouciance, and his upper-class English act earned him deference from the officials.

Others at Harvard were now taking an interest in psychedelic drugs. PhD student Walter Pahnke designed an experiment to test the theory that they could cause religious experiences using twenty divinity students from the Andover Newton Theological Seminary. Half the group would be given a dose of psilocybin the other half a placebo dose of nicotinic acid, which would cause a mild tingling of the skin but had no psychedelic properties. None of the subjects knew which chemical they were taking but would be supervised by "guides'. After initially opposing the experiment and insulting Pahnke, Leary eventually agreed to assist, providing all the guides took psilocybin and not a placebo.

The location for the experiment was a room at Marsh Chapel on the Boston University campus, the date Good Friday, both location and date chosen to ensure a meaningful setting. Hollingshead is not mentioned as being present by anyone else who has written about the experiment but in his autobiography he claims he was one of the guides, responsible for four divinity students. Thirty minutes after taking their pills Hollingshead realised that all four of his group had been given psilocybin, one of whom ripped the buttons from his jacket and declared himself to be a fish, while another slid to the floor and began to writhe like a snake. The other two students remained still while Hollingshead calmed the fish and serpent down.

There's no doubt Hollingshead was present during these early, formal psychedelic experiments with Leary, yet whatever part he played has been all but expunged from histories and memoirs of that period. Leary only touches upon Hollingshead's presence during the experiments, while his biographers fail to mention Hollingshead's presence at either of them.

Hollingshead's involvement in the Harvard scene included helping Leary, Litwin, Weil and Alpert write an article for the May 1962 edition of *The Bulletin of the Atomic Scientists (TBAS)* titled "The Politics of the Nervous System". This was a riposte to an earlier piece by Dr E. James Lieberman, correcting various fallacies, and was almost certainly the first published defence of the use of LSD for personal, non-academic, consciousness expanding, purposes. The article concluded with a statement which would underpin the future of Leary and Hollingshead's thinking about LSD, though each would interpret and practice it quite differently:

Your brain is your own. Intelligent, open collaboration can expand your mind – with words and with drugs. Only ignorance and misinformation can allow someone else to control it – with their own words or with drugs or with their imaginary fears.[18]

As word of Leary's experiments spread it became common for people to arrive at his office unannounced, to discuss psychedelics or to arrange a psilocybin or LSD session. One of these visitors was Mary Pinchot Meyer, from Washington. She asked Leary if he would teach her how to run an LSD session because she wanted to give the drug to a friend who was a very important and powerful man in public office. Leary was intrigued but Meyer would not reveal his name. She said she got the idea from hearing Allen Ginsberg on the radio, claiming that if Khrushchev and Kennedy could be persuaded to take LSD together the Cold War would end.

Leary agreed that if people in power took LSD they might become more creative and less adversarial in their approach to solving geo-political differences. As their discussion deepened, Leary invited Meyer home for dinner, which was cancelled when Hollingshead served everyone drinks and a low dose of psilocybin. Meyer accepted and before long Hollingshead was his usual entertaining self, making her laugh with tales of the bizarre things he'd experienced while tripping. Leary saw this as Hollingshead putting on a show, using his experiences as parables to show Meyer the powers and pitfalls of psychedelics and how to navigate difficult situations. Under the influence of psilocybin Meyer opened up a little, still not revealing who her friend in high office was but said, "The guys who run things – I mean the guys who *really* run things in Washington are very interested in psychology and drugs in particular"[19] and indicated she wanted to run LSD sessions with her friend to steer him away from thoughts of war and toward peace. The following morning Leary drove Meyer to the airport telling her, perhaps because he was suspicious as to her true motives, that he didn't think she was ready to run LSD sessions. Meyer was disappointed, but it wouldn't be the last Hollingshead and Leary would hear of this enigmatic woman.

Rumours about Leary's psilocybin and LSD use were reaching fever pitch at Harvard and at a meeting on 14 March he was berated for his own drug use and the effect he was having on students. Details of the meeting were made public in the *Harvard Crimson* student newspaper and the *Boston Globe*. Leary's reputation was collapsing around him and his psilocybin experiments were effectively terminated on 6 April when the head of the state drug agency told Leary and Alpert they were forbidden to administer psychedelic drugs to students unless a certified physician was present.

It was clearly time to leave, so Leary, Alpert, Metzner and others took off for the Mexican coastal town of Zihuatanejo, where they intended to start an experimental, LSD fuelled, community loosely based on Aldous Huxley's novel, *Island*. Hollingshead had other ideas. He visited the Cambridge Travel Service on 12 June and booked a flight to Jamaica, paying by cheque and giving Leary's name as a reference. The Travel Agent phoned Leary's secretary who confirmed Hollingshead worked with Leary on the Harvard research project and the ticket purchase went ahead. Three days later Hollingshead and a girlfriend named Karen flew from Boston to Jamaica. Whether it was ever Hollingshead's intention to return to Boston and the Leary circle is unclear, but he wouldn't see Leary, or America, again for almost two years.

Notes

1   Hollingshead, M. in *Sayings of Michael Hollingshead*. *Blotter* no.3 Santa
       Cruz 1979 p.12
2   Letter from S. Hollingshead to V. Hollingshead, 28/1/90
3   Stafford, Peter (ed). *Magic Grams*. Privately published. 1985
4   Watts, J. & Watts, A. *Collected Letters of Alan Watts*. New World Library
       2017 p.400
5   Hollingshead, M. *The Man Who Turned On The World*. Blond & Briggs
       1973. p.20
6   Hollingshead 1973 op cit p.23
7   Leary, T. *Flashbacks*. Tarcher/Putnam. 1990. p.119
8   Metzner, R. Email, 24/11/18
9   Dass, R. & Metzner, M. *Birth of a Psychedelic Culture*, Synergy Press 2010
       p.69
10   Ibid p.70
11   Ibid p.73
12   Ibid p.73
13   Ibid p.73
14   Ibid p.43
15   Forte, R. (Ed). *Timothy Leary: Outside Looking In*. Park Street Press. 1999
       p.285
16   The IFAS was a non profit medical research organisation established
       by Stolaroff in 1960 which ran clinical studies using mescaline and LSD on
       350 participants. It closed in 1965 when the FDA revoked research permits
       for psychedelics.
17   Forte 1999 op cit p.286
18   *The Bulletin of the Atomic Scientists*. 'The Politics of the Nervous System'.
       Vol 18, no. 5, May 1962
19   Leary 1990 op cit p.130

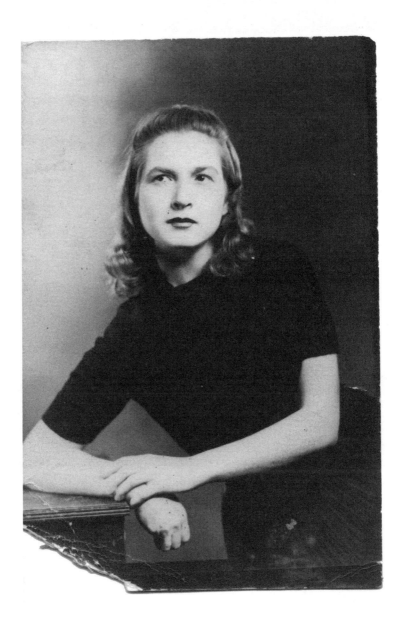

SANDOZ
Pharmaceuticals

DIVISION OF SANDOZ, INCORPORATED

*Executive Offices
and Laboratories*
Hanover, New Jersey

Chicago Offices:
2001 S. Cicero Ave.
Chicago 50, Ill.

*Medical Dept.
West Coast:*
450 Sutter Street
San Francisco 8, Calif.

Sandoz Pharmaceuticals, Laboratories and Offices, Hanover, New Jerse

anticholinergic for sustained relief

14 Monday

Saw Coffus at Heibo.
steinberg 2 cc
given bill for $56 + 4.60 ..

50 pau H - 00047

A Period Of Transition

The regret is not that LSD disturbs or shocks but that it bores.[1]

Hollingshead found Jamaica to be idyllic and a far cry from the psychedelic soaked whirlwind of the Harvard scene. He rented a beach house in the grounds of the Copacabana Club at Seven Miles and relaxed in the sun with Karen his girlfriend, restoring mind and body by swimming, surfing and walking in the jungle. But even an idyll could pall for Hollingshead and after a couple of months he was bored with the heat and landscape and longed for the variety of English weather. While he was in Jamaica The Cambridge Travel Service's Credit Manager wrote to Tim Leary complaining the cheque Hollingshead wrote using Leary as guarantor for his flights had been rejected by the bank. Mr J Everett Finch wanted to know when and how Leary intended to refund the money. Hollingshead must have known his deception would come back to haunt him but had perhaps hoped that Leary would just shrug it off as another of the Divine Rascal idiosyncrasies.

As the summer of 1962 wore on Hollingshead was running low on funds, so he wrote to his friend Eileen Garrett, President of the New York Parapsychology Foundation, asking for financial assistance. Garrett responded immediately, sending him a one-way first-class air ticket to Nice in France with instructions that a chauffeur would meet him at the airport and whisk him to Le Piol, the NY Parapsychology Foundation's HQ. At Le Piol, Hollingshead was wined and dined and spent several days discussing drugs and parapsychology with eminent academics including George Carstairs, Professor of Psychiatry at Edinburgh University. Hollingshead's account of the Harvard-Concord Prison psilocybin experiments impressed Garrett and she gave him $3000 to write a report about the research. Hollingshead used some of this money to fly to London where he joined Karen, who had returned from Jamaica, and they moved into 19a Brompton Square, a basement flat in Kensington. Before they had time to settle in, Hollingshead received a terse letter from Garrett's staff expelling him from the Foundation, explaining that Leary knew nothing about the grant Garrett had given Hollingshead to write about the prison experiments. Leary was annoyed because it was his experiment and he considered Hollingshead writing about it without his permission to be inconsiderate and disrespectful. Hollingshead was furious and wrote a sharp rebuttal to Leary claiming he *had* written to Leary in August asking him to read through his report for Garrett before he sent it to her. Either Leary never received the manuscript or Hollingshead was lying to save face, but the damage was done, and Leary was telling everyone that Hollingshead was a con man, an accusation which clearly hurt Hollingshead. Yes, Hollingshead said, it might *appear* as though he were using the tricks of the con artist to obtain money from people, but that was only how it *looked*. In desperately trying to defend his actions, Hollingshead was actually putting a con man's spin on his activities, telling Leary "However much I enjoy giving, adding, and living this image, it is not actually true"[2] and pointing out that because he lived like a "gangster" he wasn't surprised that people thought he was a con man, but in reality he had never conned anyone in the criminal sense of the term. Hollingshead was being disingenuous: at the very least using Leary as unwitting guarantor for a cheque he knew would bounce was not only a crime but a sneaky betrayal of his friendship with Leary and his generosity of spirit.

Hollingshead had been caught out and he didn't like it; the last thing he wanted was a rift with Leary, which would affect his chances of a return to Leary's research group and the opportunities that afforded. In a final attempt to turn the situation to his advantage and make amends Hollingshead finished his letter to Leary, tempering his anger with an attempt at redemption by claiming paradoxically that he was, "Not perhaps good as opposed to being bad, but a sort of goodness which encompasses good and bad at the same time".[3] Another series of house moves took place, though what prompted them is unknown, and by 20 November Hollingshead was living in Chiswick, west London from where he sent Leary a postcard. Ostensibly giving him his new address, Hollingshead was actually testing Leary's friendship by making small talk, asking how Leary's children were and letting him know he hoped soon to appear on the BBC, talking about winter holidays in Scandinavia. Just days later Hollingshead moved again, this time retreating to a large rambling house deep in the Sussex countryside at Pinefield near Battle. In the tranquillity of the early winter landscape he wrote some autobiographical material and poetry, as well as several plaintive letters to Leary. In these he tried to rekindle their friendship, waxing conversationally and eloquently about traditional aspects of the English countryside like churches, cricket and pubs. He was even bold enough to suggest Leary should completely forget the air ticket fraud and the Garrett incident, or if he couldn't do that then he might at least perhaps reframe those cons as a "spiritual exercise". Instead of raging against Leary, Hollingshead changed tack and ranted about Garrett's Parapsychological Foundation, likening their staff to the

Biblical antiheroes, Moloch and Mammon, Belial and Beelzebub, all managed by Satan himself. Leary chose not to respond.

The move from the hustle and bustle of Harvard's psychedelic community to the relative quiet of London and Sussex must have left Hollingshead feeling isolated and insignificant; the scientific and recreational use of psychedelics in Britain during the early 1960s being minimal compared to America. Whether or not others did, Hollingshead saw himself as a key player in the burgeoning psychedelic movement and realised that returning to America was the quickest way to revive his status and his friendship with Leary. It wasn't going to be easy. In the wake of the plane ticket and Garrett scams, word of Hollingshead's deceptions had spread. Al Hubbard, who had nothing but good words to say about Hollingshead in 1962, was writing to Humphry Osmond in February 1963 that Hollingshead was "thoroughly dishonest and a most convincing liar".[4] Though Hollingshead was unaware of the smears on his character, he was aware that it would be an uphill struggle to regain Leary's confidence and decided that reuniting with John Beresford was the best place to start. After a brief visit to Denmark to visit his first wife Ebba and their son Timothy, Hollingshead flew to New York in April 1963.

In his autobiography Hollingshead notes that one reason for his return to America was to set up a foundation for "mind research" called The Agora Scientific Trust, but Agora had already been in operation for several months by the time Hollingshead returned to New York and there is no evidence that he was involved in the planning stages. It was Beresford's idea in 1962 to form a group of professionals and lay people who had knowledge of psychedelic drugs and psychology. An initial donation of $100 from the publisher of the Julian Press led to Beresford instigating a six-month pilot study in 1962 under the name of the Indole Research Group. Nine people are listed as being involved, but Hollingshead is not one of them. In early 1963, following a donation of $1000 from Richard Alpert, Beresford changed the name to

The Agora Scientific Trust, Agora being Greek for a meeting or market place. Using his remaining portion of the Magic Gram, he intended to run psychedelic sessions in controlled and consistent circumstances, calibrating the results of one session against another, a variation on Leary's principle of 'setting'.

How Hollingshead became deeply involved with Agora so quickly is lost from memory, but Beresford told his partner in later life, Virginia Blyth, that he just appeared and imposed himself on them. Beresford invited PhD student Michael Corner and psychologist Jean Houston to join, and over time other psychologists and 'research affiliates' were added to the group; some of these were unusual, for instance Victor Lownes, Promotions Manager for the *Playboy* empire, who was their 'Tantric Advisor'. Agora needed an office base and in January 1963, through the benevolence of Nassau millionaire Howard Teague, Beresford acquired a flat on New York's 40 East 81st Street, comprising three rooms and a garden. The room overlooking the garden was designated as the psychedelic session room, decorated with six-inch pile Swedish rugs on the floor and colourful mandalas on the walls and ceiling. A sophisticated hi-fi with tape deck and speakers was installed as well as a strobe light, a machine that produced low frequency sound and a 'synchrotron', which alternated sound from left to right ear. The combination of these devices and the décor at Agora provided an optimum setting for psychedelic sessions where, although LSD was the primary drug used for experimentation, psilocybin and DMT were also available.

Once installed in the Agora headquarters, "Beresford's attitude was to give LSD to anyone who came to the Trust who wanted it – 'Because, there again, I didn't want to exercise any control over who might or might not have it'",[5] the only condition being that the experimenter remain at Agora until Beresford was sure they were sober enough to leave. Neither Beresford nor Houston wrote much about Agora, but Hollingshead's autobiography devotes several pages to it. He claims to have assisted Jean Houston with setting up, and writing about the psychedelic drug sessions, resulting in papers such as 'Experiments in Thought Acceleration using Psilocybin' and 'Multicentricity and Incongruity; Epistemological Significance of Recent Findings in Research Using LSD-25'.

The Agora team administered LSD and other psychedelics to several hundred people during their almost two-year existence, including a US Naval Captain, painters and a Yogi. The results of these sessions were varied and vague however and often bordered on the subjective. For instance, the Captain, who worked for the Navy's Research Department, claimed he'd solved a complex mathematical problem in his work on artificial intelligence, and the Yogi believed after just one LSD session he had jumped several stages in yogic development. Follow up contacts revealed the Captain had invented a mechanical device, but it was unclear whether it was directly connected to the insights LSD gave him, or indeed how the Yogi could demonstrate whether he had actually advanced in his training. These kinds of inconsistent results may be why Beresford decided not to publish the results of the Agora experiments. Years later he claimed that the book by Jean Houston and Robert Masters, *The Varieties of Psychedelic Experience*, written after they had left Agora, was based entirely on experiments conducted there. Although Masters and Houston's book does not mention Agora, or Beresford, it is likely Beresford's claim is, to a degree, correct.

Jean Houston, who was invited to join the Agora team because of her "familiarity with mythic and symbolic structures which regularly occurred during psychedelic sessions", wasn't impressed with Hollingshead from her first meeting, "catching on right away, although I was only around 22 or 23 at the time, that this was a character to be avoided". Houston saw through Hollingshead's faux upper-class English accent and demeanour and doubted his claims of connections with people in high places. He was, she thought, "a scam artist of the highest order,' adding she "did not find that he had anything useful to add to the research, money seemed to be his only interest." Houston left Agora within a year, believing those involved were not as serious as they had claimed.[6] Though Houston believed Hollingshead was a con man she admired aspects of his personality, summing him up with, "Michael was a master rascal of the first order and a tragic man at the same time. Such a waste of a fine mind."[7]

Beresford didn't really want Hollingshead to be involved in Agora, finding him overbearing but useful for tasks such as fundraising. But he slowly took over the Agora offices, Beresford remembering he "decided to make the office his sleeping quarters. From that time, I no longer had two rooms to work in. I had only one, because wherever he went he left an awful mess and the back room became virtually unusable. At the same time, I couldn't afford to have any kind of sheriff called in to remove him because there were so many drugs around. So, he became part of the scene. He was not asked to be and was never welcomed as being".[8] This wouldn't be the last time Hollingshead physically imposed himself on someone who believed they were his friend.

Once ensconced and unchallenged in Agora – the Trust's letterheads referred to him as 'Associate Director' – Hollingshead began to make himself known and to network with those people in New York he believed to be useful or influential. Roy Pusey, President of Harvard University's Dept. Of Social Relations, wrote to Hollingshead, congratulating him on a recent talk he'd given about psychedelics and inviting him to speak as part of their 'The Future of Man' lecture series. Pusey was impressed by Hollingshead's focus on how psychedelics could play a part in evolutionary sociology, referring to him as a pioneer researcher. He was also sending information to Frank Barron, suggesting people who might be persuaded to donate money to support psychedelic causes, a list that included doctors, judges, his old heroin addict friend, Desmond O'Brien and even one of the teachers from Red Hill School!

Hollingshead persisted in trying to repair his relationship with Tim Leary, continuing his letter writing campaign and sending him research documents he thought he might find interesting. One enclosure, 'Certain Aspects of the Phenomenology of Dimethyltryptamine', was a study Beresford conducted with DMT, research into which was in its infancy at that time. Leary wrote to Beresford, congratulating him on the paper and commenting, "I think about you and Michael often and hope that everything is going well."[9] Leary, who did not hold grudges for long, was softening.

Criticisms that Hollingshead was overly concerned with money might have been true, but he was an effective fund raiser, even if there were suspicions that it was done as much out of self-interest as for philanthropic reasons. He had been instrumental in getting the Society for the Scientific Study of Religion to fund a two-day conference, in October 1963 which included a day of discussion called 'The Application of LSD-25 to New Areas of Psychology', to be held at the Harvard Divinity School. The speakers were to be John Beresford, Jean Houston and Michael Hollingshead, whose talk was the ironically-titled 'Moral Issues in Long Term Behaviour Change'. Hollingshead wrote numerous letters to people he knew, or thought he knew, hitting them up for donations which were, ostensibly at least, for The Agora Scientific Trust. His charm worked on some but not on others. In an exchange of letters with author Bob Friedman, Hollingshead accused him of being 'stiff' in his approach to Agora, suggesting Friedman had no interest in donating. Friedman's terse response suggested he had seen through Hollingshead's schtick, remarking "I barely know John Beresford, and I don't know you...With me, I have felt you are dealing only with a distraction: 'a rich man'".[10]

Beresford's 'no-intervention' principle didn't allow him to throw Hollingshead out of Agora, but in late 1963 or early 1964, Hollingshead himself decided he was leaving. His explanation, couched in dense prose, described how it had emotionally exhausted him, the "Agora experiment was achieved at the cost of 'real' emotional contacts with other people, including at times, ourselves" and entertained the disingenuous emotional whimsy that "Perhaps it was all an elaborate form of 'self-therapy' during the tormenting time after the collapse of my marriage in 1960 and plans to reconcile with my wife and the consequent loss of my daughter…" His experiential knowledge that psychedelics rarely reveal their secrets in experimental conditions led to the insight that "…the somber doctors, scientists, technicians point only to the rigour of their particular method". Time for another change.[11]

December 1963 found Hollingshead writing from 40 East 84th Street, with a letterhead of The Excelsior Scientific Trust. The address was a fifteen minute drive from the Agora HQ and the name, Excelsior Scientific Trust (EST) almost sounds like a parody of The Agora Scientific Trust. No information exists about what the EST was, if indeed it was anything other than a Hollingshead invention to give the impression of scientific research. In his autobiography Hollingshead confusingly jumps straight from his time with Agora to moving to Millbrook mansion, leaving a gap of several months in which his activities and location are vague. Such omissions often mask time periods when he was involved in initiatives that either failed or were stepping stones between one psychedelic scene and another. As 1963 ended Hollingshead began to develop plans for an exhibit at the forthcoming World's Fair, a massive event, occupying half of Flushing Meadows Park in the New York borough of Queens and showcasing mid-20th-century American culture and technology. Hollingshead's idea for the event, to be held over two six-month periods in 1964 and 1965, was for an installation which would reflect the psychedelic experience. He thought that if he engaged the services of a professional designer he could create a huge brain-like edifice which sparkled, called 'The Pavilion of the Mind'. His plans ultimately came to nothing, one of many bold and innovative, but ultimately failed, projects.

Discussing the World's Fair in his book *Tomorrow-Land*, Joseph Tirella wrote, "Michael Hollingshead, Leary's onetime associate, tried in vain to organize a Pavilion of the Mind Exhibit at the World's Fair. He wanted to use "light, sound, color and technical innovations" to create what he called 'an exhibit both contemporary and exciting...among the many tens of millions who are expected to visit the fair.' (World's Fair executives were unimpressed with his idea.)"[12] The sentence in parenthesis may refer to one of the key organisers of the event, *Time* magazine founder Henry Luce who, with his wife Clare Boothe Luce, was an LSD aficionado who favoured keeping the drug from the general populace and adopting, as did Aldous Huxley, an elitist approach to its distribution.

In April 1964 the Agora Scientific Trust came to an end, because Beresford believed he was under surveillance by the US government, presumably the FBI. Writing to Humphry Osmond, Beresford claimed, "The actions of the American Government subtracted from one's peace of mind – several of what I considered brilliant sessions were listened to in toto by a surely puzzled band of snoopers connected with my office by a bug which I actually witnessed being installed into the telephone but which (according to the principle I practised of absolute non-interference with the progression of my work) I took no action to prevent; and for several months a team of cars was assigned to the task of following me wherever I went, to say nothing of attempts made to entrap me into selling as opposed to administering on the premises."[13]

Initially Beresford was puzzled as to who initiated this surveillance, and why, but concluded, "Much of the surveillance, I have subsequently realised, was instigated or at least provoked by the activities of Michael Shinkfield, the surname used by Michael before he had it changed by writ to Hollingshead."[14] No further explanation is given, but it is clear Beresford held this belief strongly, adding he believed Hollingshead had used his name on several occasions, for profit or gain, without his knowledge. In his autobiography Hollingshead innocently notes that one of the pieces of technology installed by him in Agora's front office was a miniature FBI-type wire recorder which, if Beresford is to be believed, was used for more than recording telephone calls to the Agora office.

On the move again, culturally as well as geographically, Hollingshead struck up a correspondence with Alex Trocchi about his new initiative, The Sigma Project. In 'sigma: A Tactical Blueprint' Trocchi expounded and explored the idea at length. Trocchi believed "a change, which might be usefully regarded as evolutionary, has been taking place in the minds of men; they have been becoming aware of the implications of self-consciousness".[15] In his thoughts about Sigma, Trocchi was presaging the cultural revolution of the 1960s to which he himself would become a contributor. He envisioned Sigma as a mechanism by which people could become aware of others who thought or created in a similar way. For example, he saw frequent small press publications as a new and vibrant way of distributing new ideas about art, literature, spirituality and lifestyle and encouraging like-minded people to feel less isolated and come together to work towards building a new society.

The name Sigma – an ancient Greek letter, in modern mathematics denoting 'the sum' – was chosen because Trocchi wanted total involvement from everyone. He was keen for people from the burgeoning LSD culture to become involved, seeing psychedelics as a catalyst for the radical cultural and social changes he hoped for. Hollingshead's connections would be invaluable in helping bring together a catalogue of "...writers, painters, sculptors, musicians, dancers, physicists, bio-chemists, philosophers, neurologists, engineers, and whatnots of every race and nationality."[16] Hollingshead was happy to be involved in yet another cultural scene that he could contribute to, and benefit from, in several ways. But in 1964, Sigma was still very much in its conceptual stage, largely existing only in Trocchi's imagination and the handful of statements he issued to interested parties.

Hollingshead would become more involved with Sigma in 1965, but for now, having extricated himself from Agora, he spent the summer and early autumn of 1964 in the wilderness, before stumbling "...out of my dark existential forest into the daylight honesty of Millbrook."[17]

Notes

1   Letter from Hollingshead to Leary, 20/1/64

2   Letter from Hollingshead to Leary, 1/11/62

3   Ibid

4   https://erowid.org/culture/characters/stolaroff_myron/stolaroff_myron_
        article1.shtml

5   Stafford, P. (ed). *Magic Grams*. privately published 1985 p.68

6   Houston, J. Email 27/12/06

7   Houston, J. Email 26/12/06

8   Stafford, 1985 op cit p.71

9   Letter to Beresford from Leary, 29/8/62

10   Letter from B. Friedman to Hollingshead 19/12/63

11   Hollingshead, M. *The Man Who Turned On The World*. Blond & Briggs,
        1973 pp.97-98

12   Tirella, J. *Tomorrow–Land*. Lyons Press. 2015 p.251

13   Letter from J. Beresford to Humphry Osmond 22/8/73

14   Ibid

15   Trocchi, A. 'sigma: A Tactical Blueprint'. *City Lights Journal* no.4 1964

16   Ibid

17   Hollingshead 1973 op cit p.98

Michael   Tim   Mary Shinkfield

Mallorca 1961

Millbrook: Far Out Or Sell Out?

Memoirs of Millbrook are rarely coherent.[1]

Millbrook mansion is the most fabled address in the history of psychedelic drugs, described by Tim Leary's friend Nina Graboi as, "a cross between a country club, a madhouse, a research institute, a monastery and a Fellini movie set."[2] When Hollingshead heard of Leary's latest venture he knew it was his next destination commenting, "although the world of Millbrook may seem nonsensical by rational standards, to the outside world it was merely another way of saying reason is not enough."[3]

Leary's International Foundation for Internal Freedom (IFIF) had lasted only a few months before being asked to leave its base in Zihuatanejo, Mexico and urgently needed a new location in which to pursue its psychedelic evangelism. William Hitchcock, brother of Leary's friend Peggy, offered Leary the sixty-four-room mansion, close to the town of Millbrook and a couple of hours by road from New York, for a peppercorn rent. Leary was impressed by the mansion with its Baroque spires and surrounding 2500 acre wooded country estate, and knew it was the ideal location for the next stage of his psychedelic explorations.

Leary and colleagues moved to Millbrook in September 1963 and IFIF was rebranded as the Castalia Foundation. The name Castalia was taken from Hermann Hesse's novel *The Glass Bead Game* in which a monastic society of elite intellectual mystics played complex philosophic games via the Bead Game, "a device which comprises the complete contents and values of our culture" which, outlined Leary and Metzner in *The Psychedelic Review*, appeared analogous to their understanding of the psychedelic experience: "groups which attempt to apply psychedelic experiences to social living will find in the story of Castalia all the features and problems which such attempts invariably encounter."[4] Leary and Metzner saw the fictional Castalia as a blueprint for their vision of what was possible via the agency of LSD.

Having made his peace with Leary over the misappropriated money from Eileen Garrett, Hollingshead moved to Millbrook in December 1964. Extricating himself from the Agora Trust and moving to Millbrook had taken the best part of a year and diverted Hollingshead from his prolific correspondences with friends in England. He had remained busy, however, appearing on radio programmes extolling the virtues of the Sigma project, LSD and marijuana and giving poetry readings at Cafe Le Metro on New York's Lower East Side, a haunt of beat poets Allen Ginsberg and Gregory Corso. Once at Millbrook he wrote to Alex Trocchi, apologising for the lack of communication, adding that he was now getting high and having great fun.

Neither Hollingshead, Leary nor anyone else has explained why Hollingshead came to be at Millbrook, or what his role there was. Based on how he inveigled himself into other scenes the best guess is that he saw an opportunity to be part of a significant psychedelic initiative and used his charisma and charm to seize it. Despite their often turbulent friendship Leary respected Hollingshead and found him useful to have around, at least for a while. Hollingshead's surreal sense of humour and faux upper-class Englishness, together with his ability to guide people through the wildest geographies of the LSD experience, bestowed on him the persona of a psychedelic court jester, a role highly valued by Leary.

On 12 December 1964 Leary married Nena von Schlebrugge, a model he met and fell in love with at Millbrook's 4 July Thanksgiving party. The wedding took place in Millbrook village at the Episcopal Grace Chapel. Leary, his best man and close associates wore formal wedding attire while the 150 guests dressed in colourful hippie finery. The wedding was filmed by D.A. Pennebaker, later to attain cult status as cameraman on Dylan's *Don't Look Back*, *Monterey Pop* and *Ziggy Stardust and the Spiders from Mars;* the fourteen-minute black and white film was later released as *Nobody Loves You Til Somebody Loves You*. Though Hollingshead doesn't appear in the film he is acknowledged off camera by Leary with a "Hi Mike", and Britta (surname unknown, previously referred to by Hollingshead as 'Karen'), Hollingshead's girlfriend of the time, is briefly glimpsed. A Swedish style buffet at Millbrook mansion followed the wedding, after which the newly-weds left for their honeymoon in India, joining Ralph Metzner. According to Hollingshead, the guests were all high on LSD and marijuana for the ceremony and the party, fuelled by LSD dosed punch, continued until dawn the following day.

Leary's wedding marked a turning point for the Millbrook community, which suddenly found itself without its leader. In Leary's absence, Millbrook split into two groups, each with their own ethos. One group consisted of those on the periphery of heavy psychedelic drug use. The other was comprised of the hard-core acid heads, including Hollingshead, Alpert, and various hedonistic visitors. According to Alan Eager "It seemed like all the other people there were unwilling participants. They wanted to be at Millbrook, but they didn't seem to want to play the game." By this he meant they didn't want to take

LSD, and when a batch of LSD arrived gave excuses not to take it. "They were claiming anything not to take LSD. Macrobiotics... and Gurdjieff."[5] While they were honeymooning in India, Hollingshead sent Leary regular tape-recorded Millbrook updates, a mixture of mundane news about Leary's children juxtaposed with accounts of interesting LSD sessions and wild nights out at events such as Salvador Dali's birthday party. These tapes served another purpose; Hollingshead used them to conceal LSD, ensuing Leary and his bride didn't run out of essential supplies.

Hollingshead was also keen to maintain his contact with Trocchi, and in January 1965 sent him a long letter, its language, content and sentence construction suggesting it was written while on acid. In it Hollingshead suggested that when he returned to Britain, Sigma, in conjunction with the Castalians, should stage an event at the Traverse Theatre during the Edinburgh Festival. This proposed 'Experiential Theatre' would attempt to replicate the psychedelic experience through sound and vision, as the aborted World's Fair exhibit had intended. Hollingshead and Trocchi corresponded about the venture during the Spring of 1965 and, although the idea faltered, it prefigured similar multi-media events Hollingshead was involved with at Millbrook and in New York, while in 1972 Edinburgh would be the location of Hollingshead's successful multi-media event 'Changes 72'. Trocchi expressed his frustration at how slowly things moved in England and how hard it was to get Sigma funded and publicised. Acknowledging Hollingshead's drive and ability to make things happen he wrote he "could use your personal collaboration...we need a sight more energy over here in England. I think it must have died out with the Plantagenets or something." In the same correspondence, Hollingshead mooted the possibility of setting up a London centre based on Leary's Castalian model, "Let's continue to explore possibilities still lacking in London. There is Victor Lownes, Desmond O'Brien, the people you know..."[6]

Structured group LSD trips were a key feature of the Millbrook calendar, with one of the participants designated as guide and responsible for the lights, the music, the taped readings and the general wellbeing of the group. These sessions were often themed, like the one guided by Richard Alpert in which everyone took a vow of silence while they concentrated on Alpert reading texts written by Indian mystic Meher Baba. After three hours, the participants who had taken 800mg of LSD, moved on to gazing into hand mirrors, watching their reflections melt into kaleidoscopic patterns, devils or former and future selves. Such an exercise can be terrifying but as Hollingshead noted it is possible to re-frame the images as mandalas and transcend them to attain Nirvana, the Buddhist state of absolute bliss. As the group descended from the psychedelic heights they worked on who they wanted to be in their re-born state, Alpert leading them on a silent sensory walk in the Millbrook woods before returning to the mansion for a simple meal of rice, wine and cheese, eventually breaking their silence.

These semi-structured trips contrasted with the behavioural exercises of Armenian mystic philosopher George Gurdjieff who designed a set of techniques, known as the 'Fourth Way', to focus attention on the moment. At Millbrook a bell rang several times during the day, the signal for everyone to stop what they were doing and answer questions on a 'Self Remembering Score Card' split into 'External' and 'Consciousness'. These headings were sub divided into the person's location, what they were doing and specifically what 'game' they were playing in both the External and Consciousness components of the exercise. Hollingshead's Score Card for 2 June describes a typical day at Millbrook for him, including references to moving furniture, gardening, reading, chatting with Leary and others and smoking marijuana.

Several counter cultural figures visited Millbrook hoping for a guided LSD session with Leary, unaware he was absent. Art Kleps, who founded the surrealist psychedelic promoting Neo-American Church was one such pilgrim. Disappointed not to find Leary in residence, Kleps was talking to Ralph Metzner and Leary's daughter Susan in the kitchen when,

"…a man with unreadable features, dressed in slacks, a sports coat and a fedora with a ribbon of photographs around the brim, came twirling into the room…as the apparition spun around the table muttering to himself, Ralph's eyes narrowed, and Susan took a deep breath and held it. He acted as though he wanted to sit down on one of the empty chairs but couldn't figure out how to do it. I pulled one out for him, which seemed to piss him off. He moved his arms angrily and sputtered. Still twirling, he moved out of the room. Susan exhaled. 'What the fuck?', I asked. 'Michael Hollingshead', Ralph said, poker faced as usual."[7]

Metzner took Kleps to one side and advised him not to take LSD when Leary was away because Millbrook had become such a crazy scene. Kleps decided to stay for a few days to observe the psychedelic circus and that night called into the Bowling Alley to find Hollingshead, still twirling, telling a rambling story about going to the Amazon to interact with alligators. Kleps was unimpressed and retired to a bedroom to talk to a female from New York, reflecting that without Leary at the helm, Millbrook was in a downward spiral. When he woke, Kleps noticed a glass of brandy that had not been there the night before and presumed it had been left by the woman he had been talking to. A seasoned drinker Kleps welcomed this liquid breakfast and drank it in one gulp, before brushing his teeth. He had barely returned to the bedroom when he realised he had been dosed with a massive amount of LSD by Metzner, and probably Hollingshead.[8]

Another notable visitor was Paul Krassner, editor of the satirical magazine *The Realist*. Relishing the opportunity to act as a guide, Hollingshead immediately volunteered his services and, having dosed Krassner with liquid LSD, led him through a spectacular psychedelic experience. Krassner claimed he could only cope with the intensity of the trip, in which he laughed so much he vomited, because of his trust in Hollingshead. Whatever else people thought about him, Hollingshead was considered an experienced LSD guide, in control and able to navigate any psychedelic storm.

During Leary's absence several new people arrived at Millbrook, some of whom were influential in the public 'Psychedelic Theatre' events staged in Spring of 1965. The first of these celebrations of the psychedelic experience took place on 5 April at the Village Vanguard in New York City's Greenwich Village, where Alpert, Metzner and Hollingshead were joined on stage by British ex-patriate philosopher and LSD advocate Alan Watts. Hollingshead introduced the evening:

Our purpose in being here is to expand our awareness. To assimilate and to see aspects of the psychedelic consciousness. To observe the phenomena of inner space. This is the Magic Theatre. By magic we mean the phenomena of inner space through which we pass most of our time asleep. Tonight, we shall be mixing auditory and visual phenomena. The brain is capable of processing all this data. It will see different images moving in random/planned fashion. Sound tracks, some of which have been cut up, will be heard. Films and light will perform. All you have to do is focus on one point. And then you will see the rest. Diversity will be unity. But do not try to understand. The brain will do all that later. Here you will have 10,000 visions. So, sit back and relax. Extend yourself to an aesthetic distance. You may have the opportunity of leaving your body. Leaving your mind. You are going on a voyage. The price of admission is your mind. For if you attempt to analyse and conceptualise you will cheat yourself of the opportunity to see things in a fresh manner.[9]

He followed his introduction with a reading of the enigmatic, scene setting Sutra 21 from the *Tao Te Ching* after which the evening's entertainments began. *The New York Times* gave the show a favourable review and similar events were staged over the following weeks at other New York venues, with more planned for the summer. With Leary still away the rift between those who wanted to stay high all the time and those favouring a sober life, deepened. Hollingshead, Alpert and others sequestered themselves in the Bowling Alley which doubled as the meditation room and for three weeks took 400ug of LSD every four hours with the ethos of "How much can we take? How high can we go? How long can we stay high for?" The intrepid psychonauts were disappointed to find that the human body quickly builds a tolerance to LSD and by the end of the experiment had abandoned measured doses and were drinking LSD straight from the bottle, unable to get any higher.

By early June, Leary had returned from India, his marriage to Nena having already disintegrated. He was dismayed to find Millbrook, once "a community of scholars and scientists," now reduced to "a playground for rowdy omnisexuals"[10] and the atmosphere tense, like an unexploded bomb. Hollingshead seemed even more wayward than usual and had taken to parading round Millbrook dressed in a scarlet cape and a Scottish kilt, dispensing his unique brand of psychedelic wisdom to anyone who would listen and many who didn't want to. Castalia was in chaos and everyone, including Hollingshead, had their hopes pinned on Leary sorting out the mess and returning Millbrook to its former equilibrium. In order to understand what was going on in his own life and the scene at Millbrook, Leary took 1000ug of LSD and retreated to the meditation house to think. He considered this session to be the wildest yet and concluded that his malaise was due to him "picking up on all the vibrations of the house". Although a veteran of several hundred high dose LSD sessions, Leary was experiencing new levels of awareness on LSD and finding it impossible to make sense of what was going on. "I was fascinated by the magic…and the power of magic and the reality of magic…There were things going on that I didn't understand." Hollingshead's influence was clearly strong, Leary noting, "And I saw a lot of black magic in it too. Particularly through Michael." This wouldn't be the last time Hollingshead's influence and behaviour would be linked to 'black magic'.[11]

Soon after Leary's return, Richard Alpert left Millbrook for France and India while Leary and Nena's relationship struggled on for a few weeks before finally collapsing. Still depressed and unable to decide on the way forward, and now missing female company, his thoughts turned to Mary Pinchot-Meyer, the enigmatic woman from Washington with whom he and Hollingshead had enjoyed a psilocybin session at Harvard in 1962. Leary hadn't heard from her in for over a year and was shocked to discover she had died the previous autumn. He shared his grief with Hollingshead who, to divert him, suggested they started work on putting together a 'new game', a sound and light installation like that used in the group LSD sessions at Millbrook, but one which they could stage in theatres for a paying audience. Leary liked Hollingshead's description of it as Neurological Art, a multi-disciplinary event designed to evoke a psychedelic experience in those who witnessed it. They decided to go to New York City immediately to speak to sound and light artists who they believed could put such a show together. There was another reason for their road trip, to discover the truth about what had happened to Meyer.

In New York City, Leary's friend Van Wolf used his media contacts to obtain a file of newspaper clippings about Meyer's death which revealed that she had been shot dead on the Georgetown canal tow path in October 1964. The press reports named Meyer's friends and social circle, and from this it was evident to Leary and Hollingshead that the 'very important man' she was hoping to administer LSD to for the good of America's future had been President John Fitzgerald Kennedy. Van Wolf immediately wanted to commission Hollingshead to write a book about Meyer's murder and her plans to turn JFK onto LSD. Hollingshead was keen but the idea came to nothing, Van Wolf claiming he had been warned off via a criminal lawyer friend who intimated that dark forces did not wish the full story to be made public.

Hollingshead and Leary put the Meyer murder behind them and set about organising the Psychedelic Exploration theatre events. Billy Hitchcock loaned them the New Theatre and the first show was staged on

14 June. Although Leary is clear in his autobiography that Hollingshead was key to these events, in 2018 Ralph Metzner claimed this was not the case, writing "No, he was absolutely not involved at all."[12] Disputes about who was involved notwithstanding, the Psychedelic Exploration events continued to spread the message and generated much needed income to ensure Millbrook's financially viability. The advertising hand-out for the events began:

The Psychedelic Theatre is a new venture in direct, non-verbal communication of states of altered consciousness...Through the use of multi-channel, mixed media presentations, involving slides, films, tapes, stroboscopes, kinetic sculptures etc.; a complete re-structuring of the sensory input is possible, permitting the systematic alteration of the usual modes of memory.[13]

These events were essentially the Happenings of the early sixties retooled as psychedelic soirees, the audience comprising a mixture of veteran trippers, those who had transcended acid and those who were yet to take it. Hollingshead wrote, "I felt satisfied with our work in New York developing the Psychedelic Theatre. Americans, the sensitive ones, were responding to the wonderful implications of LSD."[14]

There were other, far less wonderful implications of LSD at Millbrook. Hollingshead remembers LSD was left out everywhere; acid infused sugar cubes were left in bowls for anyone to take and in liquid form the drug was often kept in bottles of alcohol. For the denizens of Millbrook, most of whom had taken LSD hundreds of times, this was not a problem. For the unwitting, such as the TV crew chief who drank from a bottle of dosed port and had to be talked down from a terrifying trip, it was a completely different matter. Perhaps the most serious example of the dangers of leaving powerful psychedelics in the open came in June 1965, when Hollingshead's daughter Vanessa, now almost five years old, came to stay at Millbrook. "Women", Hollingshead wrote to Trocchi, "are a distraction too, including my own daughter, who is presently staying with me: a precocious four-year-old, trusting, loving and bright, like all American kids."[15]

Vanessa was left to her own devices at Millbrook, playing alone in the woods and mansion which she remembers as huge and cold with everyone in their own world, presumably because they were high most of the time. Though Vanessa was free to dress how she chose, play freely and eat and drink whatever and whenever she liked, she felt none of the warmth the people she lived with in New York gave her. Other children sometimes stayed with their parents at Millbrook, and Vanessa often played on the trampoline with a boy called Alex. Vanessa was fond of anything sweet and as she rushed out of the mansion to join Alex on the trampoline one day she grabbed a sugar cube from a bowl. Soon, everything seemed to be in slow motion and Vanessa tried to get off the trampoline. But when she looked down, she was transfixed with horror at the sight of "millions of fluorescent worms, squiggling on the ground. There were bright pink, purple, green and blue, they looked like huge earthworms. There were so many they covered up the entire grounds of Millbrook."[16] Vanessa had unwittingly eaten an acid laced sugar cube, giving her the dubious distinction of being the youngest person ever to have taken LSD.

Terrified and unaware what was happening to her, Vanessa screamed for help. Britta, Hollingshead's girlfriend, heard the screams and carried her into the mansion. Nothing had prepared Hollingshead or Leary for this kind of psychedelic emergency and neither knew what to do with Vanessa, who was now hallucinating strongly. Hollingshead was frightened and tried to calm Vanessa by driving her round in his car as she described the trees turning purple and her body changing shape. In desperation Hollingshead took her to Richard Alpert, who gave her a shot of Thorazine, after which she remembered nothing. Vanessa recalled, "I do remember it was one of the few times I felt my dad cared for me as much as he did and gave me that amount of attention.

I could barely make him out, but I did feel safe and protected."[17] Hollingshead was genuinely concerned about Vanessa's well-being, but he and Leary must also have worried about the serious medical and legal repercussions of a child overdosing on LSD at Millbrook.

One of the many unusual people who came to Millbrook for LSD sessions was a NASA hypnotist, who told Hollingshead that LSD and other psychedelics were routinely administered to astronauts during training to prepare them for the mental disorientation experienced in space. He claimed NASA sent him to investigate why the hippies there were having such a good time when the opposite was true for the astronauts. The answer, of course, was set and setting. In return for their help he gave Hollingshead and Alpert a quantity of JB 118, the 'space drug' used by the astronauts in training. JB 118 proved to be far more powerful than LSD, even for the experienced Millbrook trippers. Hollingshead became very high almost instantly, his body catapulted backwards by the force of the drug, his mind fired deep into inner space. For three hours Hollingshead was completely dissociated from his body, convinced firstly he was the occupant of a spaceship the size of a tennis ball, and then a bird which flew round the mansion, "Finally I was coaxed back upstairs with a piece of bread and I nested until I finally evolved back into a man."[18] To his friends, Hollingshead's avian adventures were more comic than cosmic and looked to them like a man lying face down, legs spread and arms flapping.

On Saturday nights Millbrook often hosted group LSD trips for staff and visitors. Hollingshead controlled the light show from slide projectors while Ralph Metzner took care of music and Leary sat by the baronial fireplace, directing the show with a microphone. On one trip Leary determined the scenario to be a spaceship crew with only five minutes of oxygen left before death. Everyone was asked what their final message to Earth would be and as the 'crew' confessed their sins, expressed feelings for loved ones or made jokes about their imminent demise, the lights went out and the microphone died. The trippers, too high to change fuses or hunt for candles, were wondering what to do when a light appeared outside revealing "Michael Hollingshead, whose fitful sense of humour could only be described as weird was in a kilt with a strobe light flashing on while he did naughty leaps on the trampoline, a rather startling sight and fitting end to the disrupted lecture."[19]

Hollingshead's basic needs, food and drugs, were provided at little or no cost and he was happy at Millbrook. Although not all the key players liked him, he was valued as part of the community for his contributions to the multi-disciplinary psychedelic events, his management of weekend guests, and for running LSD sessions with the ad hoc visitors who arrived on a regular basis. At Millbrook, he was freer than he'd ever been: free to do as he pleased, to amuse, entertain and be mischievous, especially when under the influence of LSD. Leary was one of the few people who understood and valued the trickster aspect of Hollingshead's personality, probably because they shared many personality traits.

Hollingshead brought an English, aristocratic, playful, elegant, party, daredevil, British explorer style to acid that was very refreshing. When everyone else was finding God or becoming rather – as we all did at times – pompous and Messianic and hyper-spiritual, Hollingshead was always there, kind of twinkling and saying, 'Well, it's all crazy, and pretty vibrations, so let's have a good time and be elegant.' And by a good time, I mean in the best sense of that – exploring and discovering and finding new delightful surprises in ourselves and the world around us.[20]

One of Hollingshead's psychedelic party tricks, literally reflecting Leary's insight, was to observe a group of visitors to Millbrook when they were tripping, waiting until they were at the apogee of the trip and in the suggestible state LSD that bestows on the unwary. Hollingshead would seize the moment and announce ominously that he knew of a mysterious tunnel deep in the bowels of Millbrook which led to a secret cave where those who dared could come face to face with "the wisest person in the world". Candles were lit and he solemnly led the group of apprehensive trippers deep into the cellars where "You'd crawl through various passageways, then come round a corner where the mischievous prankster Hollingshead had put a mirror! That was the ultimate confrontation with the wisest man in the world! Some people got freaked out by that."[21]

Britta, Hollingshead's girlfriend, left Millbrook in early summer 1965 and it wasn't long before he became involved, albeit briefly, with one of the visitors in search of their first LSD experience. Hollingshead refers to this young woman as Joan Wainscott, but her real name was Joan Westcott, an anthropology graduate from London University who had lived among indigenous tribes in Africa. As well as a career as an anthropologist and author, Westcott was also an initiated second-degree Gardnerian witch in one of Britain's oldest covens, based in Bricket Wood, Hertfordshire. Hollingshead was attracted to Westcott's air of intelligent mystery and eagerly agreed to guide her through an LSD session. When they were high, Hollingshead went into full seduction mode, reading Westcott the sensual Sutra 6 from the *Tao Te Ching*, after which they fed each other grapes before making love. Hollingshead may have believed this witchy encounter was just another psychedelic sexual conquest, but the irony is that the reverse may have been true. Westcott had a reputation for befriending and seducing famous people and, after their fling, returned to London and became psychiatrist R.D. Laing's mistress. Westcott was instrumental in encouraging members of her coven to act as a 'control group' for Laing's experiments using mescaline to treat schizophrenia.

The LSD experiments and sessions Hollingshead carried out at Millbrook were of a much more experimental nature than those conducted when working with Leary at Harvard. One of Hollingshead's pet theories was that LSD could be used to enhance athletic performance, especially in sports relying on exact timings such as skydiving or surfing. He tested this theory on himself while living with Leary, using a friend's swimming pool. In one self-experiment Hollingshead, an excellent swimmer and diver, took 250mg of LSD, and stood silently for twenty minutes on the three and a half metre high diving board until his body "seemed to independently spring off the board and perform an incredible slow-motion somersault and then land perfectly, feet first into the pool. During the experience I felt time had somehow slowed and also that I was in perfect control of every nerve and muscle in my body…"[22] The success of this experiment prompted him to run an LSD session with world-champion skydiver Jim Arender, during which he cleverly projected film of his best performances onto a large mirror to give a sense of depth, enabling Arender to analyse his technique as the LSD slowed his perception of time. Arender claimed this enabled him to improve his technique and he repeated the experiment several times. Once again, Hollingshead was unwittingly in the vanguard of a movement which, years later, would see LSD and other psychedelics used to enhance performance in sports including rock climbing, surfing, mountaineering and hang gliding.

Unsurprisingly, the unusual activities and constant comings and goings at Millbrook generated lurid rumours which attracted the attention of the press, with several newspapers and magazines despatching journalists to the mansion to find a story. Most of the media articles concentrated on the famous trio of Leary, Metzner and Alpert but *The Charlotte Observer* chose to focus on Hollingshead, perhaps because he was British. The *Observer*'s opening paragraph depicted him ominously, "'I am Michael Hollingshead,' says the man in the doorway. He is tall, thirtyish, baldish, with cold, cruel, grey eyes. 'I am your guide for the weekend. Will you follow me?' He has an English accent and a soft voice of sinister authority."[23] Hollingshead believed he had a skill that he could use for the good of others and it was his belief that, "As guide to many travellers I have taken them out of their hell and offered them at least a temporary glimpse of paradise." Aware that this might be taken as psychedelic hubris, Hollingshead qualified the statement, noting that he could not claim to be the ideal guide but "At the most I could claim to be conscious of my subject's creativity and that, in itself is a step on the road to paradise."[24] He told the journalist that he saw England, and specifically London, as being the most receptive location for his psychedelic guidance, having convinced himself that the British psychedelic scene was lagging far behind America.

The first clear hints Hollingshead was planning a return to London came in a letter to Alex Trocchi in late August in which he notes that he was in discussion with Leary and Metzner about a series of "rally-lectures" in cities including London, Amsterdam, Copenhagen, Stockholm and Frankfurt. These would be like the events at the New Theatre in New York, but on a much larger scale. Hollingshead also mentioned he was trying to involve his wealthy friend Desmond O'Brien, presumably to help bankroll these projects. He hoped he could persuade O'Brien to visit Millbrook when on business in New York to help him fully embrace the psychedelic lifestyle: "I think, really, in time, Desmond will be a great help, provided he takes a certain amount of trouble to see what is going on – have a few sessions here, meet more people, loosen some of his old imprints which are still preventing him from flowing easily, and with surety, in these areas."[25] Alex Trocchi arranged for another London visitor, the Polish expressionist painter Feliks Topolski, to visit Millbrook in August 1965, asking Hollingshead to ensure that Topolski was "'entertained', just as I would wish to be…in the satisfaction of his various metaphysical lusts".[26] The meeting went well. Topolski was suitably 'entertained' and enjoyed his first LSD experience courtesy of Hollingshead, and they formed a friendship which lasted until Hollingshead's death.

Richard Alpert returned from his European trip in early autumn and was met at Poughkeepsie station by Leary, Metzner and Hollingshead for a 'where to next?' meeting in a coffee shop. All agreed that the Millbrook experiment was coming to a natural end. The fun had gone out of the adventure and Millbrook's complex and intertwined financial, personal and ideological components were unravelling. Their collective decision echoed a statement which closed Leary and Metzner's *Psychedelic Review* article about Hermann Hesse's Castalia: "But always – Hesse reminds us – stay close to the internal core. The mystic formulae, the League, the staggeringly rich intellectual potentials are deadening traps if the internal flame is not kept burning. The flame is of course always there, within and without, surrounding us, keeping us alive. Our only task is to keep tuned in."[27] Hollingshead and the others were all set to embark on their own paths of psychedelic and consciousness exploration; Alpert was en route to reinvention as the post psychedelic guru Baba Ram Dass, Metzner was to go to New York to write, and Leary took a $10,000 advance for his autobiography, *High Priest*, which he planned to write in Mexico. Hollingshead's mission was to return to London to create a centre based on the Castalian model, where people could learn about and experience LSD. He was also tasked with bringing Leary to London at Easter 1965 for a major event at the Royal Albert Hall (or Royal Alpert Hall, as Leary punned) and other European appearances. After a later meeting Hollingshead wrote, "It was agreed that I should return to London with the idea of introducing *The Tibetan Book of the Dead* in the translation by Tim, Dick and Ralph; the cyclostyled typescript of the *Tao Te Ching* by Tim and Ralph; and the *Psychedelic Review*, a magazine devoted to the theoretical discussion of psychedelic experience."[28]

On the one hand Hollingshead's mission served Leary's purpose of an ideological beach head for the Castalia Foundation in Europe, but on the other it enabled him to dispense with Hollingshead's often chaotic presence in his life. Metzner recalled, "Tim and myself had come to think of MH as a disruptive influence and unstable. We thought of sending him back to London in UK where he was from, with a supply of psychedelics" adding, "TL, with my tacit consent, saw it as a good way to get rid of this unstable character and advance the cause in the UK."[29] Hollingshead was unaware he was viewed this way and believed he had been 'chosen', sent as the student of the master to pave the way for the Learyfication of London, England and the rest of Europe. Once his departure was finalised, a portion of Leary's book advance was used to buy him a one-way sea passage to England. On the day of his departure Hollingshead remembered Leary bringing him a piece of paper he said were his "marching orders, your instructions". Hollingshead reached for them, but Leary changed his mind, "What they were I don't know because he decided to scrap them and took a clean sheet of paper and wrote the following on it:

> *HOLLINGSHEAD EXPEDITION TO LONDON 1965-66*
> *Purpose: SPIRITUAL AND EMOTIONAL DEVELOPMENT*
> *To introduce to London the interpretation and applications and methods developed by and learned by Michael Hollingshead.*
> *A YOGA-OF-EXPRESSION BY MH.*
> *Plan*
> *No specific programme of expression can be specified in advance.*
> *The Yoga may include*
> *1. Tranart gallery-bookstore.*
> *2. Weekly psychedelic reviews – lectures – questions and answers*
> *– Tranart demonstrations.*
> *3. Radio – TV – newspaper – magazine educational programme.*[30]

On 5 October, equipped with his new instructions and luggage which, as Metzner noted, included a supply of psychedelics, Hollingshead headed for the New York City docks. But which psychedelics? This question is one of the many anomalies and inconsistencies in Hollingshead's story. In *Flashbacks*, published in 1983, and the first published record of Hollingshead's return to London, Leary notes

Hollingshead was given 1000 doses of Morning Glory seeds to take to London, and in 2018, Metzner confirmed this, "As far as I know he took Morning Glory seeds with him, which were the only psychedelics that TL and I had by that time. I know nothing about any doses of acid from Czechoslovakia."[31] Yet in his autobiography, published five years after Leary's, Hollingshead is clear he had with him, "…a quantity of LSD, about half a gram, part of an experimental batch made available by courtesy of the Czech government laboratories in Prague…"[32]

Morning Glory seeds were a useful source of LSA, a tryptamine offering similar albeit less potent effects to LSD. The seeds were widely available and easily prepared for ingestion as a psychedelic drug at the ratio of approximately 1 seed to 1ug of LSD and were often used, including at Millbrook, when LSD was scarce. But why the discrepancy in the accounts? Leary, writing in 1968, and Metzner in 2018 had no reason to lie about Hollingshead being given Morning Glory seeds to take to London, and equally Hollingshead had no reason to say he brought with him LSD from Czechoslovakia if he didn't. Neither Hollingshead nor his friends in London ever refer to Morning Glory seeds, only the SPOFA LSD. One solution to this conundrum, and perhaps a clue to darker goings on, is that Hollingshead had official connections and sources for LSD that he had not shared with his colleagues at Millbrook.

As Hollingshead boarded the MS Queen Elizabeth for Southampton, Leary and Alpert waved farewell from the quayside. Years later, Leary told Barry Miles "when Dick [Alpert] and I stood on the dock in New York waving goodbye, I said to Dick, 'Well, that writes off the psychedelic revolution in England for at least ten years'."[33] This claim echoed Metzner's belief that Hollingshead had become too chaotic and unstable to remain part of Leary's inner circle. Whether Leary's motives for encouraging Hollingshead's return to London were altruistic, self-serving or a combination of the two, the eleven months Hollingshead spent at Millbrook signified the apogee of his trajectory through psychedelic culture. Hollingshead was blissfully unaware of this, no doubt believing the connections and plans made at Millbrook represented the genesis of a brighter future.

Post-Millbrook, Hollingshead would go on to be involved with initiatives promoting LSD culture in England, Scotland, Scandinavia, America and Nepal. There would be successes and failures, but the plans he and Leary formulated for his return to England had sowed the seeds of his decline, and fall, which would play out over the following two decades.

Notes

1   Stevens, J. *Storming Heaven*. Heinemann, 1988, p.208

2   Horowitz, M, & Palmer, C. *Sisters of the Extreme*. Park St. Press 2000 p.306

3   Hollingshead, M. *The Man Who Turned On The World*. Blond & Briggs, 1973, p.99

4   Leary, T. & Metzner, R. 'Hermann Hesse: Poet of the Inner Journey'. *Psychedelic Review* vol.1 no.2 Fall 1963, p.179

5   Interview between Leary and Alan Eager, February 1967

6   Letter from Hollingshead to Trocchi 9/3/65

7   Kleps, A. *Millbrook*. Art Kleps. 2005 p.40

8   Ibid p.44

9   Hollingshead, 1973 op cit p.113

10   Leary, T. *Flashbacks*. Tarcher/Putnam 1990 p.224

11   Tim Leary interview conducted by Alan Eager, February 1967

12   Metzner, R. Email 24/11/18

13   Dass, R. & Metzner, M. *Birth of a Psychedelic Culture*. Synergy Press 2010 p.177

14   Hollingshead 1973 op cit p.144

15   Letter from Hollingshead to Leary, 4/5/65

16   Hollingshead, V. *LSD Mafia*. Unpublished ms 2013 p.17

17   Ibid p.18

18   Hollingshead 1973 op cit p.126

19   Forte, R. (ed). *Timothy Leary: Outside Looking In*. Park St. Press, 1990 p.333

20   Stafford, Peter (ed). *Magic Grams*. Privately published.
     1985 p.275
21   Leary, T. *Re/search:Pranks*. Re/search Publications 1988. p.78
22   Hollingshead, M. 'The New Secret Weapon: LSD'. *High Times*
23   *Charlotte Observer*, 1965
24   Hollingshead 1973 op cit p.143
25   Letter from Hollingshead to Trocchi, 24/8/65
26   Letter from Trocchi to Hollingshead 17/8/65
27   Leary, T. & Metzner R. 1963 op cit p.181
28   Hollingshead 1973 op cit p.144
29   Metzner, R. Email 24/11/18
30   Hollingshead 1973 op cit p.145
31   Metzner, R. Email 24/11/18
32   Hollingshead 1973 op cit p.146
33   Miles, B. *In the Sixties*. Jonathan Cape. 2002 p.87

19 MARCH 1966   2s 6d

london life

SHOCK
REPORT
ON THE

LSD
DRUG

THE MAN
WHO SAYS
BRITAIN
COULD BE
TAKEN OVER
WITH A
BRAINWASH
POWDER

PLUS: WHAT
PEOPLE (LIKE
EVA BARTOK)
ARE WEARING

PLUS: FULL
GUIDE TO
WHAT'S ON
IN LONDON

Operation London

From what I had heard in letters and conversations, the psychedelic movement in England was small and badly formed.[1]

Michael Hollingshead returned to Britain on the evening of 5 October 1965, disembarking at Southampton docks, where he was met by Desmond O'Brien who drove him straight to London. According to Hollingshead – and notwithstanding Metzner's claim that Hollingshead was given Morning Glory seeds not LSD – he had concealed in his luggage approximately half a gram of potent LSD, enough for 2500 sessions, part of a larger batch that Tim Leary had obtained from SPOFA, the Czech government laboratories in Prague.

Hollingshead had an important task; to create a London bridgehead for Leary's acid vision to spread through Britain's burgeoning LSD culture. First he needed to find a base, somewhere that London's hip and often moneyed psychedelic enthusiasts would feel at home and would reflect the gravitas of Hollingshead's undertaking. In the interim O'Brien booked him into the Berkeley Hotel in Knightsbridge, with all his expenses being covered by O'Brien.

Although Hollingshead respected few people and often had a cynical and manipulative attitude toward those he could exploit financially, he seemed to be in awe of Desmond O'Brien. O'Brien was something of an enigma on the London psychedelic scene and few people recall him or much about his friendship with Hollingshead. Yet the strength and depth of their relationship was made clear in Hollingshead's letters to Leary during the autumn of 1965. On 14 October, Hollingshead told Leary how hectic life in London was: "But the most amazing thing has been my relationship with Desmond, who is full of white magic and positive action. (indecipherable) of new learning experiences, where I simply sit back and watch this guru." This unequivocal praise was amplified with, "You know how quickly I can see the flaws in people's behaviour, how good I am at spotting others' short-cuts? Well, I've now been with Desmond everyday almost for two weeks, both of us high – but really high – and he has not only taken care of 'British re-entry' problems... but he has not hesitated to take full responsibility for my safekeeping and re-education." The letter continued in a similar vein, lauding O'Brien's ability with everything from his people skills to his ways with women, "...often two or so leaving as two or so arrive". O'Brien also provided Hollingshead with a steady stream of drugs to augment his Czechoslovakian LSD, including morphine, cocaine and hashish, which rather countered Hollingshead's claim, in the same letter, that he was trying to "get straight".[2]

After a few days at the Berkeley Hotel, Hollingshead moved to 73 St. James Street, a flat just off Pall Mall, owned by O'Brien. He had yet to find a base, but Hollingshead was already making grandiose claims about his personality and his purpose in London, telling Leary he was "only here in London to watch and share my own spiritual growth", the practise of which was "the use of LSD over many months". Hubris, to which Hollingshead was no stranger and which was amplified by the very same methods he used for his "spiritual growth", was also creeping in. He announced pompously to Leary he was now a "conscious person" and due to being in this exalted state he was unable to "bear the company of those less awake than myself" before arrogantly lamenting that his problem now was "to find anybody left who is fully conscious who will listen to me".[3]

In mid-November the search for a permanent base for Hollingshead's London activities ended when O'Brien signed a lease on 25 Pont Street, a first floor flat in Belgravia, on the fringes of Chelsea, not far from trendy King's Road. This was to become Hollingshead's home for the next few months. To give the address an air of gravitas, Hollingshead named it The World Psychedelic Centre (WPC). Shortly after moving in, thirteen boxes of books arrived from Leary, containing 300 copies of *The Psychedelic Experience* by Leary, Richard Alpert and Ralph Metzner, 200 copies of *The Psychedelic Reader* by Gunther Weil and Metzner and 200 issues of the *Psychedelic Review*, edited by Weil. Prior to this consignment books about psychedelic drugs were difficult to find in Britain, those imported from America being in short supply, only available from specialist outlets. Hollingshead intended the books to be available for visitors to the WPC and to be given away or sold to anyone deemed influential or a potential advocate for LSD.

Hollingshead immediately took some of the books to a meeting with radical LSD-using psychiatrist Dr Ronnie (R.D.) Laing and his American colleague Jo Berke. He also showed them to a journalist friend who he thought might be able to get them reviewed in British newspapers. Bob Campbell, a frequent visitor to the Pont Street flat, recalls selling copies of the books to generate funds for the WPC, although there is no evidence that the money raised was used for anything other than to sustain Hollingshead's lifestyle. London's acid heads were pleased that such books were now easily available, and Hollingshead was keen to point out that *The Psychedelic Experience* was a manual for psychedelic explorers to structure their acid trips the Tim Leary way – if they wanted to. And therein lay the problem Hollingshead and the WPC faced: prior to returning to Britain, Hollingshead had formed the opinion that "the psychedelic movement in England was small and badly informed. It appeared that those who took LSD did so as a consciously defiant anti-authoritarian gesture. The spiritual content of the psychedelic experience was being overlooked."[4] This statement could not have been further from the truth.

It was true that, compared to America, the British LSD scene in the early sixties was small, but it was well informed, and its use of LSD as an anti-authoritarian gesture was balanced by those who used it for spiritual reasons. Nor was recreational LSD new to Britain; the first recorded instance of illicit LSD in London dates to 1959 and by the autumn of 1965 vibrant psychedelic scenes existed in London, Cambridge, Edinburgh and elsewhere. Hollingshead himself had imported LSD to Britain from 1962 onwards and the drug was constantly being brought in from America, Holland and the Balearic Isles. LSD was also occasionally given out by some of the medical practitioners who were using it psychotherapeutically with their patients in over twenty-five hospitals and clinics throughout Britain, and LSD from Britain's first underground LSD lab, operated by a Camden chemist, was in circulation towards the end of 1965.

Hollingshead's belief that the British scene required – or would even welcome – the Leary method, was naïve at best, and overbearingly arrogant at worst. Leary, through his media appearances, was becoming an international psychedelic figurehead and a guru to thousands, and there is a sense from Hollingshead's writings in late 1965 that he was confident not only would the 'Leary method' be welcomed by London's psychedelic community, but as its emissary he would be hailed as much a ground-breaking figure and guide, guru even, as Leary was.

Not only were British LSD users having religious, mystical and numinous experiences prior to Hollingshead's return but their trips were less structured than Leary's method and involved a great deal of good old cosmic fun. Leary's approach to the psychedelic experience wasn't the only one in America and there was a division between

Leary's highly-structured psychedelic sessions and the far out free-for-alls advocated by Ken Kesey and the Merry Pranksters. The 'secret' to successful psychedelic experiences was simple and little more than the optimum balance of set, setting, dosage and intent; the use of guides, gurus, and tripping manuals in structured sessions could be useful, but certainly wasn't necessary and often encouraged overthinking the experience rather than going with the flow. But in the white heat of the mid-sixties psychedelic revolution there were many, including Leary and his acolytes, who believed there was a psychedelic 'way' which must be followed correctly to attain spiritual enlightenment.

The London scene's scepticism about the 'Leary way' notwithstanding, it was Hollingshead's intention to hold group LSD trips at the WPC, using the strong Czech LSD in conjunction with Leary's tripping manual *The Psychedelic Experience*. The first event was scheduled for the first full moon of his tenure at the WPC, on Wednesday 8 December. Hollingshead wrote a detailed account of the trip, giving an insight into the ritualised, sombre, way Leary prescribed for how a psychedelic session should be run. First, Hollingshead created the physical setting, ensuring the 'temple room' was suitably lit, furnished with large cushions and appropriate music, and with several chillums of hashish on hand, as prescribed by Leary's interpretation of Sutra 19 from the *Tao Te Ching*.

Let There Be Simple Natural Things During The Session
hand carved wood
uncarved wood
flowers – growing things
ancient music
burning fire
a touch of earth
a splash of water
fruit, good bread, cheese

fermenting wine
candlelight
temple incense
a warm hand
fish swimming
anything which is over 500 years old
Of course it is always best to be secluded with nature[5]

Hollingshead and his eleven companions ingested acid-infused grapes each containing a 300-microgram dose, enough for up to twelve hours of psychedelic intensity. These preliminary actions were carried out with a piety and seriousness more usually found in acts of religious faith. Hollingshead described the changes in physical and mental reaction as the LSD trip came on. At first they were subtle; an increased heart rate, occasional trembling, enlarged pupils, a dissolving of the sense of mind and body and brightening colours slowly building to a sensual crescendo ranging from euphoria to borderline alarm, before resolving into "astonishment at the absolutely incredible immensity, complexity, intensity and extravagance of being, existence, the cosmos, call it what you will."[6] As the LSD's effects intensified Hollingshead moved into 'guide' mode, ensuring pre-recorded tapes of Leary's psychedelic prayers were played at the optimum time and the psychonauts were kept in the flow. He read aloud from *The Psychedelic Experience* and played music including Buddhist chants and John Cage's *Concert Percussion*. Each of the participants was now very high, spinning through the psychedelic experience and lost in their own internal universe as Hollingshead guided them through the Bardos, or transitional states of the trip. More music, including Ravi Shankar, Bach and Debussy was played and slides of eastern spiritual and religious images projected on the ceiling to give the tripper a "demonstration and a sharing of novel energy levels and unusual forms of perception".[7]

After several hours, the drug's effect began to wane, the trippers 'coming down' and moving into the 're-entry' phase, or Third Bardo.

Hollingshead read Leary's sage advice on assimilating the effects of a mental journey beyond space and time: "Do not struggle to re-enter the denser atmosphere of routine game existence. Do not attempt to use force or will-power. Do not hold on to thoughts. Allow the mind to rest in its unmodified state...Trust your guide."[8]

Participants in these formal psychedelic experiences were discouraged from eating prior to the trip, often fasting for up to a day, in the belief that this purified the body and helped avoid nausea. To the cynical observer, or those who preferred an informal way of taking LSD, the Leary method was as an exercise in wielding control and influence over people in a suggestible state of mind. Whichever way people were using it, the quality of the SPOFA-made Czechoslovakian LSD Hollingshead brought from America was beyond compare; everyone said so. Brian Barritt had an amusing tale of his encounter with Hollingshead's latest batch of LSD. When visiting the WPC where, "the air was so saturated with acid that you only had to breath to get high," Barritt borrowed a beautifully coloured book from Hollingshead but "was at home in north London before I found it was in black and white."[9]

When not hosting LSD sessions Hollingshead was on the move, meeting and making friends, moving from party to party, networking in person and by telephone at a frantic speed. Some encounters were purely social, others sowed the seeds, often unwittingly, of future endeavours. At one party Hollingshead was introduced to Anthony Blond, co-owner of Blond & Briggs book publishers. Seizing the opportunity, Hollingshead pitched Blond an idea for a book about LSD and sex to be co-written with Ralph Metzner, an idea they had speculated about at Millbrook. Blond was extremely interested in the proposal and requested sample chapters as soon as possible. This was a big opportunity for Hollingshead, but due to the pace of his frenetic London existence nothing more came of the idea. However, and unknown to Hollingshead, the introduction to Blond was fortuitous and consequential, as it would be Blond & Briggs who published Hollingshead's autobiography several years later.

Hollingshead maintained his long-standing friendship with Alex
Trocchi, visiting him at his flat in St. Stephen's Gardens, Notting Hill,
to buy or get high on heroin and discuss how the WPC might work in
tandem with Sigma. Trocchi was an occasional LSD user but preferred
heroin, to which he'd been addicted for over a decade. Author Paul
Devereux visited Trocchi in the autumn of 1965 and, after talking to
Trocchi while he injected himself, suddenly "became aware of a thin,
angular man sitting bolt upright in a wooden chair in the corner of the
room. He was taking no notice of us at all, and was sitting motionless,
staring at the floor. 'That's Michael Hollingshead', Trocchi informed.
There seemed to be a hint of gravitas in his voice. I stared at the man
and thought he was uninteresting and with a mental shrug turned
back to our conversation with Trocchi. I didn't know who Michael
Hollingshead was. Young and ignorant, I didn't know I'd just met the
man who turned on the world."[10]

Trocchi's relationship with Hollingshead was not always smooth.
Both men had strong personalities, and both had their own agendas.
Trocchi was also good friends with Desmond O'Brien and resented
Hollingshead monopolising O'Brien's time and money. There was
friction because Hollingshead claimed the WPC had the support of
author William Burroughs and Roland Penrose, director of the Institute
of Contemporary Arts (ICA), which Trocchi doubted. Trocchi had been
present at the WPC when Burroughs told Hollingshead of his aversion
to LSD and psilocybin and thought it unfair that Hollingshead was
now claiming his patronage. This ill feeling culminated in an argument
between Hollingshead and Trocchi at a meeting on 6 December. A few
days later Hollingshead received a letter in which Trocchi accused him
of causing a rift between him and Desmond O'Brien. Trocchi no longer
felt he could work again with either of them. Hollingshead responded
tersely, returning Trocchi's letter with the threatening words, "What a
load of balls. Don't try this kind of con again – last warning", scrawled
across the top of it.[11]

Once installed in the WPC, Hollingshead's hippie friends decided he had no fashion sense, his drab outfit of jeans and sweat shirt looked incongruous compared with what his contemporaries wore, and didn't really convey the look of an acid ambassador. Colourful silk shirts, suede shoes, velvet trousers and anything embroidered or patterned, reflecting the psychedelic vision, were the fashion of the day so Michael Rainey, who ran the hip boutique 'Hung On You', was consulted and a pile of the finest hippie garb delivered to Pont Street. To Hollingshead's dismay the bill was £600, a phenomenal sum in 1965, even if it clothed the five people now living at the WPC. Although he wanted to look the part, Hollingshead's essentially conservative personality found this explosion of style and colour too much, and he quickly reverted to jeans and sweat shirt.

To spread the LSD gospel, Hollingshead published broadsheets and pamphlets which were distributed at parties, arts labs, galleries and wherever London's psychedelic elite met. *An Introduction to the Field of Consciousness Expansion with an Outline of the Effects of Psychedelic Drugs* was a slim pamphlet giving the reader a 12-step guide for taking LSD, based on Leary's principles of set and setting. Less useful was *A London Newsletter* in which Hollingshead argued that although LSD was in the news and seeping into popular culture, those who comprised the 'LSD Vanguard' were being ignored. By 'LSD Vanguard' he was referring not only to himself but to the "...tiny circle of scientists, intellectuals, theoreticians, men of letters etc who had helped bring LSD to the public."[12] Hollingshead was not receiving the recognition he believed he deserved and Leary's ideas about how to use LSD didn't seem to be catching on as he had hoped. Had this tension between the Leary method and the more relaxed British approach to the psychedelic experience not been resolved it's possible the WPC might have ended even earlier than it did.

Just before Christmas 1965, John Doyle, who was living at the WPC, suggested to Hollingshead that he meet his friend Joe Mellen, already an experienced acid-head having first taken it the previous year. Hollingshead was eager to meet Mellen to discuss trepanation, increasing the flow of blood to the brain by drilling a hole in the skull which, its proponents claimed, caused the individual to remain permanently high. Mellen had learnt about trepanning in Ibiza from Bart Huges, the first underground chemist to make LSD in Holland. Huges dubbed his theory 'brain blood volume' (often written 'brainbloodvolume' and abbreviated as BBV), and concluded that LSD caused "constriction of the veins carrying blood from the head back to the heart, thus raising the volume of blood in the capillaries from which the blood takes nourishment. This is in the form of oxygen and glucose, so if there is not enough sugar in the blood, the brain is liable to pangs of starvation, resulting in feelings of unease or horror and, as they say, a bad trip."[13] Huges called this problem 'Sugarlack' and reasoned the simple way to avoid it was to eat sugar, up to half a kilo per trip, either pure or as honey, confectionary or fruit, before and during an LSD trip.

Mellen followed Huges' advice and on his first LSD trip ate sugar lumps and lemon juice throughout the night; the experience changed his life and he began to advise everyone to make sugar a key component of their LSD trips. This contradicted Leary's advice, which was to minimise or abstain from food before a psychedelic experience. On his return from Ibiza Mellen moved into a flat on Cadogan Lane, just streets from the WPC, and John Doyle, who was supplying their scene with acid from the WPC, brought Hollingshead round to meet him. Mellen found Hollingshead's approach to the psychedelic experience radically different to his and that of many other London LSD users: "I didn't like his emphasis on mandalas and mantras and the Tibetan Book of the Dead etc. I explained to him that it was far simpler than he thought."[14] Despite Mellen explaining the BBV mechanism in detail to Hollingshead it seemed he didn't understand the idea because it didn't fit with the 'Leary method'. Hollingshead respected the Eton-

and-Oxford-educated Mellen's intelligence though, and their shared interest in LSD and consciousness expansion led to a friendship. Hollingshead visited the Cadogan Road flat several times and was impressed with, as Joe Mellen put it, "…lots of young people on acid with no one putting over a big mystery scene." Mellen believed the 'Leary method' "was the way the Americans had devised to keep people under control… It was not my idea of a good time." Although Mellen believed Hollingshead was, in a way, the antithesis of the Cadogan Road scene, he could see he had potential to change because "he was very attracted to the fact they were all young people just tripping and listening to the latest music and having a good time, and he was attracted to that and saw that perhaps he was wrong…"[15]

The WPC was always in need of funds even though the basic costs were covered by Desmond O'Brien. Sales of psychedelic literature and dealing LSD and cannabis brought in some money, but more was always needed and Bob Campbell, Mellen's friend from Cadogan Road, went with Hollingshead on several fund raising ventures including a visit to the *Playboy* empire's emissary in London, Victor Lownes. *Playboy* magazine's liberated attitude to sex and relationships extended to an interest in psychedelic drugs, and *Playboy* parties often featured LSD as a tool to amplify sensuality. Lownes was in the process of trying to set up a *Playboy* venture in London and Hollingshead thought he might be able to persuade him to donate to the WPC. Campbell's friend Maggie Roche, who organised the meeting, slipped some methedrine in Lownes' drink as an act of 'goodwill' which resulted in him donating a few thousand pounds to the WPC. Campbell also persuaded another friend, Mark Warman, who had recently received an inheritance, to make a considerable donation to the WPC. Being a methedrine user Campbell immediately noticed Hollingshead had a substantial methedrine addiction, at first using it to enhance LSD experiences then, as addiction set in, out of necessity. It wasn't uncommon for LSD users to take methedrine when they tripped because, as Campbell says, "methedrine seemed to keep the wheels moving",[16] minimising one of the effects of high dose LSD which was to distort the sense of time so a minute could feel as though it lasted for days, months, years or centuries.

Christmas 1965 found Hollingshead busy dealing with increasing numbers of visitors to the WPC, but he still found time to craft handmade Christmas card for friends and relatives. One, created during his by now daily LSD sessions, was an A3 sized multi-media collage made from Hollingshead's original abstract watercolour art, combined with text clipped from magazines and newspapers, Vedic and primitive imagery, and a demonic face topped off with a 'Viva Sativa' badge. The card was sent to his sister Janette and her husband, in Scotland, signed "A Very Merry Christmas to You All 1965 from Michael Hollingshead 25 Pont St, London SW1".

The scene at Cadogan Lane ended suddenly in early 1966, when the landlord discovered that the flat was hosting a continuous acid party. Mellen moved into the WPC, bringing with him the detailed wall scrolls expounding the brainbloodvolume concept, and persuaded Hollingshead that Bart Huges' open letter describing the BBV mechanism should be given to everyone who sold or took LSD. Hollingshead, now more receptive to a less formal approach to acid use, agreed and hundreds of copies of the letter were reproduced and distributed in London. In his autobiography, Hollingshead gives a list of notable sixties celebrities who visited the WPC to take or buy LSD or hash or just to hang out. The list, validated by Hollingshead's friends and other sources, included Roman Polanski, Feliks Topolski, Alex Trocchi, Donovan, Julie Felix, William Burroughs, Christopher Gibbs, and many more artists, writers and members of the aristocracy. Paul McCartney, who had recently taken his first LSD trip, arrived at the WPC one evening keen to check out the psychedelic scene there; Joe Mellen showed him the BBV scroll and attempted to explain the mechanism behind it. McCartney's friend John Dunbar became hostile and argued with Mellen, unwilling to accept the principles of BBV, and quickly ushered McCartney away.

Tim Wyllie, one of the original members of the Process Church of the Final Judgement, who by the mid-1960s was heavily involved in Britain's psychedelic culture, remembers going to the WPC to buy some hash and being surprised to find Mick Jagger there. Writing decades after the event, Wyllie recalled, "I can see Jagger over to my right side and slightly behind me, sitting slouched on a broken down sofa, trying to bat away the little cat while he was rolling a joint. As I think about it now, it's obvious that Michael must have been turning his pussy on and that's why she was pestering Mick for puff." Hollingshead hurried the drug deal with Wyllie, obviously trying to get back to his conversation with Jagger, but Wyllie was there long enough to make some observations about Hollingshead's personality. Although "impressed by his capacity to influence people he must have believed were more powerful than him", he concluded that Hollingshead was, "a rather ordinary chap, entranced and empowered by acid, and pimping the entheogenic experience for his own self-aggrandisement. A psychological type that became more common as time passed and which became one of the hazards of premature illumination. He appeared fully committed, even in the short time I met him, to the idea that acid would save the world, but in his enthusiasm it didn't seem to me that he had used acid to 'save' himself... I think what Michael ultimately represents is an early iteration of the primarily hedonistic aspect of the psychedelic community, more West Coast revolutionary than East Coast evolutionary."[17]

Trip after trip, party after party, Hollingshead was meeting new people daily and as was the case throughout his life, eliciting strongly polarised opinions. Chronicler of British counter-culture Barry Miles found Hollingshead "to be a good host: charming, funny, cosmopolitan, with a great fund of amusing stories about mutual friends".[18] Whether this was a genuine reflection of Hollingshead's personality or a targeted persona he affected for Miles is difficult to know. In complete contrast, psychotherapist Jo Berke, Ronnie Laing's assistant at the Philadelphia Association recalled, "I did not like him that much. I found him sort of creepy".[19] And though he liked Hollingshead, Miles harboured some doubts about both him and the WPC commenting, "...there was something I didn't trust about him...I didn't find the atmosphere there very conducive. It all seemed kind of phoney to me."[20]

Hollingshead began to adopt Mellen's ideas about how blood sugar levels affected the quality of the psychedelic experience and bowls of sugar lumps, sweets and oranges were made available to those tripping at the World Psychedelic Centre. Mellen encouraged first time trippers to visit his room where he would explain the BBV scroll and its diagrams in the hope the neophyte voyager might grasp some of the concepts and keep their blood sugar levels raised throughout the trip. Through his debates with Mellen, Hollingshead became fascinated by trepanation and in his usual manner of trying to portray himself in a favourable light, mirrored Mellen's beliefs about the procedure back to him. He told Mellen he changed his name to Hollingshead because it represented 'Hole in the head', a reference to trepanation. Hollingshead told several other people in London this was the reason for the name change, but it was a lie, contradicting the explanations he gave Leary and others at Harvard in 1962, which were also lies. Hollingshead was becoming more and more a chemical chameleon, reflecting the persona he believed people wanted to see, which was not necessarily the 'real' Michael Hollingshead.

Hollingshead was always looking for the opportunity to give acid to people in the British Establishment; politicians, aristocrats or anyone in a position of power or authority, Bob Campbell recalling "Part of Michael's grand scheme was to turn everyone on, including the Royal Family and the Houses of Parliament."[21] When he heard artist Feliks Topolski had been commissioned to paint Prince Philip's portrait, Hollingshead visited him at his studio and tried to persuade the artist to slip LSD into Prince Philip's tea as he sat for the portrait. Whether or not this happened was not recorded but the intent shows Hollingshead's willingness to dose the unwary for his own ends.

Hollingshead's zeal for giving LSD to others whether they wanted it or not extended to using it to take sexual advantage of women, basically a form of sexual assault or rape. Recalls Joe Mellen, "Michael used to put acid in the food or drink of girls he wanted to take advantage of under the influence, an unforgiveable liberty". Joe believed "Michael Hollingshead used the 'spiritual content' he often talked about as his front for what was, for him, basically a power trip. His main problem was the opposite sex, getting them to go to bed with him, and he used acid as a means to this, taking advantage of them when he'd turned them on, a VERY BAD IDEA".[22] There is no way of telling how often Hollingshead abused his position of LSD guide in this way but one trustworthy account, from Amanda Feilding (now Lady Amanda Neidpath) has come to light. Rather than relying on the usual conventions of wooing a woman, Hollingshead gave Feilding a dose of over 1000 mics of LSD. His seedy attempt at psychedelic seduction failed but the impact of the experience affected Feilding deeply and she was unable to leave her flat for several days. She describes Hollingshead as "An extremely clever man, but a black magician at heart."[23]

His manipulation of Feilding was just one example of how Hollingshead treated many of the women he had relationships with, in which he was often coercive, devious and dangerous. Acid heads considered dosing the unwitting to be abhorrent and a violation of the first of Leary's *Two Commandments for The Molecular Age*, "Thou shalt not alter the consciousness of thy fellow man". In using LSD to seduce women Hollingshead not only violated the primary principle of psychedelic use, but also revealed himself to be an opportunist sexual predator. According to one of Hollingshead's neighbours, Bob Davidson, it wasn't just women who were at risk when they visited Pont Street. Door handles and other surfaces were often smeared with LSD to dose the unwary and, for a time, an atomiser attached to the front door sprayed an LSD mist which people inhaled as they entered. This cavalier attitude to LSD resulted in over eighty people being dosed with acid infused punch at a WPC party attended by plain clothed police officers badly disguised as hippies, who reported what they saw to their superiors. It was blindingly obvious the high life couldn't continue much longer at Pont Street, but Hollingshead didn't seem to care, being "unable or unwilling to do very much about it".[24]

Hollingshead didn't take security at the WPC seriously for several reasons. LSD was still quasi-legal in early 1966. This and the WPC's location in an upmarket residential area where police raids were rare may have also added to his *laissez-faire* attitude. Even so, the suspected presence of undercover police and laws pertaining to the many other drugs to be found at the WPC should have given him cause for concern. Despite the freak outs, the twenty four hour comings and goings of people wanting to take or buy acid and hash, Hollingshead did nothing and continued to "observe the scene with complete indifference".[25]

Following the incident with the dosed punch the forces of law and order began to take a close interest in Hollingshead's lifestyle and on 25 January officers armed with a search warrant visited the WPC. Hollingshead made them wait ten minutes before answering the door, while he rushed round the flat disposing of or hiding his drug stashes, but despite his attempts the police found a quantity of controlled drugs and he was arrested, hand cuffed and taken to the police station. He was charged with possession of 16 tablets containing heroin, 137 tablets of Morphine Sulphate, 4 grains of morphine and an undisclosed quantity of cannabis (in the form of marijuana leaves). The police found the cannabis floating in the lavatory bowl where Hollingshead had tried in vain to flush it away. Under caution, Hollingshead claimed he was researching the effects of drugs on artists and writers and as such allowed people to use and keep drugs at his flat. All the drugs except the cannabis, Hollingshead claimed, belonged to a man he knew only as 'Arthur' and though he admitted allowing others to smoke cannabis in the flat he escaped a charge of allowing his premises to be used for smoking cannabis. The police didn't find any LSD, probably because in 1966 they were still naïve about LSD which, being colourless, odourless and tasteless, was easy to conceal. Hollingshead was released later that day on police bail, due at Marlborough Street Magistrate's Court on 8 March. He had been alone when the raid took place and chose not to tell anyone about the raid at the time or afterwards, there being no record of it in his autobiography. The reason for this may have been because to do so would have revealed the extent of his heroin and morphine habit which, along with his methedrine and alcohol intake, was increasing daily.

On 29 January, four days after the raid, and acting on impulse, Hollingshead boarded an afternoon flight from Heathrow to Geneva in Switzerland and then a train to Gstaad where he planned to do some skiing and forget about his impending court case. The attempted respite from his worries didn't go to plan, a postcard to Alex Trocchi noting, "Special providence continues to save me from a broken leg (too high to ski, really)".[26] Gstaad quickly bored him and he returned to London on Wednesday 2 February. The police raid at the WPC seemed to have unnerved the normally confident Hollingshead, and signs his life was unravelling began to show; his almost daily letters to Leary and others stopped and his addictions worsened.

In an uncharacteristically frank section of his autobiography Hollingshead admits he had a serious methedrine addiction and was injecting large doses of the drug up to seven times daily. He was also drinking every day, smoking hashish and marijuana constantly and taking over 500 micrograms of LSD at least three times a week, besides the increasing amounts of heroin or morphine he used to calm things down. By his own admission Hollingshead tried every chemical he was offered and even though he knew he was in a downward spiral couldn't stop. In desperation he attempted to jolt himself out of his addictions by injecting DMT, the then-uncommon, intensely powerful short-acting psychedelic. Hollingshead was hardly sleeping and was becoming increasingly paranoid but could still appreciate the irony that despite his meditation and yoga practice, the years of using LSD for spiritual purposes and the hours of philosophical discussions with people he respected, he found himself shackled to an addiction from which he could not break free.

Some of his friends saw what was going on and began to shun him. Even Alex Trocchi, who he'd known for almost a decade, was turning against him. Despite his chatty postcard to Trocchi from Gstaad in late January, Trocchi hadn't forgiven Hollingshead for the argument they had in December about Burroughs and Penrose. And when Trocchi learnt of Hollingshead's fresh negotiations with Roland Penrose to curate a series of workshops at the ICA, he decided to act. Believing Hollingshead to be disingenuous and manipulative, Trocchi wrote to Penrose outlining his doubts about Hollingshead's integrity, closing with, "It is for this reason that I feel bound, in spite of great misgivings (sincerely, I have no wish to injure Michael) to warn you."[27]

Trocchi's warning either came too late or had no influence because on 14 February 1966 Hollingshead staged the first Workshop in Consciousness Expansion at the ICA on Dover Street in London. The panel of speakers included Hollingshead, Ian Sommerville, George Andrews, R.D. Laing, and Brion Gysin. Even Trocchi, despite his tiff with Hollingshead, turned up and took a place on the panel. Burroughs also spoke, despite his misgivings about LSD; Hollingshead was hopeful he could persuade him to speak at future events, but this wasn't to be. Increasingly conscious of Hollingshead's growing addiction to methedrine, and the bad reputation of the WPC, Burroughs began to distance himself from the Pont Street scene.

Part of the problem with Hollingshead's addictions was that he had no-one to turn to for help. He had no close family members and since returning from America in October 1965 he hadn't had a girlfriend or any meaningful female relationships. This was hardly surprising considering his use of LSD as a seduction tool or his prodigious consumption of alcohol, cannabis, opiates and amphetamines. Even Desmond O'Brien was distancing himself from Hollingshead, though with his own addictions to alcohol, heroin and methedrine he probably wouldn't have been much help. News of Hollingshead's worsening predicament reached George Andrews, early LSD enthusiast and author of several books and poems about drugs. Andrews wrote to Hollingshead, admonishing him for his behaviours and pointed out that he was in possession of a potent substance which had the power of "the Void in crystal form, the lightning of the gods, the jade wine of the immortals", hinting perceptively that perhaps Hollingshead was pretending to be someone he wasn't. "In Tangier I learned to draw a very sharp line of distinction between the psychedelic guide, who is rare, and the psychedelic hustler, who is a dime a dozen". Rumours of "bad trips and flip outs" emanating from Pont Street were, according to Andrews, adding to Hollingshead's karmic load which a methedrine addiction only made heavier, "Why not lighten it instead?"[28]

In his autobiography Hollingshead indulges in several pages of drug related self-pity before concluding he was trapped in his own mind, unable to help himself, with neither psychiatry nor religion being able to offer comfort or cure. Hollingshead and the WPC were spinning into a vortex of self-destruction, with methedrine at the centre, and he was forced to admit, "The euphoria of the drug had become my refuge from the real world...The spiritual life was extinguished in the same sudden and mysterious way as it had flashed up...It was an impossible situation."[29]

In early March Hollingshead's crumbling world was further shaken when Tim Leary's lawyer telephoned from America telling him Leary had been found guilty of carrying three ounces of marijuana across the border between Texas and Mexico. The $40,000 fine Leary received was draconian, but the 30 year prison sentence was devastating. The planned visit to London by Leary and Metzner and their appearance at the Royal Albert Hall (RAH) would no longer happen. Unbeknownst to Leary, Hollingshead hadn't even booked the RAH, or any other venue, his excuse being "I had come on ahead to set it up and, like a juggler, I had several things suspended in mid-air at any one time in the sure knowledge that when Tim came he would be able to act as my 'apologist' and catch them."[30] In fact, other than turn people on with Leary's LSD and distribute his books, Hollingshead had done almost nothing regarding Leary and Metzner's proposed visit.

Hollingshead was crushed by the news of Leary's arrest. With a pending court case, serious addictions, friends deserting him and his link to Leary now lost it was hard to see how his situation could get any worse, but it did.

The evening of Friday 4 March began as a normal evening at the WPC. Hollingshead and some friends were getting high in the living room and Joe Mellen was in his bedroom, relaxing, when John Doyle and two heavily built men appeared at the door. Doyle and Hollingshead often brought acid neophytes to Mellen so he could explain the principles behind BBV to them. Mellen sensed something wasn't quite right but was prepared to answer their questions. "Have you got any drugs", asked one them. "There", said Mellen, thinking they had come to buy cannabis, pointing to a lump of hash on the table. As he did they told him, "You're under arrest". Someone had left the WPC's door open and two plain clothes police officers walked in unchallenged, presumed to be customers. The police searched the flat and found three ounces of cannabis resulting in all six people in the flat being arrested. Mellen asked the officers not to be destructive in their search of the flat and explained the BBV scroll, which seemed to defuse their enthusiasm, causing them to miss the other drugs present, including a bottle of liquid LSD in Mellen's pocket.[31]

Michael Hollingshead, Joe Mellen, John Doyle, Monique Warman, Sheldon Cholst and Mark Warman were taken to the police station where they were charged and fingerprinted. Hollingshead gave his full name of Hollingshead-Shinkfield, and his occupation as 'artist' and was charged with possession of cannabis and allowing his premises to be used for the smoking of cannabis. The others were all charged with possession of cannabis. The Pont Street Six appeared at Marlborough Street Magistrate's Court the following morning and were remanded on bail until 18 March.

The raid was the beginning of the end for the WPC; Mellen and John and Monica Doyle moved out almost immediately into a flat paid for by Desmond O'Brien. But instead of answering bail conditions resulting from his January arrest Hollingshead panicked and went on the run. A warrant for his arrest was issued. That O'Brien had assisted Mellen but not Hollingshead after the Pont Street raid is an indication of the irrevocable rift that had come between the two former friends. This rift deepened when Hollingshead saw a half-page advertisement in the *London Evening Standard* headed "LSD – The Drug That Could Threaten London", trailing an expose of the WPC in the 19 March issue of *London Life* magazine. *London Life* had emerged from the ashes of the society magazine *Tatler* in early 1965 and was considered the publication for London's hip young things. Similar advertisements for *London Life* appeared on London buses and even on TV. Hollingshead was in shock. He had been so caught up with his addictions he failed to see this media attention coming. The day the *London Life* exposé appeared, Hollingshead and co-defendants were due in court to answer charges relating to the 4 March raid. They all appeared, except for Hollingshead, and a further warrant for his arrest without bail was issued, the case against the other five defendants being adjourned to 5 April.

The WPC exposé was *London Life*'s lead story, trailed on the cover as "Shock report on the LSD drug: the man who says Britain could be taken over with a brainwash powder." When Hollingshead read the article he understood what had happened. His friend and fellow methedrine addict Hugh Blackwell, without consulting Hollingshead, had contacted the magazine when high and given them a lurid account of what went on at the WPC, leading to editor Mark Boxer tracing Desmond O'Brien to his hotel suite and interviewing him by telephone.

Although O'Brien was a high flier when it came to making money, he was naïve when it came to answering questions posed by journalists. Flattered by the attention and not understanding how his words would be nuanced and distorted to suit *London Life*'s agenda, O'Brien referred to himself as "Mr. LSD", which immediately put readers in mind of the 'Mr. Bigs' of the criminal world. O'Brien boasted he could "take control of London in eight hours" if LSD were put in the water supply of key locations such as the Houses of Parliament or Buckingham Palace. This was theoretically possible, but MP Donald Johnson's claim in the same article that cities and whole countries could be taken over if LSD was put into reservoirs was wrong: no amount of LSD in a reservoir would have any effect due to the vast quantities of acid required and the filtration processes water went through before reaching peoples' taps.

In and among these lurid claims O'Brien acknowledged that he had been involved in setting up the WPC and had encouraged the dissemination of LSD to musicians, writers and other creative types. There was no mention of LSD being used for spiritual purposes or as a tool of self-enquiry, O'Brien remarking he took it because "it is fun, quite simply fun." So much for Hollingshead's claims of spirituality and creativity enhancement at the WPC. *London Life*'s reporters were sent to hunt for LSD in London, easily finding it at several flats and a Chelsea boutique, reporting that pop stars were using the drug and there was a great deal of general interest in it. O'Brien echoed Mellen's belief that sugar should be taken on an LSD trip and insisted that the drug was relatively harmless, "We would like to see LSD available for everybody. The ideal situation would be to have it in sugar so that people could buy it with their groceries".

The piece counterbalanced O'Brien's relaxed attitude to LSD with scare stories of people who had been unwittingly dosed. These accounts were unimpressive; the best, an account of someone who had LSD slipped in their drink believing they were in Sherwood Forest with Robin Hood, probably acted more as an endorsement than a deterrent. Hugh Blackwell himself gave an account of one of his own LSD trips for the magazine, his experience of "Enormous forces of the universe pressing down on me" only serving to advertise the power of the drug to those interested in altering their consciousness.[32]

London Life wasn't the only publication to take an interest in London's LSD scene in March 1966. *The People*, a popular Sunday newspaper which delighted in exposing behaviours deemed salacious or un-British, contacted O'Brien to tell him when their reporters visited the WPC on 17 March it was deserted, the last occupants having left two days earlier. O'Brien again tried to put a positive spin on the WPC but made the same mistakes he had when talking to *London Life* journalists, referring to himself as 'Mr LSD', which didn't sit well with the claim his "interest isn't financial. I'm horrified at the way LSD is being peddled indiscriminately to youngsters by others." *The People* article painted a picture of squalor at the WPC, telling of finding syringes, empty drug ampoules and random pills scattered round the abandoned flat. A photograph showing the chaos included a bag of sugar, several psychedelic posters and items of psychedelic literature, the contents of which they dismissed as "irresponsible rubbish". Another alarmist Sunday paper, the *News of the World* ran a more general piece about LSD use, claiming Britain was under threat from the "Menace of the Vision of Hell Drug". Hundreds of thousands of people read *London Life*, *The People* and the *News of the World* and anyone either ignorant or curious about psychedelic drugs now knew what they did, how much they cost and where to get them. In trying to alarm their readers about the perceived threat of LSD, the media did more to spread the word than Hollingshead and the WPC could ever have hoped to.[33]

Hollingshead panicked again. He had six drug charges from two police raids arrayed against him and the WPC and LSD had been brutally exposed in the media. Instead of handing himself in to the police he rented a car from Hertz, stocked it with a variety of drugs, including several dozen ampoules of methedrine, and a quantity of hashish and marijuana, and set off for the northeast of England. He spent a few days in and around Durham, visiting family and his childhood haunts before paranoia struck. Convinced the Durham police were following him he headed south to Malton in north Yorkshire where he stayed with his cousin Robert Shinkfield, claiming he needed to lie low for a few days before driving west to the Lake District, avoiding the police by keeping to quiet moorland roads and country lanes.

Not knowing what to do other than evade arrest Hollingshead just drove, his growing paranoia fuelled by an ever-increasing drug intake. At times he was so high that he had to pull off the road because his vision was so blurred or he was confused when to change gear or which pedal was the clutch and which the brake. In his autobiography he remembers staying "at country hotels and leaving early in the morning", suggesting he was back to his old trick of booking into hotels and leaving without paying.[34]

This Thompson-esque road trip reached its surreal zenith one morning in the early hours as Hollingshead drove through the Lake District. A bright light appeared in his rear-view mirror; certain it must be the headlights of a police car he accelerated, driving recklessly through quiet villages and along narrow winding lanes. It was to no avail, his pursuer easily matched the pace of Hollingshead's driving and he couldn't shake them off, the light a constant presence in his rear-view mirror. In desperation he veered off the road into a farmyard and down a narrow and overgrown track for several miles before his route was blocked by a large metal gate. Fighting the urge to smash his way through, Hollingshead stopped to open the gate, which probably saved his life because the gate acted as barrier preventing cars from tumbling 30 metres into the river below. Hollingshead turned to face his pursuer, ready to admit defeat and was stunned, "the 'light' I had been picking up in my mirror and which I had believed was the light beam of a pursuit police car was only the reflection of the full moon!"[35] The impact of this radical misperception shocked Hollingshead back to reality and he reversed his car back down the track and out of the farmyard before falling asleep, exhausted, for several hours at the side of the road.

The following morning, sobered by his experience, he returned to London. But instead of handing himself in Hollingshead failed to appear in court on 5 April when his co-defendants were sentenced to fines of £50 each, John Doyle's wife receiving a twelve-week conditional discharge. Other than the few days he spent in the north of England, Hollingshead's whereabouts when he was on the run are a mystery. In his autobiography he conflates the 4 March raid and court appearance with his final court appearance in May, when he was sentenced, and gives no clue as to where he was in the interim. There is no documentation from this period of missing time, no letters to or from Leary, Joe Mellen or Alex Trocchi, his three main correspondents.

In the late 1960s Hollingshead told Paul Krassner that after he returned from the north of England he fled to Sweden, being arrested there for a minor drug offence which resulted in the Swedish police contacting Interpol and Scotland Yard sending two detectives to Stockholm to bring him back to face trial in London. Hollingshead claimed he had secreted LSD beneath his fingernails and during the flight he charmed the detectives into removing his handcuffs. On the pretext of getting the detectives a cup of coffee, Hollingshead dosed them with LSD, watching with amusement as Scotland Yard's finest giggled as they gazed into the technicolour clouds. Hollingshead quickly left the plane when it landed, waiting until he passed through customs before letting Scotland Yard know where they could find their missing detectives. A tall story perhaps, but Hollingshead repeated this account to several people at different times in his life, and knowing his predilection for dosing the unwitting it is possible the escapade did take place. Hollingshead enjoyed a few days of freedom in London before handing himself in to the police on 6 May, appearing at Marlborough Street Magistrates Court on 7 May and being remanded in custody until 9 May when he was remanded again, for sentencing, until 24 May.

Word of Hollingshead's activities in London filtered back to Tim Leary and rumours, truths perhaps, quickly gained traction. In early May, Art Kleps visited Millbrook to catch up with Leary and to ask what happened to Metzner, Alpert and Hollingshead. "I keep getting reports on him that are hard to believe, Arthur. He's in England now and I hear he is doing all kinds of diabolical things. Like turning people onto LSD and then turning them in to the police", Leary told Kleps. Kleps responded by telling Leary he thought that Hollingshead had surreptitiously dosed his glass of brandy in 1965, but Leary wouldn't believe him; yet another instance where Leary chose to either ignore or disbelieve his friend could do such things.[36]

Hollingshead chose not to have legal representation in court, deciding instead to represent himself. To heighten an already a surreal experience he took LSD and under cross examination about the search of Pont Street on 25 January made a joke about attempting to flush marijuana down the toilet. His resulting sentence of twenty one months imprisonment, harsh for such relatively minor crimes, was probably exacerbated by his levity in court and his having jumped bail on multiple occasions. High on LSD and stunned by the court's decision Hollingshead was led to the cells where he awaited transport to one of Her Majesty's prisons. Operation London was well and truly over.

Notes

1   Hollingshead, M. *The Man Who Turned On The World*. Blond & Briggs 1973, p.144

2   Letter from Hollingshead to Leary 14/10/65

3   Letter from Hollingshead to Leary 22/10/65

4   Hollingshead 1973 op cit p.144

5   Leary, T. *Psychedelic Prayers*, University Books, 1966, p.5

6   Hollingshead 1973 op cit p.151

7   Ibid p.154

8   Ibid p.155

9   Barritt, B. *The Road of Excess*. PSI, 1998, p.8

10 Devereux, P. Email 11/2/18

11 Letter from Trocchi to Hollingshead 8/12/65

12 Hollingshead, M. London Newsletter, December 1965

13 Michell, J. *Eccentric Lives and Peculiar Notions*. Adventures Unlimited, 1999 p.147

14 Mellen, J. *Bore Hole*. Strange Attractor Press, 2015 p.76

15 Ibid p.77

16 Campbell, B. Interview 7/3/07

17 Wyllie, T. Email, 7/10/13

18 Miles, B. *In the Sixties*. Jonathan Cape, 2002 p.176

19 Berke, J. Email 9/3/07

20 Savage, J. *1966: The Year the Decade Exploded*. Faber & Faber, 2015 p.117

21 Campbell, Bob. Op cit 7/3/07

22 Mellen, J. Email 1/8/18

23 Neidpath, A. Email 28/11/06

24 Hollingshead 1973 op cit p.169

25 Ibid p.169

26 Postcard from Hollingshead to Trocchi, 31/1/66

27 Letter from Trocchi to Penrose, early 1966

28 Hollingshead 1973 op cit p.162

29 Ibid p.162

30 Ibid p.169

31 Mellen 2015 op cit p.78

32 *London Life Magazine*, 19/3/66

33 *Sunday People* 20/3/66

34 Hollingshead 1973 op cit p.167

35 Ibid p.167

36 Kleps, A. *Millbrook*, 2005 p.81

" .... SIX MONTHS IN PRISON ...
NEVER LATE, NEVER SICK, NEVER
ON REPORT, AND WORKS HARDER
THAN ANYBODY ELSE. WHAT'S YOUR
LITTLE GAME, EH, 596 SHINFIELD-H

A Giant Alarm Clock

There's a noise to prison. The metallic noise itself. You know, it's like living inside a giant alarm clock.[1]

On May 24 1966, Michael Hollingshead, now Prisoner 4380, was driven from court to HMP Wormwood Scrubs (aka The Scrubs) to begin his 30 month custodial sentence. In 1966, The Scrubs was the main destination for prisoners sentenced in London courts, who had further trials or appeals pending or were awaiting allocation to another prison. Hollingshead glimpsed the grimy Victorian edifice with its crenelated walls and gothic towers looming over him as the prison van drove through the gates. As he walked through the doors he was instantly aware of the prison atmosphere, heavy with the odour of old food, perspiration and stale urine.

As officials went through the paperwork and induction formalities in Reception Hollingshead noticed that his prison records gave 'waiter' as his occupation, rather than writer which was the occupation he gave when charged. This amused him both because he would be waiting in prison until his release and because he believed he was "continually placed in the wrong category by outside observers".[2] His amusement didn't last long. As he was led to his cell the sights, sounds and smells of the prison made him feel "as if I were entering the bowels of the earth. I don't think I have ever been quite so depressed as I was for those first few minutes in prison. My soul turned grey, if such a thing is possible. I felt drained of all light in this netherworld place in which it was impossible to imagine how anything had ever been young or beautiful."[3]

Hollingshead's accommodation for the next few months was a single person cell, the walls and ceiling of which were painted such a bright white Hollingshead quipped he needed sunglasses for comfort. As his first night behind bars drew closer his aesthetic sensibilities shut down, the psychedelic intensity of his life in swinging London replaced by the starkness of his cell and the soundscape of footsteps, jangling keys and clanging doors punctuated by the shouts and wails of prisoners. Hollingshead had endured some dark days, but this was a new low. After a better night's sleep than he expected, Hollingshead's natural resilience and curiosity kicked in as he started to come to terms with the new game he found himself in. Dressed in coarse and itchy striped prison shirt, jacket and trousers, with thick socks and heavy boots accessorised by a black tie his identity was reduced to just another of Her Majesty's prisoners, dead as "a stick, a stone, a zombie".[4]

After a plain but filling breakfast of porridge, sausage, bread and margarine, he returned to his cell to await his appointment with the prison Governor, who liked to see each new inmate. The Governor must have been puzzled to find that, although Hollingshead had not been a prisoner before, he had been involved in running psilocybin sessions with prisoners in the Concord Prison Experiment in the early Sixties. But his former status counted for nothing in The Scrubs, and after their chat Hollingshead was allocated to the laundry room, where his tasks included washing the prison nurses' underwear and ensuring they weren't stolen by inmates for personal use. Physical labour didn't suit Hollingshead and he was moved first to the ironing room then to the book bindery. He failed hopelessly, possibly intentionally, in each of those duties and was eventually relegated to the cliched prison job of sewing mail sacks where at least he could sit down.

Hollingshead adapted quickly to life in The Scrubs. He wasn't happy to be there but he was pragmatic enough to realise the opportunity his temporary incarceration offered to read, paint and write. Leary sent him a copy of the newly published *Psychedelic Prayers* and he immersed himself in books on Hindu and Buddhist practices found in the prison library. Writing poetry and corresponding with Leary, Trocchi, Mellen and other friends also helped pass the time. As the late spring of 1966 blossomed into Britain's first summer of widespread LSD use, increased police action against people found with hash or acid led to several others from the psychedelic scene being remanded in custody. Nik Douglas the painter, Hugh Blackwell the writer, Hugh Landsdowne the poet, Robert Fraser the art gallery owner and John 'Hoppy' Hopkins, editor of *International Times*, all passed through The Scrubs during the summer of 1966 and Hollingshead was pleased to see these old friends for conversation, chess and the exchange of news. Suddenly, prison didn't seem so bad.

Hollingshead had no problem obtaining hashish and LSD during his sentence and cannabis was smuggled in using several methods, including packed down the barrel of felt tipped pens. Drugs were not a big problem in British prisons in the Sixties and prison staff were naïve about cannabis and almost totally ignorant of LSD which was easily smuggled in, soaked onto letters or the pages of books. One of Hollingshead's visitors was Richard Alpert, his friend from the Harvard and Millbrook days, who brought with him, to Hollingshead's delight, a bunch of LSD infused grapes. Alpert's visit gave rise to one of the many anomalies in Hollingshead's autobiography, where he claims Alpert was accompanied by Augustus Owsley Stanley III (aka Bear), the legendary American LSD chemist. Stanley acknowledges he was in England with Alpert at that time but denies having visited Hollingshead or having even heard of him until years later. Though hash and acid were easily available in The Scrubs, methamphetamine, heroin or alcohol were not and Hollingshead was able, at least while he was in prison, to keep these addictions at bay.

The only surviving records of Hollingshead's time in prison are the letters he wrote and, seven years later, recollections in his autobiography. Many of the events and people he writes about from this time can be verified, but we only have his assertions for others. One puzzle concerns George Blake, the MI6 double agent, sentenced to forty-two years in May 1961 for being a Russian spy. Blake served part of his sentence in Wormwood Scrubs, where Hollingshead claims he met and befriended him, finding him an excellent conversationalist and chess player. Blake was intrigued by Hollingshead's LSD stories and expressed a desire to take the drug in prison, with Hollingshead as guide. Until then Hollingshead had been cautious who he gave LSD to in The Scrubs, restricting it to prisoners he knew or those already experienced with the drug. He made an exception to this rule for Blake and planned a session for a Sunday afternoon, when there was a minimal staff presence and cells were left open for socialisation.

Hollingshead chose Blake's cell for the trip as it had curtains and carpets, a stock of books and even a short-wave radio. Blake took an unknown dose of acid and calmly settled down to wait for the drug to take effect. It's unclear if Hollingshead took LSD as well, he usually did when acting as a guide, but he certainly advised Blake what to expect and how to manage the experience. As the LSD began to take effect Blake became agitated and paranoid, accusing Hollingshead of being a Secret Service agent who had tricked him into taking a truth drug under the pretence of it being LSD. The irony that in the 1950s MI6 spent several years trying and failing to develop LSD as a truth drug was almost certainly lost on both men. Blake's paranoia continued to grow, and he threatened Hollingshead, telling him he would be assassinated within the next twenty-four hours. Hollingshead was unaccustomed to this kind of extreme reaction and was beginning to regret turning Blake on, concerned a prison warder might overhear his panic and intervene. He decided the best way to deal with the potential freak out was to remain calm and to keep reassuring Blake that everything was alright and allow his paranoia and anxiety to pass. The approach worked and once past the peak of the trip Blake became quieter and thoughtful but remained anxious, expressing his fears about the years of prison ahead of him. Hollingshead's description of the trip with Blake sounds plausible, but did it really take place, or was it a literary fantasy, implying communion with a notorious character who was as opposed to the consumer driven status quo as he was?

Hollingshead only ever mentions the Blake trip once, in his autobiography, which was written over six years later. None of Hollingshead's letters to Leary from prison mention the incident which, if it did happen, is odd because Hollingshead liked to boast of any achievement which might impress his friend. Nor did Hollingshead relate the story to Joe Mellen, who visited several times and maintained a correspondence for the full term of his imprisonment. And there is damning evidence that the trip didn't take place from two sources, one close to Hollingshead and one very familiar with Blake's life. Kristof Glinka met Hollingshead in Nepal, two years after his prison release, and they became close friends. Kristof was also the ghost writer of Hollingshead's autobiography, with access to his diaries and other personal documents, yet he has no recollection of being told about Blake and suspects the story is a lie, added by Hollingshead to the final draft of the book before it went to the publishers. Roger Hermiston, Blakes's biographer, has serious doubts about Hollingshead's claim too, writing, "I find it hard to believe that he (Blake) would forsake his controlling, somewhat puritanical character to dabble in drugs. He may well have made friends with Hollingshead, as he did with men from all backgrounds in the Scrubs – but drug experimentation doesn't seem likely."[5] Blake escaped from The Scrubs not long after the alleged trip, later surfacing in the USSR.

Taking everything into consideration the likelihood is that Hollingshead made the story up for literary effect, just as he later falsely claimed to have turned on several of London's psychedelic luminaries. Whether true or not, the tale of George Blake's trip exemplifies the difficulties we face in accepting many of Hollingshead's claims, not least because some of them *were* demonstrably true.

Within weeks of arriving at The Scrubs, Hollingshead appealed against his three convictions relating to the possession of morphine, arguing that as he had been refused legal aid and was not allowed to call witnesses he had been denied the right to a proper defence. The court report in the newspapers, following the 11 October hearing, noted Hollingshead had been "thrown over" by two firms of solicitors prior to his trial in May which explains why he chose to present his own defence. In his autobiography he portrays this as an act of defiance against the system, whereas in reality he was denied legal aid and couldn't retain paid representation. Against strong opposition from the prosecution, Lord Parker concluded there had been a miscarriage of justice and quashed the three convictions. Hollingshead didn't contest the conviction for possessing a small amount of cannabis and Lord Parker ordered the sentence to be reduced to a still draconian 18 month prison term.[6]

Hollingshead was pleased at the reduction in his sentence and even more pleased on 13 October when he was transferred from The Scrubs to HMP Leyhill, an open prison in Gloucestershire to which prisoners considered a low risk of escape were sent. Leyhill had no security fences or walls and Hollingshead was delighted to be surrounded by nature, his senses flooded by the sights, sounds and smells of the English countryside in autumn. Leyhill did have its downside though.

The accommodation at The Scrubs was bleak and basic but Leyhill's was even less salubrious and on arrival at Leyhill Hollingshead was allocated a bed and storage locker in a dormitory shared with thirteen other men. It was there he met musician Pat Ryan who was serving time for possession of hashish. Their chance meeting led to a long friendship which would prove to be of musical significance for Hollingshead several years later. Hollingshead also met HMP Leyhill's Governor and discussed a wide range of subjects with him including the poetry of Robert Burns and Ella Wheeler Wilcox. The Governor was keen for inmates at Leyhill to get involved in as many activities and interests as possible and suggested Hollingshead might like to join the prison Bridge Club and Debating Society – both of which he did – and perhaps apply for a course in fish ecology at Bristol University or even start a flying club. Quite how the flying club idea worked in the context of a prison environment was never explained, but it was a measure of Leyhill's progressive approach to the problems of incarcerating intelligent young men that they had discussions of that kind. Or, it could have been yet another of the untruths Hollingshead's autobiography is peppered with.

Just as he did at The Scrubs, Hollingshead quickly got the measure of HMP Leyhill's system and the 'rules' of the game. His immediate concern was what job he would be allocated. Sewing mail bags at The Scrubs was easy, but a demeaning waste of his talents and ingenuity, so it was with satisfaction, and a degree of irony considering his miswritten occupation on entering The Scrubs, that he was sent to be a waiter at the adjacent Prison Officers' Training School. In this role Hollingshead became one of the first prisoners trainee staff encountered and he exploited to the full the opportunities this allowed. As he waited tables, Hollingshead gained the confidence, trust and even affection of the trainee warders, and was soon being given the occasional bottle of wine and allowed to use their billiard table, among other freedoms unavailable to other inmates. Hollingshead was regarded by Leyhill staff as a model prisoner, but his intelligence and demeanour also meant he was treated with suspicion. Their attitude was summed up by Hollingshead in a cartoon he drew and sent to Tim Leary, showing a balding, large nosed Hollingshead clad in an arrow covered prison jacket being asked by a Prison Officer, "...six months in prison...never late, never sick, never on report, and works harder than anybody else. What's your little game, eh, Shinkfield-Hollingshead?"[7] Part of Hollingshead's 'little game' was simple; he kept a low profile, caused no trouble to staff or inmates and served his sentence quietly. As Pat Ryan remarked years later to Hollingshead's daughter "Michael had the run of the prison, worked in the kitchen and manipulated even the hardest criminals, they all got a kick out of him."[8]

One of the best ways for any prisoner to get through their sentence was to fill the long days and nights with as much interest and activity as possible and Hollingshead threw himself into several projects. In the course of their correspondence, Leary agreed to compile a book of Hollingshead's writings and artwork, for which he would write the Foreword, and find a publisher. Most of Hollingshead's prison writings are lost but it's possible from his letters to Leary to work out the kind of things he was collating. For instance *The Ballad of Wormwood Scrubs* was a long poem about his time there, the title based on Oscar Wilde's *The Ballad of Reading Gaol*.

When Hollingshead was first sentenced, he lied to his parents, telling them his absence was due to him touring Canada and Scandinavia. When his mother discovered he was in prison she was disappointed but probably not surprised at either his predicament or his lie. She might have been more concerned had she known her son was seriously considering drilling a hole in his head. This idea stemmed from letters and conversations about trepanation with his friend from the WPC Joe Mellen, whose mentor Bart Huges had drilled a hole in his head in January 1965 to reduce his brain blood volume and thus, hopefully, remain high forever. Hollingshead wrote at length from prison to Leary about Mellen, trepanation and BBV, debating whether he should be trepanned. BBV was a brief sensation in the mid Sixties and Mellen wrote 'Brain Blood Volume', a song which folk singer Julie Felix recorded on her 1966 record, *Changes*. However, even the promise of a permanent high was not enough to persuade many people to drill a hole in their head and only a handful, including Mellen and his wife Amanda Feilding, actually carried out the procedure.

As 1966 turned to 1967, Hollingshead wrote a melancholic letter to Leary, enclosing the finished version of the *Ballad of Wormwood Scrubs*, and making the observation – certainly true in Hollingshead's case – that, "The psychedelic experience increases our wisdom but doesn't reduce our follies".[9] There's no record of most of Leary's replies, but it's clear there were often lengthy gaps between responses. As Hollingshead was busily working on the book with Leary, these delays in communication worried him. Writing on Valentine's Day 1967, Hollingshead opened with, "In case you don't quite recall me, dear Timothy, I'm the cheerful little widowed lady you met in London with the headaches, that never complained".[10]

When Hollingshead became eligible for home leave he asked his sister Janette to send him a selection of train times between Gloucester and Edinburgh between 4 and 10 April 1967. He also told Leary he would soon be writing from Edinburgh and not Leyhill, noting that another major piece of writing, a short book entitled *Walden III*, or *The Confessions of an English Marijuana Smoker* was well underway. Hollingshead's home leave passed without incident other than the car he was driving being issued with a parking ticket in Edinburgh's Charlotte Square. This didn't bother Hollingshead as the car was borrowed from his brother in law, who received the court summons and had no choice but to pay up.

Leary responded with uncharacteristic speed to Hollingshead's letter, enclosing a draft of his forthcoming book *High Priest* for comment. Hollingshead wrote back, being generally complimentary about the manuscript and clearing up a few minor factual errors, suggesting

Leary refer to him as Shinkfield-Hollingshead rather than Hollingshead as the inclusion of his birth surname would lead to better sales figures in the north of England and Scotland where his family lived. He was somewhat annoyed at Leary's description of him as "Michael with his half bald head and his angelic gross face, pink-veined from alcohol, chain smoking Camel cigarettes." Hollingshead argued that his face wasn't pink-veined and the suggestion it was caused by alcohol "did not fit the picture I had of myself at that time". He suggested a somewhat poetic description, "...with his half bald head and his angelic gross face, sunlit and tranquil, indicating its (indecipherable) slowly to the waning sea unrippled, far below: a face in which nothing replies, whose silences are one more meditation for the rose."[11]

At the prison Governor's behest, Hollingshead became heavily involved with Leyhill's debating society; opposing, and winning, such debates (proposed by the governor) as 'This house is of the opinion that ladies are more important than gentlemen'. He was also writing, Paradise Lost – The True Story, a psychedelic revisioning of Milton's poem, assisted via letter and visits from Joe Mellen. Milton's original text was added to and altered so, for instance, the opening line became, "There was war in heaven. Satan lost – flipped out on prolonged Sugarlack".[12] Hollingshead persuaded several prisoners to help him create a multi-media 'Happening' interpretation of Paradise Lost, presenting his reworking of the poem as he believed the original might have been. At the first meeting of those involved in the play Hollingshead consulted the I Ching and threw the hexagram K'un, The Receptive, which he interpreted as an encouraging sign. Plans were made for a mime element in the show and designs drawn up for large geometric mobiles and masks. Inmates worked on constructing a strobe light and new music was written to accompany John Dowland's Elizabethan compositions. This included a couple of the songs Joe Mellen had written for Julie Felix, 'The Great Brain Robbery' and 'Brain Blood Volume', the latter featuring verses and chorus of:

It's what the pipes have been smoked for
Witches have been cloaked for
Headstands have been done for
The whole thing was begun for
It's what the world was made for
The price must be paid for
Brainbloodvolume[13]

When the Prison Chaplain heard about this new version of Paradise Lost he attended one of the planning meetings and described the production, unsurprisingly, as 'godless'. This only encouraged Hollingshead and he was delighted to report the criticism to Leary and Mellen. His letters to Leary were now almost entirely about the play and brainbloodvolume, several pages of tiny, closely written and barely intelligible handwriting and dense with content, much of which was obscure and only clear to those who understood the concepts behind trepanation. His fascination with LSD seemed, for the time being at least, to have been subsumed by the possibilities of BBV, with Hollingshead finding Mellen's philosophy, "...very restful, satisfying and hopeful". One reason for this hiatus of interest in LSD might have been because in HMP Leyhill Hollingshead didn't have the same access to the drug as in The Scrubs. Quoting the manuscript of *Walden III* to Leary, Hollingshead notes, "The only subject I won't write about is LSD. I'm doing myself brain damage, honestly. Talking about the LSD scene damages the mind."[14]

The summer of 1967 was hot and sunny and when he wasn't working on the play, his writings or correspondence, Hollingshead passed the time playing cricket and bird watching. Being on the cricket pitch topped up his sun tan while he was able to observe the weather and bird life from his cell and from helping with the prison gardens. Hollingshead wrote long descriptions of all the aspects of the natural world he experienced at Leyhill and it's obvious his observations stimulated his mind and gave him great comfort. But this nature-inspired peace of mind was often interrupted by his frustration at what he saw was happening in the media. An avid reader of newspapers and radio listener, Hollingshead was picking up on what he called, "the new spate of armchair psychedelia, which threatens an incredulous public as surely as it jolts those of us who 'know'". In the 21st century there are thousands of published books dealing with every aspect of the psychedelic experience and its culture but prior to 1967 there were only a handful. Citing Houston and Masters' *Varieties of Psychedelic Experience*, Andrews' and Vinkenoog's *The Book of Grass*, Bestic's *Turn Me On Man* and Lawrie's *Drugs*, Hollingshead, who knew the authors personally, wrote to Leary, "What on earth can one say in the face of all this nonsense?". According to Hollingshead, 98% of what was written in these books was nonsense, the 2% that wasn't being apparently some quotes from Errol Flynn in *The Book of Grass*.[15]

The media attention given to the World Psychedelic Centre at Pont Street, the police raid, and Hollingshead's imprisonment appeared to have ended his relationship with Desmond O'Brien, Hollingshead's last communication with the Old Etonian banker and psychedelic entrepreneur being in March 1966. O'Brien is never mentioned again until 1973's *The Man Who Turned On The World*. Perhaps, after the *London Life* debacle, as he had done with other friends and acquaintances when they annoyed him or he felt threatened by them, Hollingshead decided he had no further use for O'Brien, and he was simply dropped from Hollingshead's friendship circle. O'Brien vanished completely from the psychedelic scene and in 1969 died of an overdose in the grounds of his country estate in Cheshire, surrounded by hundreds of ampoules containing heroin, morphine and methedrine.[16]

As Hollingshead's prison sentence entered its final six months, he began to worry about the future; what he would do when released and, more importantly, what he would do for money. Other than a few trunks containing writings, ephemera and artefacts picked up on his travels, stored in Edinburgh, Hollingshead had no money or assets and his employment prospects looked bleak. He hadn't been conventionally employed since living in Denmark in the 1950s, although it had always been his long term ambition to carve out a career as a writer. Now, even the book of poems and other writings Leary said he was collating and brokering on his behalf seemed in doubt, but Hollingshead clung to the idea and was so convinced it would come to fruition he sent Leary a Prologue entitled *Omne Meum, Nihilistic Meum*, literally "tis all mine and none mine".

On 19 August 1967, Hollingshead wrote again to Leary, expressing his hopes and fears for his future when he was released on 13 September. Though he longed for freedom, Hollingshead was worried he might fall back into the kind of drug abuse which had led to his imprisonment. Now disillusioned with his self-styled role as a public advocate for LSD he told Leary that his future was as a writer and he was excited about the novel he was writing. But to finish the novel, and establish himself as a writer, Hollingshead needed money and somewhere to write. He'd had quite enough of Britain, telling Leary, "Quite honestly, I'm not happy at all at the thought of staying in this country". He boldly asked for a $300 advance on royalties for their book, claiming it would give him, "a little freedom from games immediately I come out and a chance to get out of the way for a bit". It is unclear whether Leary ever forwarded the money to Hollingshead but it seems unlikely as the book never found a publisher.[17]

Prior to his imprisonment Hollingshead's idea of prison had been a mixture Nazi concentration camps and the Alcatraz fantasies of American B movies. By the end of his sentence he realised the British prison system was considerably different. Hollingshead was incarcerated at a time when there was little violence between prisoners and, by and large, inmates were treated with respect by the prison guards. His physical liberty had been constrained but Hollingshead had found the freedom to express himself creatively through his writing. Prison, he wrote, was "a feeling, a subjective as well as a purely physical thing... Prison is some kind of other place in which I would never wish for anyone to have to live out their simple life or death."[18]

On 13 September 1967, Hollingshead walked free from HMP Leyhill. His first port of call was to visit his sister Janette in Scotland. He stayed for a while at the Roxburghe Hotel in central Edinburgh and set about raising funds for his next venture. Still half-heartedly hoping Tim Leary was going to publish his prison essays and poems, he wrote a plaintive letter, sending some more content for the book. Leary's lack of response to Hollingshead's queries clearly irked and upset him, reflected in comments such as, "Shall we ever meet again in this lifetime? I wonder; and feel quite sad that one should have to entertain such thoughts at all."[19] Leary's response, if indeed he did respond, is not known.

Hollingshead was free, but times had changed. He had no London base, no income and his British friends seemed unconcerned about him. Worse still, his parents had stopped sending him money. Desperate for funds, he approached his 96-year-old grandmother for financial support and in doing so inadvertently displayed the callous side of his nature. His grandmother was in hospital and, according to Hollingshead, "... spending her fortune on medical services to reach the age of 100 and thus receive a telegram from the Queen."[20] The doctors, perhaps having been informed of his manipulative nature, denied Hollingshead access to his relative.

In serving sixteen months of his eighteen month sentence, Hollingshead missed being able to participate in Britain's 1966 and 1967 'summers of love'. But he'd had enough of Britain and, after the failure of the World Psychedelic Centre, had no reason to stay there, nor was there anything for him in America. He had tired of their psychedelic scenes and wanted a fresh start, somewhere he could refocus after prison, somewhere he could get his mind together, write and plan what to do next.

Notes

1   Stafford, P. (ed), *Magic Grams*. 1985, p.165
2   Letter, Hollingshead to Trocchi, 8/9/66
3   Hollingshead, M. *The Man Who Turned On The World*. Blond & Briggs, 1973, p.172
4   Ibid p.172
5   Hermiston, R. Email 10/1/2018
6   *The Guardian* 12/10/66
7   Letter, Hollingshead to Leary, 28/10/66
8   Hollingshead, V. email 20/1/07
9   Letter, Hollingshead to Leary, 29/12/66
10   Letter, Hollingshead to Leary, 14/2/67
11   Letter, Hollingshead to Leary, 19/4/67
12   Letter, Hollingshead to Leary, 25/5/67
13   Ibid
14   Letter, Hollingshead to Leary, 8/6/67
15   Letter, Hollingshead to Leary, 20/6/67
16   *Daily Express*. 'Banker Who Died Next To Secret Drugs Hoard'. 20/9/69
17   Letter, Hollingshead to Leary, 19/8/67
18   Hollingshead, M. *The Man Who Turned On The World*. Blond & Briggs, 1973, p.184
19   Letter, Hollingshead to Leary, 25/9/67
20   Ibid

THE CELLIST
Charoux 1958

Removed
for
RESTORATION

Fly Me To The Moon

I like Michael very much, but he sure seems mixed up.[1]

On 30 September 1967, Michael Hollingshead boarded the MS Blenheim at Newcastle in the north east of England for the voyage to Oslo in Norway. After the heat of the summer and his foetid prison accommodation Hollingshead felt unfettered as he watched England recede into the distance. He was returning to an area he felt an affinity with, "For I am at heart a Northerner, most at home in my Scandinavian Kingdoms of the snows; essentially a Tundra type."[2] After disembarking in Norway Hollingshead rented a small farm above the tree line of the Gudbrandsdal Valley a few miles from the town of Lillehammer. Thousands of feet above Lake Mjoesa, Hollingshead felt isolated but content in the prehistoric landscape chosen by playwright Henrik Ibsen to be the home of his wandering hero, Peer Gynt, to whom Hollingshead, in his autobiography, had the imagination, some might say audacity, to liken his own peripatetic life to.

For the first few weeks Hollingshead did little, enjoying the passage of clouds as they drifted across the rock strewn hillside. For intellectual stimulation he started making notes for his autobiography and began translating Norse sagas into English. This latter work helped him to regain his fluency in Norwegian and acted as an aid to concentration, putting him in a meditative state of mind. Hollingshead saw his time in the Gudbrandsdal Valley as a period of waiting and hoping, although for what he doesn't say, while getting on with mundane tasks. It was not in his nature to remain isolated for long though and, besides his daily writing discipline, he befriended a group of poets in Lillehammer where he was invited to a counter cultural poetry reading. On the evening of the event as he walked down the mountain, Hollingshead fortified himself with several joints against what he expected to be a drab evening. His fears about the counter culture in rural Norway were confirmed when he had to endure several sincere but dull anti-Vietnam war poems, one comparing the Vietnam war to the coming of motorways to Norway. Hollingshead was the final poet of the evening and to create a dramatic atmosphere he dimmed the house lights and lit candles to create a flickering penumbra before adopting the half-lotus position and in perfect Danish intoning Leary's translation of Sutra fourteen from the *Tao Te Ching*.

> *Gazing, they do not see it*
>   *they call it empty space*
> *Listening, they do not hear it*
>   *they call it silence or noise*
> *Groping, they do not grasp it*
>   *they call it intangible*
> *But here*
> *We spin through it*
> *Electric, Silent, Subtle*[3]

The audience reaction isn't noted, but Hollingshead's swift return to his mountain fastness suggests Lillehammer wasn't ready for his level of psychedelic intensity.

The hermit's life soon lost its allure for Hollingshead and he began to visit Copenhagen in Denmark, intending to look up old friends and find gainful employment. It was in a student bar there one evening in late October that he met Bodil Birke, a twenty-year-old student at the university. Hollingshead charmed Bodil with his soft voice, his smile, intelligence and sense of humour and she fell in love with him. The feeling was mutual and before long Hollingshead stayed at Bodil's flat when visiting Copenhagen, eventually moving in. When she asked what he was doing in Norway and Sweden he told her he was writing his autobiography, poems and translating old Norse sagas.

Psychedelic drugs were scarce in Scandinavia in 1967 and Hollingshead initially found them elusive until he befriended a group of wealthy bohemians. Some of them lived in big houses near the sea to the north of Copenhagen, and Hollingshead would visit them to smoke hash and take acid and occasionally DMT. Hollingshead had first met one of the group, Karl Eskelund, when he lived in Sweden during the 1950s. Eskelund was a travel writer and had been to Mexico where he took peyote with the Huichol tribe and wrote of his experiences in *The Cactus of Love*. Eskelund's peyote experiences led him to a wider interest in consciousness expanding techniques and he was fascinated by Hollingshead's descriptions of Joe Mellen's trepanation and brainbloodvolume theories. With Hollingshead's help, Eskelund wrote an article about trepanation for a newspaper but it was rejected, before being re-written and published in *Information*, a small circulation newspaper for intellectuals.

In December 1967, for the first time in years, Hollingshead met up with Timothy, his son from his marriage to Ebba. Timothy was home from boarding school for his fourteenth birthday and Hollingshead took him out for a meal, writing proudly, "He is a wonderful person. I bought him a pipe, which was all he really wanted, much to my delighted surprise."[4] It is not known if Hollingshead contacted his ex-wife on this visit to Copenhagen, but as he chose not to tell Bodil of the birthday outing with Timothy it's likely Ebba was there.

For a few months during the winter of 1967/68 Hollingshead was content, enjoying life in Scandinavia and his relationship with Bodil. Hollingshead's previous relationships had been fraught with his drug and alcohol abuse and his infidelities. His relationship with Ebba had disintegrated within a few years, and he treated his second wife, Sophie, badly, being violent and unfaithful on several occasions. With Bodil, however, he seemed to have found a woman he genuinely loved and who he treated, by and large, with respect. Writing to Joe Mellen just before Christmas 1967 Hollingshead noted, "...I am currently kept high by a love affair, which is becoming the most beautiful experience of my life; for only the love of a woman can make an honest man of me..."[5] Hollingshead and Bodil spent most evenings in Bodil's flat making love, reading and listening to music. Hollingshead was a voracious reader and among his favourite books during this time were Aldous Huxley's novel, *Island*, Maurice Sendak's hallucinatory children's tale, *Where the Wild Things Are*, Saul Steinberg's *The New World*, Anais Nin's *Collages* and the Norse Sagas. The Beatles, Cream and Jefferson Airplane, among other hip bands of the time, provided a soundtrack to their idyllic existence and he was also fond of listening to cassette tapes of poetry, particularly that of his friend Joe Mellen.

Bodil's parents were unhappy with their daughter's new relationship, not least because of the sixteen-year age gap between the two, so when Bodil went to stay at Christmas Hollingshead thought it better to remain in Copenhagen. Though she was only away for a week Hollingshead sent her love letters every day and dedicated a lengthy poem to her. Other than a few weeks in September and October at the isolated farm above Lillehammer, Hollingshead had moved in with Bodil although he noted enigmatically to Joe Mellen, "Girls provide me with dinners and beds, so any male business is only conducted at night";[6] an observation which reflects the casual misogyny of the times and perhaps also hints at infidelity. Hollingshead was also cautious where his mail was sent to and rather than having it delivered to Bodil's home, he paid for a Post Restante service in Copenhagen. Money was a perennial problem; being out of work in Scandinavia meant that he relied on money borrowed from his family, Bodil or friends. In January 1968, using his fluency in Danish, Hollingshead began to work four hours a day as a messenger at one of Copenhagen's daily newspapers, but money was still tight, and he had to give up smoking and drinking. Although living with Bodil and ostensibly in love, for some reason Hollingshead chose not to tell her about his new employment.

Through his friendship with Karl Eskelund Hollingshead met the Danish millionaire Simon Spies who had made his fortune by buying his own airline and developing cheap package holidays for Scandinavians. Spies was a flamboyant character who boasted of his sexual appetites, which included bacchanalian orgies at his spaceship-like mansion and having sex in public with the star of *Bordellet* (The Brothel) at the film's premiere. Spies was also interested in ways of altering his consciousness, being familiar with meditation and yoga, even employing his own personal Indian mystic. In the late 1960s Spies was becoming curious about the potential of psychedelic drugs but like Hollingshead had found LSD hard to find in Denmark. Knowing of Hollingshead's reputation Spies asked him if he would obtain a large quantity of LSD for him and his friends, offering him a fee and return air fare to London to do so.

This was exactly the kind of work Hollingshead liked best and he accepted the offer. Spies entrusted Hollingshead with a substantial amount of cash with which to buy the LSD and in late January 1968, Hollingshead flew alone to London. He asked Bodil to accompany him, in the belief travelling together as an apparently 'straight' couple would minimise attention from customs officials, but she declined, fearful of the possible consequences. She had no reason to think Hollingshead wouldn't return quickly to Copenhagen but when several days passed and he hadn't come back or phoned she began to worry something bad had happened. Some weeks later, in late February, she received a letter from Hollingshead containing her flat keys and an apology in which he noted, without giving details, that he was having a difficult time and that things had turned out very badly. Bodil never saw or heard from Hollingshead again.

There is a possibility that though the deal to buy acid for Spies wasn't made until early 1968, Hollingshead may have been planning the scam for some time, as he had been thinking about a move to America, and eventually to Tonga, for a while but his "... fears and doubts were overcome somewhat by Christmas..."[7] In his autobiography Hollingshead gives a completely different version of life in Scandinavia and his reason for leaving. There is no reference to his time in Copenhagen with Bodil, or of his friendship with Eskelund. Nor is Spies or the arrangement to buy a large quantity of LSD for him mentioned. Other than some perfunctory details about the weeks spent at the farm above Lillehammer the chapter *Where the Wild Things Are* is a romanticised, airbrushed version of reality. Here Hollingshead claims he wanted to remain in Norway but didn't because "however one tries to understand oneself and sort out one's priorities for happiness, reality is forever getting in the way",[8] without explaining that the 'reality' he refers to was that he had stolen money from a wealthy, influential businessman in a carefully-calculated scam. Writing to Bart Huges later, Karl Eskelund added a postscript confirming Hollingshead had conned Spies and others, "Joe's friend, Michael Hollingshead, made a vanishing act with a fairly large amount of money belonging to other people. It is a strange story. I like Michael very much, but he sure seems mixed up."[9]

Returning to Scandinavia and Bodil was not an option, so after a few weeks in London Hollingshead returned to America to catch up with Tim Leary and Richard Alpert and pursue his dream of being a writer. Hollingshead said farewell to his friends in London and used some of Spies' money to fly to Boston where he had arranged to stay with Gunther Weil in Cambridge, close to the airport. He and Weil spent several hours that night catching up with news about their mutual friends and Hollingshead was surprised to discover the American psychedelic scene had changed considerably since he was last there in 1965. The main wave of LSD experimentation had passed; fewer people were using psychedelics and instead were exploring techniques and spiritualities such as astrology, the Tarot, Meher Baba, yoga, and Gurdjieffian practice. This shift was brought home to Hollingshead the next morning when he rang round his old circle of acquaintances and found Al Cohen, Rolf von Eckartsberg, Paul Lee, Stanley Krippner, Frank Barron, Richard Alpert and others he once took LSD with were now pursuing paths of personal development without psychedelics.

Their change in allegiance puzzled Hollingshead. He sampled some of the easily available illicit LSD and was unimpressed, believing it to be impure and nowhere near the quality of the original Magic Gram. This, he believed, was because since LSD had become a controlled substance, synthetic rather than organic precursors were used in the drug's synthesis. Hollingshead concluded that the 'street acid' now available in America "lacked that invisible non-pharmacological factor – the magical, spiritual component that was what acid was all about".[10] He debated this issue at length with Leary, who disagreed and thought the quality of acid was more or less the same. In a 1975 interview Hollingshead expounded his ideas to American psychedelic historian Peter Stafford, claiming "I had listened to many people who told me they had taken LSD, but from their description it was a completely different journey".[11] The essence of Hollingshead's unsubstantiated belief was that the original consignment of Sandoz LSD had come from one very particular batch of ergot used by Albert Hofmann, and that this gave users a different psychedelic experience to all the subsequent batches. That LSD had fundamentally changed was a bugbear of

Hollingshead's which he would raise several times in the future. Further investigation was clearly needed, but for now his immediate problem was finding employment.

Hollingshead made one last visit his old stamping ground of Millbrook mansion, now only occupied by a few diehards. Art Kleps and his girlfriend Wendy lived in the gatehouse and were just about to go to bed in the final days of January 1968 when a car pulled up. "It's Michael Hollingshead", Wendy said, "He's got a girl with him and he wants to talk to you". Kleps was not a fan of Hollingshead, and had no intention of letting him through the gates unless it was an emergency of some kind. Kleps went downstairs to meet him and found him to be "extremely strung out, as usual, but at least quasi-rational". The purpose of his nocturnal visit was to retrieve something he had stashed under a rock over three years earlier. Hollingshead wasn't interested in talking to Kleps, only in looking under the rock. He didn't say what he was looking for but Kleps presumed it was drugs of some kind. His search proved fruitless and Hollingshead drove off into the night without even thanking Kleps for his help. Kleps was sceptical about the whole experience, "His stash was not under the fucking rock, and maybe it had never been under the fucking rock and maybe there never was any fucking stash", he concluded.[12]

Using his contacts at Harvard, Hollingshead found work there as a trainee librarian in the University Library. His fluency in Scandinavian languages secured him the role of assistant curator of Scandinavian Acquisitions, with a two-year training course and a potential career. Hollingshead spent his days learning the skills of a librarian and in his spare time running poetry workshops at The Readeasy in Nutting Road, Cambridge. This brought him into contact with the area's thriving counter culture, which ensured that he soon had a ready supply of drugs, including opium and high-quality marijuana. His new found stability on the East Coast lasted barely a month before it was shattered at the end of March when Tim Leary arrived in Boston on a lecture tour.

Within hours of their reunion, Leary had undermined Hollingshead's promising career as a librarian with an invitation to return to Berkeley with him. Hollingshead was overjoyed at the chance to be with Leary again and at the end of April resigned his post, flew to California and moved into The Embassy, Tim's Berkeley home.

In San Francisco, Leary took his friend to visit Eldridge Cleaver and Ken Kesey which he found interesting, but Hollingshead was happy just hanging out at Leary's house talking to the procession of counter culture foot soldiers and luminaries who passed through on a daily basis. Besides Leary, the person whose views seemed to chime most with Hollingshead's was the Grateful Dead's Jerry Garcia who said, "Acid has changed consciousness entirely. The US has changed in the last few years and it's because the whole psychedelic thing meant, 'here's this new consciousness, this new freedom, and it's here in yourself'."[13]

Meeting up with Leary again gave Hollingshead the chance to ask about progress with the book he'd been writing in prison which Leary had said he would find a publisher for. Leary had been true to his word and tried his best to find a publisher, managing to get William Targ of New York publishers G.P. Putnam's to read Hollingshead's letters and poems. Putnam's were soon to publish *The Politics of Ecstasy* and Leary had an excellent relationship with them, but even that couldn't sway Targ to publish Hollingshead's book. He had read Hollingshead's writings and considered Hollingshead "...an extraordinary man (and mind), working in quiet chaos and frenzy...One of the problems I see is repetition. There is an over preoccupation with certain matters and after a while one gets a feeling of repetition – and frustration." Targ wasn't totally negative though, writing he would like to see more of Hollingshead's material and commenting, "Perhaps it will jell in my mind when I see more of his work". Hollingshead was disappointed at not being offered a contract but heartened by the interest in his writing and became determined to continue honing his craft until he could get a book deal.[14]

Most of Hollingshead's writing from this period is lost but one piece survives, a 350-word article from April 1968 called *Freud Beats the Fuzz*. Targ's comments to Leary may have just been polite, because if the quality of *Freud Beats the Fuzz* is representative of the material he was sending Leary, Hollingshead would be lucky to get anything at all published. Hollingshead's writing hope now rested on his proposed autobiography, parts of which could already be discerned in letters to friends sent from prison and Scandinavia. To complete his autobiography Hollingshead needed the luxury of solitude and money to support himself during the writing process, neither of which were offered by life in American psychedelia's fast lane. Hollingshead's writing ambitions and projects were temporarily shelved in favour of embedding himself in Leary's retinue, although he contributed to issue one of *Harbinger*, a one-off successor to the defunct San Francisco *Oracle*. Hollingshead's submission to the 24-page tabloid was called *Introduction to "Lightshow"* and he was in good literary company, with Leary and Alan Watts among the other contributors.

With his court case looming, Leary was feeling the pressure and desperately needed some respite from the media. John Griggs from the Brotherhood of Eternal Love came to the rescue and in mid-June flew to Berkeley to invite Leary and his wife to stay at the Brotherhood's ranch in the picturesque San Jacinto Mountains, not far from Palm Springs. Leary seized the opportunity and moved into a secluded cottage where he intended to sit out the legal storm, avoid the media and do some writing. Hollingshead also moved to the ranch for the summer, to be near his friends and to help the Brotherhood repair buildings, level dirt roads and build a sauna which was often used for communal hashish smoking. Each month, Hollingshead and others would trek into the high desert mountains for a full moon LSD session, loosely based on Indian Peyote ceremonies, held in a cave in which they lit a large fire. Guitars, drums and rattles were played and under the influence of an average dose of 1500 ug LSD, the tripped-out group would sing and dance and watch the skies for flying saucers. It was in that cave where Hollingshead, on LSD, read Carlos Castaneda's contentious first book *The Teachings of Don Juan: A Yaqui Way of Knowledge* while it was still a doctoral thesis. His wry comment on Castaneda's books, was, "Some of the best fiction I have read recently. I think they're very good".[15]

In September, Leary received notification his appeal would be held on 28 October at the Supreme Court in Washington. Hollingshead thought it would be a good idea to raise public and media support for the trial using celebrities connected to LSD like Paul McCartney, Donovan, the Rolling Stones and the Moody Blues, who had recently recorded 'Legend of a Mind (Timothy Leary's Dead)' for their *In Search of the Lost Chord* album. Hollingshead wrote to Barry Miles, asking him to be an intermediary, suggesting a meeting of the musicians at the Brotherhood's Ranch, and pointing out that the Stones had tried to find the property recently but got lost. If the musicians could coincide their visit with the full moon Hollingshead said they would be welcome at the monthly full moon LSD ceremony in the mountains. There was no response from Miles or any of the musicians.

Life in California with Leary and the Brotherhood was, even by Hollingshead's standards, chemically high octane and the paranoia associated with extensive drug use began to set in. Drug fuelled or not, paranoia isn't always unjustified or imaginary and several events caused Hollingshead to be worried the Ranch was being watched by the police. On one occasion, the Brotherhood outed a wandering Jesus-like hippie as an undercover narcotics agent from Oakland, and when Hollingshead was taking part in a group acid trip at the mineral springs near Laguna, a police helicopter appeared overhead, causing the Brothers to scatter and hide. His paranoia came to a head when he stumbled across several tons of unconcealed marijuana in a barn. He was exhausted, having "… met too many people in California, heard too many things, maybe even taken too much acid".[16] Hollingshead again longed to be alone to take stock of his situation, and within weeks of celebrating the full moon in the San Jacinto mountains he left the Brotherhood's ranch unaware that it was that same moon which would soon provide him with a brief film appearance and, more importantly, money.

The name Scott Bartlett is little known outside of avant garde film circles, but in the late sixties he was fast becoming one of the leading experimental film makers of his generation. Using a variety of methods and equipment including negative images, polarisation, kinescopes and signal processing, Bartlett developed a technique of hallucinatory film making which chimed with the emerging psychedelic culture and the drugs that fuelled it. His 1967 film, *OffOn*, featuring kaleidoscopic mandalas, was regarded as a key work of psychedelic cinema, and he was invited to provide light show backdrops to bands like The Grateful Dead and Jefferson Airplane at the legendary Fillmore West and Avalon concert venues. Bartlett was obsessed with the American space programme and its intention to land a man on the moon and, with the help of seven young men, each involved in the arts, Bartlett made *A Trip to the Moon*, a 16mm black and white 30-minute film. He opted for a cosmic, spiritual interpretation of a journey through space, having the men discuss the I Ching and astrology over electronically treated images of the moon and spacecraft. Hollingshead, his barely discernible face and voice mixed deep in the audio and video effects, was one of the seven men involved and was paid a substantial fee for his contribution to the film, which had a limited release. Bartlett went on to make a colour version, *Moon '69*, which impressed film makers George Lucas and Francis Ford Coppola, who supported Bartlett's filmmaking throughout the Seventies. *A Trip to the Moon* was just another stop on Hollingshead's journey through the counter culture, but his fee enabled him to escape America, Leary and the Brotherhood and travel to his next destination.

Tonga had been on Hollingshead's mind for a while and on 11 November he made the two day journey to the remote island from San Francisco, via Fiji, arriving on 13 November with a three-month visa.

He had mentioned his urge to visit Tonga in a letter from prison to Leary but gave no reason for his interest and it is odd he set his mind on such a relatively obscure location. Tonga was an island paradise and Hollingshead waxed lyrical in his autobiography about its beaches and the diversity and beauty of its flora and fauna. After checking in to a hotel in Nuku'alofa, the island's capital, he went for a walk before settling down to watch the spectacular sunset. Gazing over the jungle his senses were filled with the sounds of gulls wheeling above him and the drone of the cicadas beneath him. He watched an old fisherman walking home with his nets against the tumult of the crashing waves and a great peace came on him, he thought "Here should I be; and free from myself".[17] Hollingshead was constantly trying to be free of himself without realising the fundamental truth that wherever you go, that's where you are.

Hollingshead found Nuku'alofa too busy for his liking and studied the map of Tonga's 150 islands to find an even more remote spot in which to rejuvenate himself. He settled on Vava'u, a long boat journey from the main island. The potential isolation appealed to Hollingshead and he telephoned the Governor to ask permission to stay there while he concentrated on writing his autobiography. Charmed by Hollingshead's Englishness, the Governor sent a Land Rover to pick Hollingshead up from Vava'u's pier and take him to the thatched hut which was to be his new home. Hollingshead once again thought he had found the perfect location, somewhere he could unwind and try to unravel the loose ends of his life in the heart of nature where he felt inclined to, "…sink down every morning before the beauty of the place in fervent gratitude".[18] This idyll lasted just over a day. On his second morning he woke to the sound of rock music which he traced through the island's dense countryside to a primitive hut occupied by three Americans from the 120 strong Peace Corps contingent carrying out voluntary work on Vava'u. Hollingshead was invited in and offered a bag of locally grown grass from which he rolled a joint. Jefferson Airplane, one of Hollingshead's favourite bands, and the Grateful Dead's *Anthem of the Sun* and *Aoxomoxoa* albums were playing on the cassette machine and he was soon as stoned as his hosts. Hollingshead quickly established his LSD credentials and was surprised to find his new friends had never tried it but would like to. Hollingshead had 100 doses of the Brotherhood of Eternal Love's potent Orange Sunshine acid with him and suggested that he run an LSD session with them on one of the uninhabited islands off Vava'u's coast. The only record of this group LSD trip exists in Hollingshead's autobiography and, although he tries to make light of the event, it's clear that this was one of the few occasions where his legendary abilities as an LSD guide failed badly.

On the three-mile motor-boat journey out to the island, Hollingshead tried to prepare the acid neophytes, giving them an idea what to expect and how to deal with paranoia by chanting a Hindu mantra. The session got off to a good start; the weather was sunny and other than the sound of the waves and the birds there were no distractions to the volunteers' first trip. Instead of keeping a watchful eye on his charges Hollingshead began to meditate as the LSD's effects took hold, unaware that one of the group was experiencing serious problems dealing with the onset of the drug. An occasional effect of LSD is that it gives some people a messiah complex, whereby they believe they are a saviour of others and even the entire human race.

One of Hollingshead's charges loudly declared himself to be Jesus Christ and everyone else his disciples. Hollingshead tried to talk him down from his delusion, but to no avail. As the trip intensified so did the claims of the Messiah who ranted about his imaginary ministry, variously displaying anger, laughter, dismay and fear. A bad trip can be contagious if not carefully managed and the messiah's behaviour began to panic the others. Some of them wandered off into the surrounding jungle, others sat transfixed as their colleague expounded upon the world's evils, insisting they join him on a crusade to save humanity. Now lost in his own trip and without consideration for the welfare of the newly deranged messiah or the rest of the confused group, Hollingshead wandered down the beach alone for several hours. When he returned the group were huddled round a small fire and slowly coming down from the LSD. The messiah had ceased his religious proclamations and, after a night round the fire, was able to laugh at his reaction, but word of the group's disastrous LSD experience quickly spread. The authorities had long suspected that the Peace Corps were using marijuana on Vava'u and had tolerated it, but rumours of LSD caused them to act. The British Consul contacted Hollingshead to ask him what the nature of his business on Tonga was and detectives landed on Vava'u to search for rumoured marijuana plantations. Hollingshead could see a storm brewing, one which could end up with his arrest and possible imprisonment and, wise enough to know the net was closing, returned to San Francisco.

Hollingshead believed his return to America in 1968, after his prison sentence and subsequent disastrous time in Scandinavia, would put him back in the heart of the psychedelic culture. But hooking up with Leary again had only led him back to drug excesses and life in Leary's shadow. The police were persecuting Tim Leary and The Brotherhood of Eternal Love and others from the Millbrook and Harvard scenes had turned to natural ways of altering their consciousness. His own writing career had floundered, with success always tantalisingly out of reach, and he was once again at a dead end in his life's journey. His thoughts turned to the stories he'd heard from travellers returning from India, Nepal and the Far East. Leary, Alpert and others from the Millbrook and Harvard circles had all made the journey to the East in pursuit of spiritual enlightenment, excellent hashish and stunning landscapes. Now it was Hollingshead's turn; it was time to move on again.

Notes

1	Letter from K. Eskelund to B. Huges, 11/6/68
2	Hollingshead, M. *The Man Who Turned On The World*. Blond & Briggs, 1973, p.185
3	Leary, T. *Psychedelic Prayers*. University Books, 1966, p.17
4	Letter from Hollingshead to Mellen, 5/12/67
5	Letter from Hollingshead to Mellen, 7/1/68
6	Letter from Hollingshead to Mellen, 5/12/67
7	Ibid
8	Hollingshead, 1973 op cit p.192
9	Letter from K. Eskelund to B. Huges, 11/6/68
10	Hollingshead, 1973, op cit p.197
11	Stafford, P. Interview with Michael Hollingshead. *High Times*, Winter 1975, p.21
12	Kleps, A. Millbrook, *The Original Kleptonian Neo-American Church*, p.206
13	Hollingshead, 1973, op cit p.211
14	Letter from William Targ to Tim Leary, 2/4/68
15	*High Times*, op cit 1975, p.21
16	Hollingshead, 1973, op cit, p.213
17	Ibid p.213
18	Ibid p.215

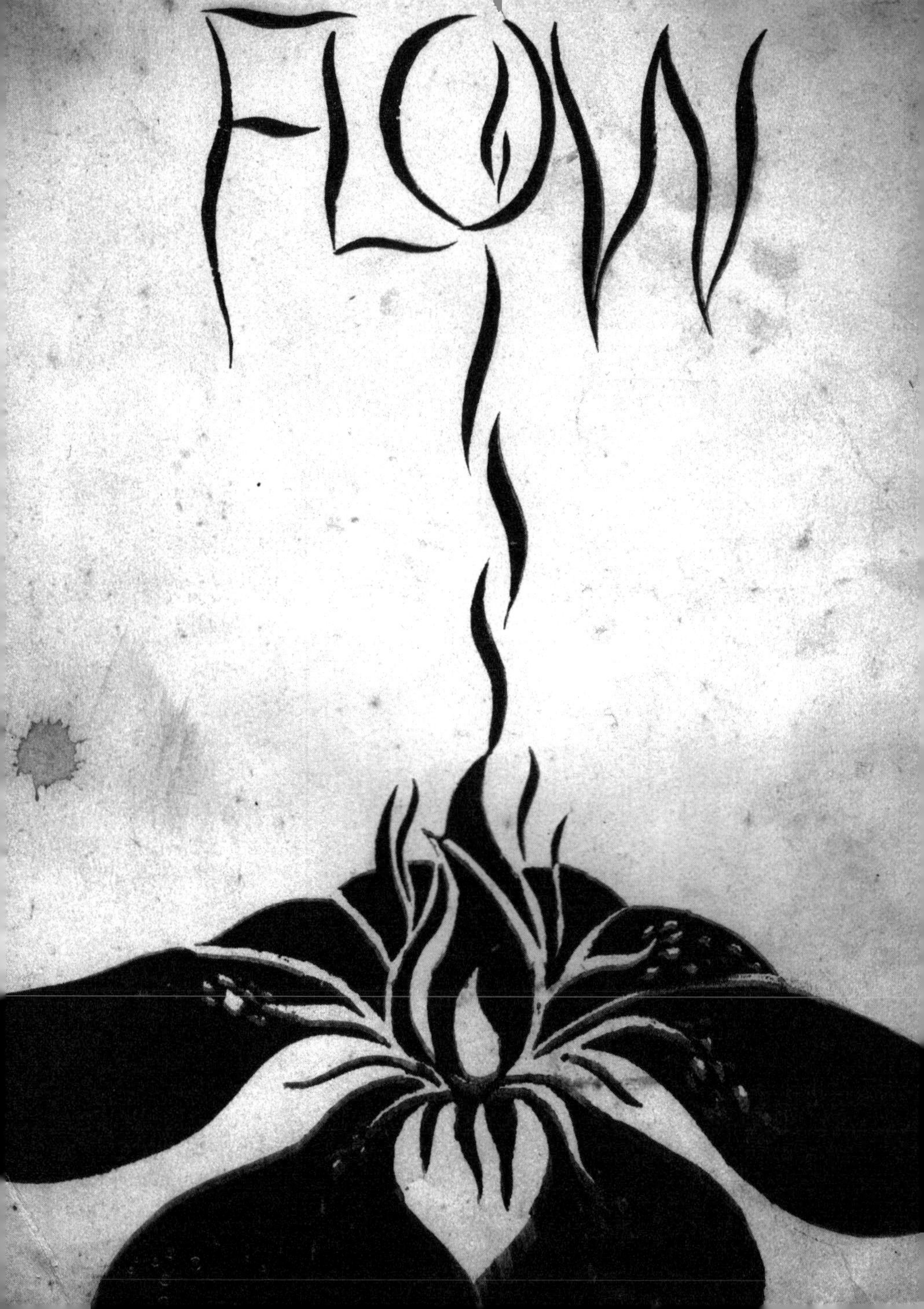
FLOWN

The Journey To The East

Similar to the role Tibet had played in the Western imagination forty years earlier, by the late 1960s – with Tibet closed and Nepal now open – Kathmandu became the home of utopian otherness for a new generation of counter-culturists.[1]

It was an auspicious day for travelling. On 16 July 1969, as Apollo 11 exploded from Earth's atmosphere on its journey to put the first men on the moon, Michael Hollingshead flew into Kathmandu aboard a DC-9 airliner. He travelled light, carrying only his typewriter, hand luggage and a few hundred doses of California 'sunshine' LSD, given to him by the Brotherhood of Eternal Love. He also had about $1000 in cash, the remainder of his fee from the *A Trip to the Moon* film. Any fantasies Hollingshead entertained about breathing in fresh Himalayan mountain air were quickly dispelled by the heat and humidity of the imminent monsoon. A wave of doubt as to his purpose in Kathmandu swept over him in the taxi from the airport and he had to fight off thoughts of heading to Bangkok or Australia. Instead, he checked into a cheap hotel and smoked a few chillums of hash to get his head straight. It had the desired effect.

> *The spell of the Himalayas was upon me. The beauty of my surroundings began to penetrate a hardened carapace, for these mountains had begun to exercise a magic thraldom of their own. And now I was part of it.*[2]

For travellers in the 1960s, air travel to Kathmandu was a luxury. Nepal was usually reached by an arduous overland journey combining hitchhiking, cheap buses, trains and local transport, with journeys often taking several months. Many believed the journey itself was an integral part of the Kathmandu experience, but as usual Hollingshead took the quickest route not only between travel destinations but between states of mind. But however you got there, and however long you stayed, Kathmandu was one of the great hippie destinations of the 1960s.

What exactly drew Hollingshead there is unclear but seems to have been partly a spiritual quest, partly a psychedelic pilgrimage. The religious impulse engendered by high dose LSD sessions had led many psychedelic users to embrace Hinduism or Buddhism as an adjunct to their psychedelic practise, or as a means of integrating their powerful experiences. The *Tibetan Book of the Dead* and other eastern spiritual texts had always been on hand during the high dose LSD sessions at Harvard and Millbrook, and the search for god-head, spiritual awakening or enlightenment, however that state was expressed, was a key driver in the psychedelic circles surrounding Leary. Hollingshead, Leary and others had visited numerous ashrams in America, to which early psychedelic explorers including Bhavani (aka Yvonne Neal, a former senior member of the League for Spiritual Discovery) had retired, and a sense of questing for spiritual truths obtained by other-than-psychedelic means was afoot. Metzner, Ginsberg and Leary had already made the pilgrimage to India, returning with tales of wide-eyed wonder, spiritual insight and a vision of a way forward without drugs. But all, except one, came back as themselves, the exception being Richard Alpert, one of Leary's original Harvard tripping crew, who went east and came back a changed person.

In America, Alpert had glimpsed the kingdom of heaven many times when on LSD, but each time he came down the LSD inspired insights and spiritual states of mind vanished and he was the same old person playing the same old games. This constant return to the quotidian distressed Alpert and as a result, '...an extraordinary kind of depression set in – a very gentle depression that whatever I knew still wasn't enough.'[3] Alpert visited India and Nepal in 1967 and in Kathmandu's Blue Tibetan restaurant met an enlightened American hippie *sadhu*, Bhagwan Dass, who took him to meet his guru, the Indian Neem Karoli Baba. Alpert was overwhelmed by this meeting, not least because the guru consumed a staggering 915 micrograms of LSD, swallowing it in front of Alpert with no apparent effect. The impact on Alpert was dramatic; surely anyone who could handle that amount of LSD could master anything the universe could throw at them. He took the name Baba Ram Dass (meaning servant of god) and returned to America a different man, spiritual practises replacing LSD binges. Alpert went on to write *Be Here Now*, one of the key hippie books of the 1970s, and is to this day a respected spiritual teacher, advocating a drug free path to enlightenment. For a guru, or indeed for anyone, to take 915 micrograms of LSD and remain unaffected is a remarkable event. Remarkable, that is, if true. Clark Heinrich, author and authority on psychoactive fungi, was told by Baba Hari Dass, head of Karoli's ashrams, that Karoli had not taken the LSD pills but had simply palmed and crushed them.[4] Sleight of hand tricks such as this are common among gurus and shamans and there is a delicious irony in the fact that Alpert was at first fooled by the trickster Hollingshead and later by Karoli.

Perhaps it was Alpert's path and example that Hollingshead wished to follow; journey east to find escape from the jaded Michael Hollingshead game, a chance to reinvent himself as a new spiritual being and the possibility of returning to the west as a spiritual, rather than psychedelic guru. Maybe Hollingshead, reflecting on his bumpy friendship with Leary throughout the '60s, could even see the opportunity for a bit of one-upmanship to Leary's guru game?

If spirituality was one lure to Nepal, then drugs were another. Prior to 1973 and the hippie backlash, cannabis was cheap and legally available, even sold in Government-run shops. Many of Kathmandu's hotels catered specifically for the western traveller in search of hash and high times; at Camp Hotel for instance, the management always kept a free chillum in circulation. Others, like the Cabin Restaurant, had psychedelic décor and a stereo playing the latest western rock music. One Nepali noted 'There is so much charas being smoked here that you could just get stoned by sitting here.'[5]

But the underlying and unspoken reason Hollingshead went to Nepal may have been much more prosaic. During 1968 and '69, while in New York, Hollingshead had again acquired a serious heroin habit. Kathmandu he thought, might provide the fresh air, exercise and opportunity for spiritual practise that would straighten him out again. He hinted at this to Leary noting, 'I am arranging my life now in such a way that everything I do is done consciously and with a view to finding my own centre, which I nearly lost during this last sortie into New York City'.[6]

On his first full day in Kathmandu, the vestiges of his hashish reverie echoing in his jet lagged mind, Hollingshead set off to find appropriate clothes and more hash. He made his way through the bustling medieval streets and alleys to Rana's teashop, where he accepted a chillum offered by a group of westerners. Despite being an experienced cannabis user, Hollingshead almost fainted: "The hash was the strongest I'd ever had and completely immobilised me... Rana, the dapper young Nepalese owner of the place, would come over every now and again and ask me if there was anything more that I wanted... I merely shook my head and continued just sitting in my utter stupor.'[7] Hollingshead bought 8 grams of hash for today's equivalent of 20p, and returned to his hotel to sleep off the high.

The next day he renewed his acquaintance with Narayan Shrester, private secretary to Nepal's Crown Prince, who he first met several years earlier at Harvard. They talked at length, Hollingshead outlining his intentions while in Nepal, including starting a poetry magazine called *Flow*. Hollingshead tried to persuade Shrester that he should view the inundation of western hippies not as long-haired layabouts but as spiritual seekers following in the footsteps of the wandering Hindu holy men or *Sadhus*. There were more mundane reasons for the meeting with Shrester, namely the matter of Hollingshead's visa. The authorities in Kathmandu were cracking down on visa applications, some being issued for as little as two days with six weeks being the average duration granted. Hollingshead's friendship with Shrester paid off and the following day he was issued with an extendable one-year visa. After the meeting Hollingshead spent a long, stoned, afternoon in Nepal's National Museum, the religious artefacts transporting him from the present to the timeless spiritual past of the Himalayas. He felt his consciousness shifting to a mode in which he believed he would, '... never feel "alone", which is to live in my own spiritual reserves, that the body-mind was capable of being filled up again with the light through the simple process of looking. How easy it all seemed.'[8]

Hollingshead soon identified the key people in the Kathmandu hippie and spiritual scene and began to befriend them. Whether by giving them LSD, engaging them in his various schemes or just by hanging out with them, Hollingshead quickly became a well-known figure among the city's hippie population, his charisma and presence ensuring everyone was aware of him, making him a local legend. Chronicler of the hippie trail Rory MacLean recalls, 'Michael Hollingshead, the Englishman who had introduced Timothy Leary to LSD, swept along Freak Street pontificating on the aspirations of the great psychedelic revolution.'[9]

One early visitor to Hollingshead's hotel room was Madhusudan Thakur, a Brahmin from Northern India and keen Sanskrit scholar. Thakur was translating Nepalese poetry into English and had also written a sympathetic article about the influx of hippie visitors for Nepal's English language magazine *The Rising Nepal*. Hollingshead was impressed with Thakur and the pair formed a partnership which was eventually to lead to the publication of issue one of *Flow*. Other ideas were mooted including a centre at which spiritual seekers from all points of the globe could meet and learn Sanskrit. A written proposal for this initiative was drafted, and the Crown Prince's secretary, Shrester, informed of the plan by telephone. He too was keen on the idea and immediately arranged for Hollingshead and Thakur to visit renowned poet and Vice President of the Royal Nepalese Academy, Balkrishna Sama. After Hollingshead had, as was his practise prior to any meeting, smoked a chillum to aid his creative processes, he and Thakur visited Sama to discuss the project. The stumbling block was the start-up costs which Sama estimated at around $595,000, an unfeasibly large sum of money to raise in 1969. *Flow*, however, was a different matter. Sama was enthusiastic about the magazine and Thakur translated and read verses to Hollingshead from one of Sama's latest poems, *To Soma*, which had been inspired by the recent Apollo 11 moon landing.

Hollingshead couldn't believe his luck. Not only had he found two noted Nepalese poets to contribute to *Flow* within days of his arrival in Nepal, but there was also a synchronicity of the first poem he was offered being about the Apollo 11 launch which had happened as he flew into Kathmandu. Surely these were propitious signs? Balkrishna Sama certainly thought so. He looked directly at Hollingshead and told him this was a most auspicious omen. Hollingshead agreed and wondered if, perhaps, he'd finally found the guru he had been searching for. But, for the time being at least, LSD remained Hollingshead's chemical guru and he wasted no time in distributing his Brotherhood of Eternal Love's California 'sunshine' to anyone in Kathmandu who wanted it, helping to facilitate some spectacular group LSD experiences. In August he took a group of nine hippies to the summit of a mountain in the Kathmandu Valley where they took LSD in a stunningly beautiful sacred landscape, surrounded by Tibetan Stupas, Buddhist shrines containing religious relics. Hollingshead noted several of the Stupas were vaguely mushroom shaped and wondered if they represented Soma, the divine mushroom mycologist Gordon Wasson had shown him slides of in America a few months earlier. 'But of course, we all got too high to hunt the mushroom and everyone went off into their own trip, assembling late in the afternoon with great tales to tell and discoveries to make.'[10]

In another adventure Hollingshead wrote of a night trek he undertook alone, aiming to reach a mountain peak by sunrise, when he was captured by robbers who took him to their camp and demanded his shoes, clothes and meagre travelling possessions. The bandits were unimpressed by Hollingshead's claim of friendship with people in high places and the situation looked bleak until he escaped by throwing a teapot at the bandit leader, kicking away a tent pole and outrunning his pursuers. This is one of those stories for which we only have Hollingshead's written account as evidence and, bearing in mind his self-mythologising tendencies, this escapade may have been fabricated to impress Leary!

Hollingshead was keen to share with Leary his joy at being in Nepal; "I think I may have finally found the happiness I have missed for all these years of harum-scarum activity. Indeed, I have. I really have you know."[11] The content of his letter was the usual mixture of self-obsessed thoughts, 'I have undergone some profound and significant changes, making my life seem rational and sincere",[12] gossip about the hippie scene in Kathmandu and plans for the future, including obtaining permission to visit the remote kingdom of Mustang and attempts at getting fit enough to attempt the trek to Annapurna. Leary had heard of the recent spate of problems caused by westerners in Kathmandu; hippies freaking out and assaulting each other or running naked through streets and temples; Hollingshead's view was that this was caused by a lack of LSD and the easy availability of heroin, morphine and alcohol. This was contradicted by some commentators on the Kathmandu scene who believed it was the *presence* of LSD that caused the freak-outs. But for Hollingshead LSD was as much a currency as it was cause and effect, the oil with which he initiated and lubricated connections, solidifying his self-styled status and reputation as 'Man Who Turned on the World'. He complained to Leary the supply of LSD he brought to Nepal was almost exhausted, "This sunshine I have is the first significant amount seen here for several years. Cannot we always arrange for a small amount of each batch to reach these distant outposts? I will try to contact one or two people and have them send me some. But a word from yourself would be helpful here, I think. Everyone here wants some. I have enough for perhaps another 50 sessions. If we are going to live as a community and undertake pilgrimage, then the Sacrament should be available.'[13] Four years later in his autobiography he contradicted himself, saying there was lots of LSD. In view of this contradiction it's tempting to interpret his account of freak-outs being caused by a *lack* of acid was a subtle form of emotional blackmail, intended to persuade Leary to use his influence on the 'people' Hollingshead alludes to.

Not all those Hollingshead befriended in Kathmandu were acidheads or hippie travellers. And nor were the hash cafes, full moon parties and monasteries the only places Hollingshead could be found. Kami Kanetsuka, who had lived in the city since 1966, met Hollingshead at a British Embassy garden party held to celebrate a visit by Prince William of Gloucester. Chameleon-like, Hollingshead had shed his usual hippie garb and reinvented himself for the event in a smart grey suit, which he referred to as his 'uniform' for such occasions. Kanetsuka and Hollingshead became good friends and he visited her at home and spent time with her at parties in and around the city. He was impressed because the Kanetsukas owned a fridge, a scarce item in Kathmandu at that time, but Kanetsuka's husband, who opened the first Japanese restaurant in Kathmandu, didn't like Hollingshead because he persistently stole items destined for the restaurant from the fridge. Kanetsuka was never directly aware of Hollingshead's LSD use but remembers, "At some gatherings where he must have taken acid, I would be talking with him and then he would go off into some place that was completely incomprehensible to me."[14] Unlike the experience many women had of Hollingshead, Kanetsuka's was a positive one, 'I think I thought of him as a kind of crazy man, but he was always kind to me.'[15]

In September 1969, Hollingshead moved out of his hotel and rented two floors of *Shangri-la*, a large house near to the Swayambhunath temple in Kathmandu's Bijuswari suburb. Here he established a daily routine of breakfast, followed by a chillum of hash, after which he worked on editing issue one of *Flow*. Hollingshead discovered that permission from the Nepalese Prime Minister was required for a foreigner to publish a magazine in Nepal. This potentially serious obstacle didn't daunt Hollingshead because, as he often did, he knew someone who knew someone who could open the necessary social door. In this case the someone was Soorya Bahadur Singh, a contributor to *Flow* and a Nepalese government official whose brother was private secretary to the King of Nepal. Hollingshead utilised these connections to arrange an audience with the Prime Minister. According to Hollingshead the Prime Minister liked him immediately, a conviviality which came about not least because of the laughter generated by Hollingshead's formal Nepalese attire, which was from another century in that country's sartorial history. During the hilarity at this fashion faux pas, the Prime Minister signed the necessary document allowing Hollingshead to publish *Flow*.

The *Shangri-la* house became the focus for many of Hollingshead's LSD transactions, a constant stream, by his own account, suggesting the diminishing stash he bemoaned to Leary had been replenished, possibly from some of the many Californians visiting Kathmandu. The increasing availability of LSD, together with the rising number of freak-outs and Hollingshead's obvious connection to the LSD scene, led the editor of Kathmandu's English language newspaper *The Rising Nepal* to ask him to write about the influx of hippie travellers. Hollingshead was keen to oblige and penned *The Divine Mutants*, a lengthy piece which referenced Leary's aphorism "Turn On, Tune in and Drop Out" and explained the hippies' dissatisfaction with the encroaching forces of western conformity. He wisely avoided direct mention of LSD, instead stressing his belief that those flocking to Kathmandu were, as he had told the Crown Prince's private secretary, a new wave of spiritual pilgrims. The editor of *The Rising Nepal* was impressed and commissioned Hollingshead to write a twelve-part series on Tantra for the paper, called *Old Art in the Hands of New Artists*.

Spirituality was very much on Hollingshead's mind toward the end of 1969 and he believed he was close to a breakthrough: 'My life in the West is over on 31 December, 1969. My pact with the Spirit Mercurius is now over, and I shall now consider myself then free to perhaps retire into the Buddhist hierarchy.'[16] Hollingshead's reference to Mercurius is intriguing and meshes with the analysis of his personality being that of a Trickster. Mercurius, or Mercury, is the Roman god of financial gain, eloquence, communication, travellers, boundaries, luck, trickery and thieves. He is also the guide of souls to the underworld. Hollingshead saw himself skilled in all those qualities and could thus have easily identified with Mercurius. What or who Hollingshead intended to identify with after Dec 31, 1969 is not mentioned, and New Year's Eve passed without comment.

While in Nepal, Hollingshead became aware of the problems faced by those on the hippy trail arrested for possessing or smuggling hashish. From Greece through Turkey, Iran, Pakistan, India and Nepal, hundreds of young people were being arrested and thrown into jails and

forgotten or ignored by their own countries. Hollingshead encouraged
Leary to contact the relevant embassies and obtain the names of those
imprisoned for 'psychedelic offences' so that they could raise awareness
of their plight. The idea didn't progress further than discussions in their
letters, but it was a subject of great concern to Hollingshead and one
which occupied his thoughts a great deal while in Nepal.

Hippy traveller Jasper Newsome flew into Kathmandu in October
1969 and immediately made his way to Swayambhunath, known as the
Monkey Temple because of its simian occupants. A friend there brought
him up to date with the city's hippie scene; 'In brief, many people,
much acid, some incidents.'[17] Newsome's friend told him there was a
man named Michael Hollingshead in Nepal who had some acid called
'Sunshine'. Newsome had met Hollingshead many times in London,
but hadn't seen him since the spring of 1966. Jasper listened as his
friend told him about Hollingshead's crazy ideas: he wanted to employ
hippies to construct a sewage system in Bhaktapur to help rid the town
of cholera; he was starting up a literary magazine called *Flow*; he was
writing his psychedelic autobiography and, to cap it all, he was helping
a princess found a monastery. Even better, Hollingshead had become
friendly with the Crown Prince of Nepal and could apparently arrange
visa extensions for the chosen few.

Newsome sought Hollingshead out and they met, reminisced
about old times and took acid. Something – no one knows what – went
disastrously wrong during the trip, leaving Jasper upset and irritated.
After brooding about the disappointing psychedelic experience, the
following morning Jasper decided to renounce all drugs forever. This
was a common course of action for many who experienced a psychedelic
dark night of the soul, but Newsome wanted to take it further and
wanted to blacken Hollingshead's name. In a rage he strode off to the
Kopan monastery run by Hollingshead's friend Zenaïde Rachevsky, to
berate her about Hollingshead's shortcomings, calling him 'a pernicious
character doing untold damage to the human race for the sake of his

own gratification.' Zina exploded with laughter, saying 'dear Michael takes himself so seriously, but he's such a child'. For once, it seemed, someone had got the measure of him!

After a few days of drug free deep meditation Newsome forgave Hollingshead, who was characteristically unreceptive and refused to take any responsibility for the bad trip, telling Newsome he had '...just been projecting his own fears onto him' during the experience. Newsome was angry again and couldn't bring himself to ask Hollingshead to use his contacts to arrange a visa extension, instead heading to the hippie enclave in Goa. On hearing Newsome was leaving Nepal, Hollingshead remarked condescendingly, '... when or if I returned in spring, I would find those who had spent the winter in Kathmandu so much higher than those who had gone down to Goa.'[18]

Also in Kathmandu was Billy Forbes, who had last seen Hollingshead in 1968 in Arizona at the Sri Ram ashram, and bumped into him occasionally at the house of a mutual friend. But because of Hollingshead's reputation as a "...snitch and a junkie – two psychedelic sins",[19] Forbes and some of his friends preferred not to get too involved.

Though many travellers were keen to partake of Hollingshead's high-quality LSD, the same could not be said for his Nepalese friends, with the notable exception of poet and philosopher Rama Prasad Manandhar, who expressed his desire to have a psychedelic experience. Hollingshead agreed, explaining about the possible dosages and their likely effects. Manandhar decided on a 300 mcg dose, a high one for an acid neophyte. The ensuing session went without incident, Manandhar apparently 'getting' the psychedelic experience perfectly, announcing at one point, 'We must try to expand the 'moment' into infinite duration!'[20] The experience was so profound that Manandhar spontaneously composed a poem called *The Moment and The One-Ment*, which Hollingshead published unedited in issue one of *Flow*.

Hollingshead's flirtation with Himalayan spirituality led him to meet the Buddhist monk and saint Gyalwa Karmapa (aka the sixteenth Gyalwa

Karmapa), who was visiting the monks at Swayambhunath. Rama Prasad Manandhar was a friend of the saint and arranged for Hollingshead to meet him as the sun rose at the monastery. Hollingshead stayed up all night to prepare for the meeting, tripping on acid and consuming chillums of hashish, framing this practise in spiritual terms as 'performing chillum and acid Sadhana'.[21] Sadhana is Sanskrit for an ego-transcending spiritual method to accomplish something, though the cynical might see it as just getting stoned before doing something. Hollingshead was very high by the time meeting took place and hallucinated light emitting from the area of the Karmapa's 'third eye', on his forehead.

Hollingshead expounded his belief that spirituality in America would be strengthened if eastern Lamas opened a discourse with the leaders of the Arizonian Hopi Indians. Karmapa summoned him closer and touched the centre of his head, at which point, in his autobiography, Hollingshead claims he experienced a moment of *Samadhi*, the state of intense concentration usually achieved only through intensive meditation. He felt '...utterly and completely cleansed, as though the divine thunderbolt had gone through me like a million-volt charge',[22] and believed his life to have been permanently changed by Karmapa who was widely held to be a living god.

Issue one of *Flow* was published in Kathmandu in February 1970 and retailed at five rupees. Due to a dispute with the printers, who increased their costs at the last minute, it was only half the originally-intended length, but was nonetheless quite an achievement. A copy annotated with 'Please take care this copy to reach Timothy Leary in one piece.' was sent to Leary for his comments and approval. What Leary thought of *Flow* is unrecorded, but it was an impressive affair, a mixed bag of poetry, prose, philosophy and counter-cultural speculation from westerners, Nepalis and Leary himself. Knowing exactly how to get the best results from those he knew in high places, Hollingshead printed a dedication in issue one

TO HIS ROYAL HIGHNESS THE CROWN PRINCE OF
NEPAL AND HER ROYAL HIGHNESS ON THE OCCASION OF
THEIR MARRIAGE

KATHMANDU   FEBRUARY 27, 1970

In his own contributions to *Flow*, Hollingshead waxed lyrical
about his proposed Himal Centre, and contributed an impassioned
elegy to an unidentified Spanish woman and love interest, *I Love You
Linda, M.* But his most pertinent and vibrant contribution was *The
LSD-Communarium: The Situation of The Present – 1970*, his position
statement on LSD, contrasting the mind-blowing nature of psychedelic
religious revelation with the problems of trying to integrate those states
of mind into everyday life. Part three of the article railed against the
substance itself, claiming the quality and purity of LSD was dropping,
possibly because of the amount of 'counterfeit acid' that was beginning
to appear; LSD made by less pure synthesis or substances sold as
LSD. His concluded that 'The best defence always is to hesitate, use
common sense, and realise that what you buy 'on the streets' is not
LSD-25 – whatever you are told.'[23] The issue also contained a letter
to Hollingshead from Leary written almost two years earlier in which
Leary asks Hollingshead to write a Foreword to his forthcoming book
The Politics of Ecstasy. Hollingshead was overjoyed to be asked, but his
text was never used.

However, Leary's letter is noteworthy for other reasons. That Leary
asked Hollingshead to write the Foreword for what would be Leary's
most famous and influential book demonstrates the continuing strength
of their friendship despite their many conflicts. In the letter Leary also
makes his position in psychedelic culture very clear, condensing the
thrust of *The Politics of Ecstasy* into two pages with statements such
as, "I assume (why would anyone assume other) that I am sent here
to become the wisest, most illuminatory being that the world has ever

known." Leary also claimed that "The key to the evolutionary process at the present stage is LSD" but that to become an LSD saint it was also necessary to become adept at one of the many – Leary lists 21 – yogas, with the end result being "I expect that any saint will be able to take 1000 gamma or drink a quart of whiskey with me and find God." The letter concludes with more hyperbole:

> I am able to contact secular power with ease, win the Nobel prize – stop the war, make a million, become a movie star, because I have accepted the basic energy formula – all energy is available to him who knows that it must not be grabbed, held possessed or used for any purpose except spiritual. I have no interest in fame, in the success of my books – thus I become more and more famous.[24]

One evening, tired and hungry after his explorations, Hollingshead visited the Bakery Ashram, one of Kathmandu's more notorious hash cafés, where he heard a young man reading a love poem. This was Kristof Glinka, a Polish poet who Hollingshead decided was a verbal magician, someone who could play a key role in the future of *Flow*. When he learnt that Kristof, later a crucial player in the organisation of Britain's free festivals of the '70s and '80s, had a degree in Sanskrit from Oxford University, the meeting seemed heaven sent. Kristof was in Kathmandu on a one-year visa, producing a play of *Dr. Faustus,* and had made numerous literary connections in the city. Once again, Hollingshead had met the right person at the right time and he and Kristof became close friends, working together on *Flow,* which Kristof took over as editor. With his knowledge of Sanskrit, issue two of *Flow* expanded its circulation and grew to over eighty pages, filled with poetry from some of Nepal's finest creative writers and poets, as well as his own poetry and that of western writers such as George Andrews. Hollingshead remained on board as Interplanetary Editor.

Kathmandu and its surroundings were fast becoming the place for disillusioned westerners to set up their own spiritual retreats and Zenaïde 'Zina' Rachevsky, often referred to as a 'Princess', was one such person. Zina wasn't a real princess, but an ex-New York socialite from a wealthy family who used the 'princess' tag to add glamour to an already glamorous existence. Zina had hung out with the beat poets in San Francisco and had met Hollingshead at Millbrook. She was only the second western woman, after Alexandra David Néel, to study with Tibetan lamas, and her wealth and interest in eastern spirituality led her to Nepal where she founded a Buddhist retreat and study centre at Kopan, overlooking the Kathmandu Valley.

Zina told Hollingshead about her spiritual training with the lamas and how spiritual teaching could be directly transmitted between guru and acolyte. Her description of '...the essence of transmission being telepathy or more exactly *darshan* — a kind of 'flash' or vibration that is transmitted in the guru-chela relationship'[25] intrigued Hollingshead and reminded him of some types of psychedelic experience. Hollingshead decided to stay out at Kopan for a while, where he was photographed looking old and weather beaten, talking to Zina at a festival. The photographer, Age Delbanco, who was in Nepal on the trail of Richard Alpert's guru, met Hollingshead at Kopan in June 1970 when they agreed to share a room together. Delbanco soon discovered that Hollingshead, who was undertaking a vow of silence for a few days, was at the monastery not for spiritual reasons but because he was trying to kick a heroin habit.

Hollingshead's vow of silence appeared to be optional and Delbanco soon found him to be a "pain in the arse", pestering him with written requests to be passed to Zina or the monastery cook. When Hollingshead broke his vow of silence he told Delbanco he had been the voice of Denmark at the BBC during WWII; another of his fantasies as he would have been only fourteen at the end of the war! Returning from a visit to Kathmandu one day, Delbanco found that Hollingshead had filled their room with his writings, leaving nowhere to sleep. He insisted to Zina that Hollingshead vacate the room and, though visibly angry, he was clearly under Zina's spell and complied.

Hollingshead's visa was due to expire in July 1970. He could have easily obtained an extension through his friends in the Nepali government, but he rarely stayed in one place for long and was getting restless again. He had learnt a lot in Kathmandu, about himself and about the hippie culture he was indirectly responsible for inspiring. The monastery experience had impressed him deeply and he formulated a plan to create a monastery in Britain, one where travellers returning from the East could chill out and re-integrate into western society.

It was time to move on and so, boarding another DC-9 airplane he flew to first to Calcutta and then on to London. On the flight Hollingshead mused about what he had learnt in Nepal, concluding that the bland, consumer driven way of life in the west was having a corrosive effect on people, preventing genuine personal, social and spiritual improvement. Something needed to be done, and in the closing pages of his autobiography Hollingshead writes that man must take control and endeavour to live life as exemplified in Aldous Huxley's novel, *Island*, "a very imaginative effort to protect a way of life based in nature, that is lived organically as a flowing growing process."[26]

Similar thoughts to Hollingshead's were already being shared by thousands of others in the western counter culture, prompted by psychedelics and spiritual practise. If Woodstock had encapsulated the hippie dream in August 1969, the chaos and death at Altamont just weeks later had exposed the darker side of the story. The widespread use of psychedelics was losing focus and psychedelic culture was being commodified and monetised. Good quality LSD was becoming harder to find and psychedelic drugs were being counter-balanced by the increased availability of heroin and amphetamines.

What, in the early years of hippie culture, appeared to be the golden road to unlimited devotion now seemed tarnished and directionless; as Bob Dylan sang, the times were 'a changin' and another chapter in Hollingshead's enigmatic life was about to begin.

Notes

1   https://digitalcommons.macalester.edu/cgi/viewcontent.
     cgi?referer=&httpsredir=1&article=1287&context=himalaya p.19
2   Hollingshead, Michael. *The Man Who Turned On The World*, Blond & Briggs
     Ltd, 1973 p.221
3   Alpert, R, *Be Here Now*, Hanuman Foundation, 1978
4   Heinrich, C. Email 23/3/19
5   http://citeseerx.ist.psu.edu/
     viewdocdownload?doi=10.1.1.1014.5985&rep=rep1&type=pdf
6   Letter from Hollingshead to Leary, August 1969
7   Hollingshead, Michael. *The Man Who Turned On The World*, Blond & Briggs
     Ltd, 1973 p.223

8   Ibid p.225

9   MacLean, Rory. *Magic Bus*. Viking, 2006 p.275

10   Ibid

11   Letter from Hollingshead to Leary, August 1969

12   Ibid

13   Tomory, D. *A Season in Heaven*, Thorsons, London, 1996

14   Kanetsuka, Kami. Email 21/2/14

15   Ibid

16   Letter, Hollingshead to Leary, September 1969

17   Tomory, D. *A Season in Heaven*, Thorsons, London, 1996 p. 117

18   Ibid pp.120, 122, 123

19   Forbes, W. Email 5/3/14

20   Hollingshead, M. *The Man Who Turned On the World*, Blond & Briggs, 1973
       p.245

21   Ibid p.247

22   Ibid p.248

23   Hollingshead, M. *Flow* no.1 Kathmandu, February 1970

24   Leary, T. in *Flow* no.2 Kathmandu, Spring 1970

25   Hollingshead, Michael. *The Man Who Turned On The World*, Blond & Briggs
       Ltd, 1973 p.251

26   Ibid p.254

You Take The High Road

Michael Hollingshead wanted to have his own kingdom, an enterprise he called 'the Free High Church of the Isles.' At its centre would be 'acid', LSD. Acid would be a kind of sacrament[1]

The name 'Rosslyn' conjures images of the delicately wrought, enigmatic stone carvings in the 15th century Rosslyn Chapel. Made famous by Dan Brown's book and subsequent film, *The Da Vinci Code*, the chapel (actually a small cathedral) stands in the village of Roslin in Scotland's Midlothian region. Thousands of people visit the chapel each year to marvel at the carvings, wondering if tales of the Holy Grail concealed in the chapel's architecture could be true. In the early 1970s, however, Roslin was much quieter, the chapel tourist free, but other forces were at work and the town was to become the key location for Michael Hollingshead's next undertaking.

In August 1965 Roslin's former miner's welfare institute became the base for The Fraternity of the Transfiguration (FOT). Named after the transfiguration of Christ on Mount Tabor, when his disciples witnessed him shining with the brightness of the Holy Spirit, the FOT aspired to a simple monastic life and to help people in crisis. Led by Father Roland Walls, regarded as something of a Christian guru by his followers, the FOT house at Roslin became well known as a destination where itinerants could find sanctuary from their problems. At Roslin they would be welcomed and supported in a non-judgemental environment and could stay as long as they chose. Although Roslin was already in a rural area, Father Walls and his colleague Father John Halsey wanted a more remote location in which to become self-sufficient and develop the FOT as a spiritual community for those who needed it. Their desire to retreat from 20th century life was echoed by the hippies' 'back to the land' movement which had led to hundreds of self-sufficient communes appearing across Britain, Europe and the USA. It was the dream of many hippies to find a group of like-minded individuals with whom they could live communally, cultivate their own food and share a simple life, with or without drugs, depending on their beliefs.

Hollingshead was concerned that many young acid heads who returned from travelling in the East found it difficult re-integrating with western society in a way that enabled them to assimilate their often life changing experiences. "They found coming back to the west after years in the Himalayas just a very bad trip because there you've opened yourself out and then you have to come back to all this shit."[2] Hollingshead's answer to the problem was to found a commune where returning hippies could decompress and reflect on their experiences before re-entering society. Such a secluded, self-sufficient commune would also, Hollingshead thought, be the perfect place for him to get down to writing his autobiography; all he needed was the location.

Janette, Hollingshead's younger sister, had recently moved from her home town of Darlington to the village of Polton in Midlothian, and one day in the late summer of 1970 she was surprised by Michael knocking on her door, freshly returned from Nepal. His thin, gaunt physique and long straggly hair and beard shocked her. But while his appearance might have changed since Janette last saw him, his personality had not, and the intervening years of drug use, prison time and frugal Himalayan life had further magnified the distance between him and his family. To Janette it seemed like her brother had come from another planet and, culturally at least, he had.

"He had come to visit her and spent all day talking without interruption and she did not know what to do with him",[3] was how FOT chronicler John D. Miller described the meeting. Even those used to Hollingshead's long and often manic rants found them difficult to endure and the effect on Janette was dramatic. She didn't want him in her house a moment longer and suggested he went to the Fraternity of the Transfiguration in Roslin. Roland Walls had baptised Janette's child and she knew him to be kind and a sympathetic listener who might even be interested in her brother's wild stories. Hollingshead agreed to go and received a warm welcome from Walls and Halsey when he arrived. They spent the afternoon deep in conversation, Hollingshead telling the two monks about his trip to Nepal and the spiritual doors he had opened with LSD. Whether Hollingshead was just passing the time or whether it was his ideological entrée to suggesting he join the monks at Roslin is uncertain; but he never acted without purpose and it's likely he understood that forging a meaningful link with the monks could be useful in the future.

In the late afternoon Hollingshead bade farewell to his new friends and departed, telling the monks he was heading south, presumably back to London. Literally minutes later, as the monks were discussing their unusual visitor and his LSD philosophy, there was a sharp knock on the door. It was the police:

'Have you had a visit from this man?' they asked, showing a
photograph of Hollingshead.

'He's just left us.' they replied.

'Do you know where he has gone?' the police continued.

'He didn't say.'

'Interpol would like to see him.'[4]

Interpol will not discuss their interest in Hollingshead but
presumably an offence committed overseas had caught up with him.
Although Hollingshead never referred to this event anywhere or told
anyone about it, Miller records Hollingshead re-appearing at their
Roslin base several months later, clean shaven and with short hair
telling them he "had spent the intervening months in custody".[5] He
was welcomed by the monks who invited him to come with them to the
Tibetan Buddhist community at Samye Ling in the Scottish Borders.
This was a stroke of luck as 'English Robin' and David Smith, friends of
Hollingshead's from Nepal, were there. When he arrived he was excited
to find English Robin's cousin was the Earl of Glasgow, who had just
given the FOT access to the huge garden and annexe at the Isle of
Cumbrae's Cathedral of the Isles, a move also supported by Richard
Wimbush, Bishop of Argyll and the Isles.

Hollingshead's brain went into overdrive. Synchronicity was at work
and he knew that he should seize the opportunities it presented. The
FOT monks had been waiting for instruction from the Lord before
starting their self-sufficient spiritual community and Hollingshead was
also looking for a place to start his own. Suddenly, the future was clear.
The two tribes would form a joint community, each representing a facet
of disaffection with the modern world. This was the hippie dream writ
large and the answer to Hollingshead's frustrations. Everything seemed
set for success yet, before he could move to Cumbrae, Hollingshead
once again vanished for a while, the only trace of him during the
winter of 1970 being a short *Daily Mirror* piece in which he announced

he was starting work on his autobiography. He also made an appeal for British universities to begin controlled research into "real LSD", complaining that the key component, ergot, was now synthetic not organic. The article noted that he was "in retreat with the Fraternity of the Transfiguration".[6]

Meanwhile, even before the *Daily Mirror* article, other members of the counter culture seeking an alternative lifestyle were being inexorably drawn to Roslin. Flashback to 19 September 1970 when Kevin Hebrides and his friend Treebeard attended a small one-day festival called Glastonbury Fair, the first of the legendary Glastonbury Festivals. Hebrides and Treebeard remained in Glastonbury where they met Hollingshead's friend David Smith, who had recently returned from India believing he was the reincarnation of John the Baptist. Smith invited them to join a proposed multi-faith experimental commune on a Scottish island. The idea was vague but appealed to Hebrides and Treebeard who, like thousands of other hippies in Britain, were 'on the road', travelling with just a sleeping bag, personal possessions and essential items such as a copy of the *I Ching*. Smith told them about the Christian monks at Roslin, and their plans to move to an island and, eager for new experiences and excited by the idea of a commune with a spiritual element, Hebrides and Treebeard hitchhiked to Roslin. Walls and Halsey agreed they could join the commune. The FOT's chronicler recalled, 'These new arrivals felt that they had gained access to a spiritual dimension of life through the use of hallucinogenic drugs. Now they wanted to make a link with others who had a different path to the spiritual realm.'[7]

A friend of Father Halsey observed, 'The hippies seemed to be anxious to try and start living some sort of life. I'm not sure quite what sort of life. Because when they came to Cumbrae with John they didn't really do anything much at all. But it was a good thing to do, to give them a chance to see how they would get on.'[8] With Sam and Mike, two more hippies recently returned from the east, Hebrides and Treebeard drove from Roslin to Cumbrae in a Bedford van. Father Halsey travelled with them and Father Walls a few days later. The commune's new home was the cathedral's eight-bedroomed annex, basic but sufficient for their needs, consisting of a communal room, bathroom and several smaller rooms used as bedrooms. The monks elected for a more spartan existence, using wooden huts in the Cathedral's grounds as monastic cells.

Initially, the hippies worked closely with the monks, cultivating the soil, planting seeds and eating vegetarian meals together in the cathedral refectory. Hollingshead arrived in mid-March and, despite the commune being set up to be leaderless, through subtle manipulations and by virtue of his reputation and worldly experience, he soon became its *de facto* leader. He was also, at 39, by far the eldest, most of the communards being teenagers or in their early twenties. Hebrides hints at Hollingshead's leadership ambitions when he says, 'I think it was the second part of the year that some of Michael's ideas were more manifest and even then there was no obvious power play.'[9] Kevin also recalls Hollingshead was using some of his time on Cumbrae to write a book, as also noted in the *Daily Mirror* report.

The hippies adorned the large room of the cathedral's annexe with altar cloths and embroidered church hangings borrowed from the cathedral, as well as a painting of Buddha showing the chakras. This provided a space for a variety of purposes; a shrine for dropping acid and smoking chillums, a workshop and general lounge. The chillum smoking ceremonies were carried out with great gusto and accompanied by chanting from Kristof, a later arrival, and commune member Jamie Wormauld. The monks lived a more basic lifestyle, sleeping in their wooden huts and dressing in tunics fashioned from blankets. They worked the land every day and expected the communards to join them in their labours, which at first they did. Miller's history of the FOT records that two of the communards were keen to fit in with the monks' way of life and intended to permanently settle on Cumbrae, but they were in the minority. This early rift within the commune was also noticed by the Dean of the Cathedral who was able to negotiate with some commune members but not with Hollingshead who, rather than become part of the Fraternity of the Transfiguration, "Wanted to have his own kingdom, an enterprise he called "the Free, High Church of the Isles".'[10]

Hollingshead's Cumbrae commune became known by two names. Initially it was called The Free High Church, a play on words of the ultra-conservative Free Church of Scotland and the concept of 'church' as a psychedelic 'high'. Later, they referred to themselves as The Pure Land Ashram. As a wilder contingent of hippies arrived in the long hot summer of 1971 there was a marked change in relationships between the commune and the monks. The hippies either failed to arrive for work with the monks or simply left early for more interesting activities, their initial enthusiasm and optimism fading when confronted with the realities of hard physical labour. But word of Cumbrae's existence had spread through the growing commune movement and a steady stream of visitors began to arrive, some bringing cannabis and LSD, further undermining the commune's initial aspirations.

The influx of new visitors and the partners of those living there also altered the sexual dynamics and relationships were forged and broken, with the resultant emotional fall out adding to the commune's problems. As Hebrides explained, "Sex was pretty free and easy there",[11] but although Hollingshead tried it on all with all the women living there, he was unsuccessful. Animals arrived too and the commune acquired a few pets including a dog called Tander and two kittens, Arfa Key and Fanny Trip. Although the monks and hippies had a superficially shared interest in spirituality and communal living, the hippies' lifestyle was essentially inimical to that of the Christian brothers and, not long after Hollingshead's arrival, the rift between the two ideologies began to irrevocably widen. Whether this was directly caused by Hollingshead is unclear, but it follows the pattern that whenever he arrived on a 'scene', that scene and the people in it began to change, and not always for the better.

Hebrides has some interesting points to make about Hollingshead's personality on Cumbrae and, though many who came within his orbit found him manipulative, overbearing or controlling, Hebrides remembers him as fundamentally easy going, with a wry sense of humour. This feeling was shared by the other communards, suggesting that Hollingshead was temporarily free of his reliance on alcohol and hard drugs and enjoying the freedoms of being part of a small group of like-minded people. Despite his apparent contentment, Hollingshead slowly and subtly began to distance himself and the communards from the Christian monks. The monks had initially supported the communards in several ways, providing food and tools as well as money for tobacco and other essentials until Hollingshead decided they should be independent of hand-outs. This seemed like a positive move and the communards generated money by taking on casual gardening and agricultural jobs on Cumbrae or exchanging their labour for food. Being responsible for their own food enabled the communards to eat separately from the monks but this further isolated them from the Christian community who had originally encouraged and welcomed them.

In retrospect, Hebrides believes the monks were naïve and trusting in their belief the hippies would adapt to the austerities the monks aspired to. Conversely, he accepts the communards, average age twenty-two, were too young and lacked the maturity necessary to make the venture a success, allowing a fantastic opportunity to slip through their fingers: "Looking back, we kinda blew it, a good opportunity, but we were into the anarchy and we were young and restless and wanted to be young and wild."[12]

Kristof had also returned from Nepal and was working as a producer for Jack Bond Films, who were making Jane Arden's experimental film *The Other Side of The Underneath*, near Abergavenny in South

Wales. After a dispute with Bond over a shared female interest Kristof 'borrowed' the film crew's motorcycle and headed north to Cumbrae to join the commune. His arrival gave Hollingshead the chance to interact with an older person of a similar intellect whom he knew well. It was also the start of the full moon LSD sessions. There is some dispute among surviving members of the commune as to whether LSD was used at all on Cumbrae, and if so in what circumstances. When Kristof arrived he and Hollingshead were, "...a bit more hard core than the rest. Maybe it was their suggestion that the new name of the group should be The Free High Church of Cumbrae and that the principle would be that everyone should drop acid on the occasion of the full moon."[13] Hollingshead had picked up the practice of taking LSD at the full moon from the Brotherhood of Eternal Love in California, and later in Kathmandu. Some former communards don't remember these events, but Kristof, Hebrides and others are certain they took place.

Hebrides remembers LSD becoming increasingly available as the year progressed, usually brought in by visitors or friends, while others recall Hollingshead always having a supply of potent LSD, probably the Brotherhood of Eternal Love's California Sunshine. Hebrides remembers, "We built drums and had instruments for music, and we cleaned out a broken-down ruin in the woods and would meet under the starlight for almost tribal sessions... At some point we built two big drums out of old whisky barrels and we cleared a broken-down building in the woods where we could light a fire to be used for full moon acid ceremonies. This was Michael Hollingshead's idea I think. Full moon was considered important."[14] Although tolerant of what they saw as the hippies' dissolute lifestyle, at one full moon event Father Halsey was offered cannabis, causing him to 'freak'. Selected people were ordained into the Free High Church by a faux serious ceremony involving reading *The Proclamation of the New Heresy*, smoking a chillum of hashish and chanting:

Ayahuasca Lopophora Rape
Ololinqui Salvia Tiltlitzen
Sophora Datura Coleus
Tenonacatl Marijuan
Psilocybe Teyhuinti
I ordain you a servant of the most high
And you in turn, ordain the rest

"The chillum is then passed round 3 times, each time it passes the sacrifice the chant is uttered, the certificates of ministership are given out."[15]

Toward the end of the summer, Tim Hargreaves and his twin sisters arrived at Cumbrae in their 1940s Bedford truck with an introduction to Hollingshead through English Robin. Tim Hargreaves felt Hollingshead's "...idea of peace and tranquillity on the island had already foundered by the time we arrived, we certainly didn't help matters. There was a lot of chillum smoking complete with ritualistic Indian Sadhu chanting, drumming, but no acid as, ostensibly, this was a post-acid retreat."[16] Cannabis was brought to Cumbrae by short-term visitors or by commune members who had been to festivals or to friends in Glasgow and Edinburgh. Hebrides believed it was more essential than LSD, "Hash was the most prevalent. When there was stuff to smoke it was equivalent to good times. Other times were considered flat". Cannabis was also grown, "Using our new-found gardening skills... we planted seeds and grew our own plants".[17] Kristof too remembers massive cannabis plants in the greenhouse there and on one occasion a visitor to the commune ingested the juice of a whole cannabis plant and had a religious epiphany in the chapel, raving that he'd seen Jesus.

Judy Hargreaves remembered a lot of fun at the commune, but there was a very clear gender division when it came to work. Women did most of the cooking with the "Serious work of getting stoned, writing poetry and deep thinking" being very definitely the men's work. Hargreaves' sisters both held Hollingshead in extremely low esteem. "They thought ideas about women's liberation meant nothing to him and he exhibited sexist manipulative tendencies."[18]

The younger hippies were on Cumbrae ostensibly for culturally ideological reasons but were more interested in pushing the envelope of reality; sex, drugs and communal living overshadowing any initial spiritual pretences. That they were being manipulated in this direction to some degree by Hollingshead may well have gone completely over their heads, or they may just not have cared. Whatever view the communards had of themselves, from the perspective of the older, world-weary and experienced monks, it was clear that Hollingshead was the driving force behind the Ashram. Judy Hargreaves' memories confirm this. She and her sister only intended to stay at the commune for a while, but Hollingshead persuaded them to stay: "fresh blood, girls to do the chores?" Others present weren't too happy at the division of labour between the sexes but "Hollingshead had control and the final word on everything." Hargreaves also noticed Hollingshead "held tightly onto the young people who came from rich families, Kevin and Jaimie, etc."[19]

The full-on hippie lifestyle also encompassed divination using the I Ching, which played a major role in life at the commune. Hollingshead and Kristof were both impressed and influenced by the ancient Chinese oracle and most people at the commune had their own copy of the text. The traditional method of divination was practised, involving multiple throws of subdivisions of 49 yarrow stalks to arrive at the characteristic hexagram. Kristof's memories placed the I Ching at the centre of the communal LSD sessions: "It was used for our little sessions of taking LSD because it was thrown at the beginning and by the time you get to read the hexagrams things were getting wobbly, but it used to set the scene and so the I Ching was quite useful, much more so than what I call the psychedelic Bible, Leary's *Book of the Dead.* That was used a few times, but people preferred the Ching"[20]. Some of the younger commune members, however, used the venerable oracle for slightly less spiritual purposes: "We all loved the I Ching and it was often used... Mainly to ask questions about girls."[21]

It was the I Ching which stimulated the next major event in Hollingshead's life, an idea which arose after commune members paid an impromptu visit to the Edinburgh Festival in September 1971. Tim Hargreaves and three other commune members gave a spontaneous performance at the Traverse Theatre, singing doo-wop behind a 14-year-old guitarist who couldn't play the guitar! This followed virtuoso violinist Yehudi Menuhin's somewhat earnest musical support to an opera singer performing traditional Scottish folk songs, "Menuhin's face as he left the stage showed total incomprehension and rage."[22] Hollingshead and Kristof had links with many of Edinburgh's counter culture movers and shakers, among whom was art gallery owner Ricky Demarco, to whom they pitched the idea for an interactive art and divination installation centred on the I Ching, the full story of which is told in the next chapter.

Hollingshead occasionally left Cumbrae, sometimes on his own, sometimes with others. Some absences were of a mysterious nature and were not questioned. Other excursions were made to Edinburgh where he was making connections among the artistic and hippie communities, or to visit communal living experiments elsewhere in Scotland, including the embryonic Findhorn Community on the north-east coast. Findhornians eschewed drugs in favour of a strict ethical and moral code, underpinned by meditation and a vegetarian diet and spiritual workings with Devas, the elemental spirits of vegetation. More cult than commune, Findhorn was a far cry from the anarchic social experiment taking place on Cumbrae and the communards mocked Findhorn as being a bunch of whimsical New Agers living a soft life in caravans. Other visits included a trip to the beatnik author of *The Warp*, Neil Oram, at his commune in the mountains above Loch Ness, and at least two trips to the Incredible String Band's community on a country estate near Peebles. The String Band had been early LSD devotees and Hollingshead was keen to get its leader, Robin Williamson, to support his psychedelic vision. But by 1970 they had left drugs behind, exchanging psychedelics for the dogma and clean living prescribed by L. Ron Hubbard's Scientology.

By late Summer 1971, eleven people were living permanently at the Cumbrae commune so, to alleviate the overcrowding caused by new arrivals and visitors, plans were submitted to the Cathedral Trustees for the construction of a simple dwelling in the Cathedral grounds. The plans were rejected; the Trustees realising that if they did not deal with the commune now, more hippies would arrive and their existing problems would multiply. Matters came to a head when the Earl of Glasgow's wife visited the Cathedral and was appalled to see her hippie cousin having nits picked from her hair by her boyfriend. This was the last straw, and the Earl told the commune they must leave. A flurry of meetings between the Dean of the Isles and the Cathedral's Trustees were convened to discuss how to evict the commune. On 9 September the Dean announced, "…at the meeting of the trustees it was unanimously decided that the community be discontinued, and you have to leave by next Wednesday"[23] (15 September). Bishop Wimbush, one of the commune's original supporters within the Church hierarchy, was in Sri Lanka and the commune send a telegram to him, pleading for his intervention.

We appeal to you Father that you may intercede on our behalf so that we may continue our work here. And to say that we would like the opportunity to meet with you to discuss the matter and the reasons we have been told to leave. This experiment has seen a lot of sympathetic interest from friends in Britain, including many ministers, and it would be a severe blow to our movement if we had to leave under circumstances which prevail at the moment and we are at a loss to understand.

This letter is signed by the people presently living at the Ashram. We are a group of people trying to live outside the 'system', with money as our lowest priority. We really cannot afford to leave just like that, and we would have nowhere to live, not as a group.

> *Thank you, Father, for your kind and loving interest in our work*
> *and we look forward to hearing from you about a possible meeting on*
> *your return to Scotland and the Diocese.*[24]

But the Bishop was no longer supportive of the commune and his response to their plea was brief and brutal, "I endorse the Trustees Eviction Order. Would support legal pressure without waiting for my return."[25] This was the beginning of the end. The Argyll & Bute police visited the commune in mid-September and told Hollingshead the Dean of the Isles had asked them to return on 29 September and arrest them under the Scottish Trespass Act. Feeling under pressure and with nowhere to move to, the communards somewhat belatedly began to consider their future. It was a tense time as the commune members waited to see if the police would carry out their threat, and in an effort to raise public awareness of the commune's plight, Hollingshead approached the media, garnering support from *Time Out*, who reported:

> *Just over a year ago a group of young people brought together by Michael Hollingshead formed a living commune in Scotland. With the help of the Bishop of Argyll, Richard Wimbush, they were given a house next to the church in Cumbrae. Hollingshead was looking for a quiet life to write a book.*
>
> *Over the year the house was cleaned up and decorated and a successful crop planted. Now, however, with the Bishop of Argyll away in Ceylon the other two trustees, Bishop Neil Russell and the Earl of Glasgow, have given the commune notice to quit.*[26]

The *Time Out* demographic was culturally and geographically remote from the drama being played out on Cumbrae however, and Hollingshead's plight was just an abstract news item. On 20 September a film crew from BBC Scotland spent the afternoon filming the commune for a documentary about alternative societies, bringing with them several newspaper reporters. Hollingshead had engineered the timing of the film crew's visit, hoping it would help stay the hand of eviction. Miller's history of the FOT suggests this was the case, noting that after the initial eviction order was served the hippies, "…were seen coming out of the annexe in a long line, with gardening tools – spades, hoes and rakes – on their shoulders. They were striding out it seemed, to work on the land. What could this be? Next, off the ferry came TV cameras and reporters and photographers from the press. Here were these poor, hard-working members of the cathedral's harmless commune, being put off the island by the wicked earl. Despite ingratiating themselves with the sympathetic media, the Hippies found that they were no longer welcome within the cathedral precincts."[27]

The 29 September deadline passed without incident and the communards relaxed. The following day was Hollingshead's 40th birthday and celebrations were called for. *The Book of Cumbrae* recorded, "Thursday 30 Sept. Michael's birthday. The Church takes off on a rocky hill with sunshine. Tree and Sam do breathing exercises while the Buddha watches the scene til dawn."[28] "Takes off" and "sunshine" in this context obliquely refer to the commune taking a group LSD trip on the California Sunshine LSD Hollingshead was so fond of. The Scottish press present during the film crew's visit reported on the Church's attempts to evict the commune, one news piece quoting the Dean of the Cathedral, "The young people who came here at first were splendid. But they have all been cast out by the ones who are here now." That wasn't strictly true but echoed Tim Hargreaves' comments about the commune's plight when he arrived in late summer. The Dean wouldn't comment on the specific reasons why the commune was facing eviction but made it clear that they had to be gone by 12 noon on 3 October. Commune member Sam McDonald summed up the hippies vs authority stand-off with, "He says we are filthy and live immorally. We are just trying to be independent and get away from the rat race."[29]

In another newspaper report the Dean claimed the hippies were 'undesirables' who were no longer welcome because there were too many of them, their alleged vandalism "...a source of irritation to me and the trustees of the Cathedral" and warning, "Don't get the impression that they are penniless. Most of them come from well to do families and can quite easily lay their hands on money."[30] This wasn't true but added to the perceptions of many newspaper readers of the era that anyone living an alternative lifestyle was supported by financial hand-outs from parents. Hollingshead realised the eviction was imminent and in an effort to at least delay it so they could find somewhere to go, sent an urgent telegram to a hippie lawyer friend, Tom Forsyth, asking if he could help. On 28 October there was a final showdown between the communards and the authorities. The Very Reverend George Douglas, 84-year-old Dean of the Isles and the Isle of Cumbrae's Chief of Police met with Hollingshead, Kristof and others in the Shrine room of the annexe. The meeting was recorded and written up in *The Book of Cumbrae* as *Reality Is The Stuff Of Fiction*.

The Dean told them they had to leave the island on the 5.00pm to Largs on the following day, 29 October. The requirement to leave also extended to the two monks from The Fraternity of the Transfiguration. Hollingshead vigorously protested they hadn't had enough time to find a place to spend the winter, but his pleas were ignored. The Dean told them if they didn't leave by Friday, they would all be arrested for 'lodging without consent' and the Chief of Police backed this up with, 'I will order other men to come up here and apprehend everybody'.

An argument developed, and quickly escalated, about whether the charge of lodging without consent existed or not. Tom Forsyth, the lawyer, challenged the Chief of Police, pointing out the disputed situation was a civil not criminal matter. The meeting descended into chaos, with raised voices and people talking over each other. The Dean tried to exert his authority, telling the Free High Church if they didn't agree to his requirements, he would have them arrested there and then. This caused further uproar and hilarity and the argument continued with neither side making either sense nor headway. Finally, the Dean gave in, saying, 'I am going to give you a concession. I shall see you again at twelve o'clock tomorrow, that is, if you are in your right senses', backed up by the Chief of Police's terse, 'Twelve o'clock tomorrow, right?' and punctuated by Kristof's sarcastic, 'Same time, same place.'[31]

Hollingshead put his own spin on the commune's eviction, throwing the problem back at the Cathedral and the Trustees who originally granted permission for the commune to live in the Cathedral's grounds. Biting the hand that feeds was one of Hollingshead's specialities. If he couldn't get his own way, or if his plans failed, as they often did, it was always the fault of others and never him. Interviewed after the eviction, Hollingshead's analysis was: 'After all the promises here we were, living in the middle of it and seeing a lot of hypocrisy and a lot of trouble dealing with shady politics, half-truths and sometimes downright lies. And we were getting progressively shocked by the behaviour of those church fathers. We sensed their growing animosity. But one day the Dean came to have tea with us and the local police chief and it was all smiles, and we thought, 'Oh boy, the pressure's off' – then three days later, they turn up again, faces like granite and we have three days to leave. So then we had to consider – what was the church? What was religion? Why were those people doing this?'[32]

After the final confrontation Hollingshead accepted they had overstayed their welcome and there was no choice but to leave. The commune wanted to remain in Scotland, preferably on an island, but nowhere could be found at short notice. Kristof's girlfriend Liz Davies came to the rescue, offering the Free High Church the opportunity to move into her ex-husband's house in Archway, north London. The offer was gratefully accepted, and the commune quickly packed their van and set off for London, stopping for the night at the Incredible String Band's community of cottages at Glenrow. Although Williamson and the band had eschewed psychedelics, Hollingshead still believed there was some value in another visit. Perhaps, he mused, the Ashram may be able to set up camp alongside the Incredible String Band's communal endeavour?

His hopes were dashed when he found the Incredible String Band were on tour. Tim Booth, of Irish psychedelic folk band Dr Strangely Strange, was looking after the Row in the band's absence and it fell to him to entertain. Disappointed at not meeting Williamson, Hollingshead chatted to Booth who explained the ISBs current position on psychedelic drugs, which Hollingshead understood but was still mystified by. Accepting that his quest to convert Robin Williamson was futile he chatted with Booth into the night over several joints. Booth remembers, 'It's all a bit vague, there may have been exotic and bewitching Polish girls, gauzy tendrellic dresses and sparkling eyes...No. Just Michael looking for enlightenment. He came to the wrong place. He was an interesting conversationalist, but I got the feeling he did not really want to be having the conversation with me'.[33]

The following day they drove to the Fraternity of the Transfiguration's house at Roslin, but this was overcrowded so they continued on to a Benedictine monastery somewhere in the Scottish Borders, where they overnighted, and then south for London. They had reached the outskirts of Sheffield when the van's engine failed, leaving them stranded on the hard shoulder of the M1. 'And it came to pass that, on a secluded spot by an overpass, the Lord moved the machine and it spoke forth with oil and pieces of metal, which was interpreted as an omen of ill fortune'.[34]

A broken-down van full of long-haired, flamboyant hippies was bound to attract attention and before long the local drug squad arrived and searched everyone. Luckily the police found nothing to detain them further and after some assistance from two commune members travelling separately by car, a van was hired, and they continued south. To break the journey, they stopped at Hilton Hall near Huntingdon in Cambridgeshire. The 17th century hall had been a haunt of literary doyens Virginia Woolf, D.H. Lawrence and T.E. Lawrence, but was now occupied by Steve Abrams, a leading counter-culture figure. Staying with him at the time was, among others, poet and novelist Thom Keyes. Hollingshead knew Abrams and Keyes were never short of drugs, having worldwide LSD links and, at that time, connections to the British chemist Richard Kemp, who would become infamous for his role underpinning the Operation Julie LSD manufacturing and distribution ring. On arrival, in keeping with psychedelic hospitality, the group were offered not tea and sandwiches but strong psychedelics as part of a 'psychological experiment'.

Those words rang alarm bells and not everyone indulged. But most did, and they first insufflated a line of crystals described to them as a 'new propellant', which Tim Hargreaves believes was DMT, followed by a drop of liquid acid they were told was pure Sandoz LSD. Although those who took this combination were experienced LSD trippers, they were unprepared for its potency. Tim Hargreaves recalls, "Treebeard attempted to mount the huge colour TV downstairs and was slipped and tied into a sleeping bag for his own safety. I recall hanging onto a rose bush and crying inconsolably."[35] Hebrides, who had stopped taking psychedelic drugs, observed the event, remembering 'It all went terribly wrong and they thought we were going to wreck their house and their reputation locally. It nearly came to that."[36]

This psychedelic disaster was later recorded in the *Book of Cumbrae* as *The Incarnation at Steve's Hilton Hall*, part of which read:

'*Man he say it's crystalline, you gonna have fun*
We say: CHURCH
He say: HIGH
Two hours later
Time to die'

The *Book of Cumbrae* account of the experience noted 'No effect, that stuff'. This was the commune's in joke on the effects of any strong psychedelics or hash, as in, "You are tripping and are passed a chillum, take a toke and say 'absolutely no effect!'"[37]

The following day, somewhat worse for wear, they set off south again, this time without further incident. 'Well, we made it to London, cautiously driving through a thunderstorm and sneaked into the pad in Archway.'[38]

Notes

1   Miller, J. *A Simple Life*. Saint Andrews Press 2013 p.105
2   Los Angeles Free Press, 'We're a natural little community...', 25/2/72
3   Miller, J. *A Simple Life*. Saint Andrews Press 2013 p.104
4   Ibid p.105
5   Ibid p.105
6   *Daily Mirror*. 'Drug Man Goes Into A Monastery'. 10/11/70
7   Miller, J. *A Simple Life*. Saint Andrews Press 2013 p.104
8   Ibid p.105
9   Hebrides, K. Email 5/3/07
10 Miller, J. *A Simple Life*. Saint Andrews Press. p.104
11 Hebrides, K. Email 11/3/14
12 Ibid
13 Hebrides, K. Email 5/3/07
14 Ibid
15 *The Book of Cumbrae* 1971
16 Hargreaves, T. 10/9/13
17 Hebrides, K. Email 11/3/14
18 Hargreaves J. Email 14/10/14
19 Hargreaves, J. Email 11/8/18
20 Glinka, K. Email 24/11/13
21 Hebrides, K. Email 11/3/14
22 Hargreaves, T. Email 10/9/13
23 *The Book of Cumbrae* 1971
24 Ibid
25 Ibid
26 *Time Out*. 'Commune Evicted'. 24-30/9/71
27 Miller, J. *A Simple Life*. Saint Andrews Press. p.105
28 *The Book of Cumbrae* 1971
29 'We stay – isle hippies', undated, unnamed newspaper, September 1972

30   *Daily Express*, 'Hippies say 'We stay'',

31   *The Book of Cumbrae* 1971

32   *Los Angeles Free Press*, 'We're a natural little community...,' 25/2/72

33   Booth, T. Email 24/9/13

34   *The Book of Cumbrae* 1971

35   Hargreaves, T. Email 10/9/13

36   Hebrides, K. Email 5/3/07

37   Glinka, K. Email 13/4/19

38   *The Book of Cumbrae* 1971

Changes

Perhaps the age of the electronic computer and specialised sciences such as neurology will paradoxically bring about a new application of the ancient Oracle of Change.[1]

On a winter's day in late December 1971, "Strolling down the Portobello Road, ruminating on luck, coincidence and synchronicity", Brian Barritt bumped into Michael Hollingshead, who he'd not seen since he visited the World Psychedelic Centre in 1966 to buy LSD. "He's been in Nepal putting out a mag called *Flow*", wrote Barritt, "now he's the guru of a commune in North London. They are shortly going up to Edinburgh to tell fortunes by computer and the I Ching."[2] Before they parted, Hollingshead invited Barritt and his girlfriend to visit him in north London.

At 40, Hollingshead was over 20 twenty years older than most of his followers and though his friends were all part of the counter culture, he had more in common socially and culturally with Barritt than with members of the Pure Land Ashram. Hollingshead and Barritt also shared a close friendship with Tim Leary. In 1968 Barritt and Liz Elliot travelled to Algeria to meet Leary who was being sheltered by Eldridge Cleaver's Black Panther Party after escaping from prison in the USA. The three became good friends, tripping partners and more, Elliot and Leary falling in love and having an affair which lasted until Leary took up with Joanna Harcourt-Smith. Barritt and Elliot enjoyed a long and productive relationship with Leary; Barritt co-wrote Leary's *Confessions of a Hope Fiend* and worked with him on his 'Eight Circuit' model of consciousness and they were all involved in the acid-drenched recording session for the Ash Ra Tempel LP *Seven Up*. Despite being Leary's closest British friends, Hollingshead, Barritt and Elliot have been almost completely written out of American psychedelic histories or biographies of Leary.

Elliot had not yet met Hollingshead though she was aware of him through Leary and Barritt. Friends or not, both men were often disparaging of Hollingshead's character, "They were like, 'Oh, Michael', you know, like he was a con man, he didn't care for anybody, he just went about his own business and got what he could out of it, like basically he was a hustler. But they were all hustlers, so I don't know why they talked about him like that. He was probably just a bit better at it than they were." Hoping to see more of Barritt now they were both in London, Hollingshead invited him and Elliot to visit him at the commune.[3]

Hollingshead's new home was 15 Tremlett Grove, a large terraced house in Archway, North London, which belonged to the estranged husband of Liz Davies, Kristof's partner. It was more communal house than commune, each person having their own room and carrying out repairs and improvements in exchange for rent-free accommodation. Barritt and Elliot paid a visit later in December, Elliot remembering that she found Hollingshead being the centre of attention, sitting in a raised position, surrounded by acolytes and clearly playing the guru game.

Barritt, as another elder statesman of the British hippie community, joined in and everyone listened to "the two great men, talking".[4] Elliot thought Hollingshead needed Barritt's friendship and approval for the same reason he needed Kristof's – they were closer to Hollingshead's age and of a similar intelligence; she could also see that Hollingshead, like Leary, was drawn to young people because he was stimulated by their energy. Hollingshead immediately ordained Barritt into the Pure Land Ashram and encouraged him and Elliot to come up to Edinburgh to help with their planned I Ching event.

The idea had originally come about in August 1971, while Hollingshead and Kristof were living at the Pure Land Ashram's commune on the Isle of Cumbrae. The I Ching was part of daily life there, frequently consulted on anything from girlfriends to questions about the meaning of life, as well as being an integral part of their full moon LSD ceremonies. Hollingshead and Kristof were intrigued by Alfred Douglas' speculation, "Perhaps the age of the electronic computer and specialised sciences such as neurology will paradoxically bring about a new appreciation of the ancient Oracle of Change",[5] which prompted Hollingshead's decision to tangibly combine the I Ching's mystical predictions with the logic of computing.

Exactly how this concept could be brought to fruition puzzled Hollingshead until he met with gallery owner Richard Demarco, on a visit to Edinburgh in the early autumn of 1971. Hollingshead pitched the idea as being something which would, "translate the archetypal imagery of the I Ching into an audio-visual, tactile environment, such that a one-to-one correspondence exists between a given image content of a given hexagram and the range of stimuli in the environment".[6] Demarco thought the idea unusual but innovative and worth taking a risk on. He immediately offered Hollingshead the use of the Richard Demarco Gallery (RDMG) between 30 January and 6 February 1972.

Hollingshead had been intrigued by the I Ching since his time
with Leary in the early Sixties. The west had its own divinatory system
in the form of the tarot but the I Ching became widely used in the
counter culture mainly as part of a broader adoption of eastern spiritual
practises, but also because it was simple and portable. A tarot reading
required a pack of 78 professionally made cards, whereas the I Ching
could be cast simply, using three coins, or in its more complicated form
using 50 short sticks. Kristof remembered the I Ching "was used a lot.
It seemed like a very useful thing compared to the Tarot, which was a bit
heavy you know, sometimes you'd get the Death card and you couldn't
sleep!"[7] In London during 1965 and '66, Hollingshead noticed the
interest in the I Ching among London hippies and later, in Nepal and
America, he observed hippies treating it as if it was a holy text. Even
the Beatles were fans: George Harrison wrote 'While My Guitar Gently
Weeps' while thinking about the I Ching and how "whatever happens
is meant to be, and there's no such thing as coincidence – every little
item that's going down has a purpose."[8] The band's enthusiasm for the I
Ching was taken to ludicrous extremes in 1968 when, at John Lennon's
behest, their multimedia business, Apple Corps, paid an astrologer
£50 a week to use the I Ching in business decisions. Alfred Douglas
explained "The I Ching was created at a time when man's links with the
deeper levels of his own psyche were stronger and deeper than they are
today. It is a power house of psychic images which can act as a bridge
between conscious minds and the depths of the unconscious."[9]

Now they had a venue and a time scale to work with, Hollingshead
and Kristof asked the I Ching to comment on their undertaking.
Their question was answered with Hexagram 8, 'Holding Together',
its commentary noting "Holding together brings good fortune".[10]
Treebeard and Kevin Hebrides cast a second consultation and received
Hexagram 11, 'Peace'. Detailed analysis of both Hexagrams by Kristof
convinced Hollingshead and the others that the Oracle's answers were
fortuitous and they should, "proceed sincerely, not waste time, avoid

easy solutions and concentrate on the inner aspects of the work... of doing justice to the I Ching and the Tao that pervades it. For is not the I Ching a gift of heaven and earth?".[11] The title of Kristof's note was 'Changes 72' which became the name of the event when it was launched at the RDMG.

The word 'event' didn't adequately describe Hollingshead's vision. It was to be in a gallery, but it wasn't really an 'exhibition' as it was participatory. Nor was it a 'happening', which suggested a one-off, perhaps spontaneous, event, whereas Changes 72 was intended to run for a week. The most apt description would have been 'installation' but in 1971 that word was not in common use, so Kristof created the portmanteau word 'exhibion', melding 'exhibition' and 'exhibit'. The Changes 72 press release announced, "This series of experiences is obviously not an 'exhibition' in the accepted sense of the word, nor is it exactly a happening, lecture, religious service or fun-fair, although it contains elements of these. Accordingly, a new word has been invented to describe it – E X H I B I O N."[12]

The creation of Changes 72 was a staggering mental and physical feat of translating imagination into reality. LSD might have been responsible for the creative impulses responsible for Changes 72 but besides cannabis smoking, psychedelic drug use was in abeyance during preparations for the exhibion. Conceptualising the idea and physically equipping the RDMG was one thing, finding a computer firm who wanted to be involved and who understood the work's requirements was something else. Hollingshead eventually found a company called Systemshare who took on the project as a way of publicising its services. The binary nature of the I Ching was well suited to becoming the world's first computer-based interactive divinatory system and Systemshare was easily able to fulfil Hollingshead's needs.

Before Changes 72 opened, Hollingshead and Kristof published issue three of *Flow*, the first since their return from Nepal; its eighteen, odd-sized single sided pages printed on a treadle driven letterpress owned by Liz Davies. The first page featured a sketch of members of the Pure Land Ashram, including Hollingshead, drawn by Feliks Topolski as part of a session involving all the ashram members. A painting of Hollingshead from the same session became part of Topolski's huge 'Hundred Hippies' canvas which now hangs above the bar next to his gallery on London's South Bank. Among the contributions was *The Praises of Mary Juan*, Kristof's paean to cannabis, and several short poems by Morning Flower, celebrated simply in Hollingshead's only offering, *essence poem for morning flower* (Myra Coppersmith, see p.219)

> *our essence*
> *our being   our karma*
> *our doing[13]*

Several newspapers and magazines gave Changes 72 advance publicity, notably the London-based underground newspaper *Frendz*, which devoted three quarters of a page to the Pure Land Ashram. Hollingshead gave a definition of the Pure Land Ashram's vision, "The Molecular Church answers that we have bypassed reasoning, destroyed the nuclear family and substituted tribal feedback systems. The Church didn't start on Cumbrae, it begins right here at the point of love when the 3rd eye perceives chaos and the wreck of the western world and the phoenix rises from the ashes…in times of political struggle for liberation the church exists as a network of organic cells joined together by the full moon rites."[14]

In mid-January 1972 Hollingshead and Kristof, along with eight of the PLA, drove to Edinburgh to publicise and set up the Changes 72 exhibion. Demarco provided free accommodation but when Hollingshead saw the tiny flat on offer he rebelled and booked everyone into a 5-star hotel, charging it to Demarco who was in America on business, oblivious to the deception. Before Changes 72 opened, Hollingshead threw a dinner party at the hotel for the PLA, extending the invitation to friends from Edinburgh's counter culture community, all at Demarco's expense. The lavish, multi-course dinner was not without incident. Poet Alan Bold was so drunk he had to crawl out of the restaurant on his hands and knees and one of the Pure Land Ashram's cats was given its own seat at the table. The cat refused the oysters it was served and was not satisfied until the waiter returned with River Trout Meuniere. Scams such as this led Pure Land Ashram members to nickname Hollingshead Professor Ripovich, an epithet which must have caused Hollingshead a wry internal smile in the knowledge the PLA had no idea about his previous scams.

In advance of the opening, Hollingshead was busy with last-minute publicity and contacting the press to drum up interest. One press release was enigmatically titled 'When is an Art Gallery not an Art Gallery? Answer: When it's an Oracle'. The title of another even more enigmatic, 'The Oldest Book in The World Interpreted by The Newest Device'. Journalists were let into the secret that the mysteries of the I Ching would be interpreted by the "largest and most complicated computer in Scotland", which was "always right". Tempering the ancient and mystical divinatory process with science, the press release explained how the I Ching had been influential in the discovery of binary mathematics.[15]

When Barritt and Elliot arrived in Edinburgh they found chaos. Hollingshead's girlfriend Morning Flower (aka Myra Coppersmith), a Californian hippie he met in Nepal, had turned up in London before he set off for Edinburgh and was now part of the team. Trying to balance his love life with his obligations, Hollingshead was "running around" trying to set Changes 72 up from virtually nothing. "This was the thing I liked about him – it seemed to me that he'd just grabbed the idea of the gallery and just made it up as he went along",[16] remembered Liz Elliot. Barritt and Elliot did what they could to help; Barritt obtained some photographic slides from the city's art school, and with everyone working flat out and all hours, Changes 72 began to take shape.

Although Hollingshead could be misogynistic, and many women felt uncomfortable in his presence, Liz Elliot didn't have a bad word to say about him. "I think I was seeing him as a hustler, which I can groove with, and other people can't. Michael talked to me like I was a real person and didn't ignore me and was quite gentle and nice to me and didn't overdo it, so that I felt totally comfortable with him." Of course, this could simply have been because Hollingshead knew and respected her partner, Brian Barritt, but it demonstrates how his attitude and demeanour toward women varied widely.[17]

Despite the problems in setting up the gallery, Hollingshead and Kristof, with the aid of the PLA and friends, brought Changes 72 to fruition on time and more or less exactly as they had envisaged it. Liz Elliot might have thought Hollingshead made it all up as he went along and pulled it together at the last minute, but behind Hollingshead as front man, two key PLA members were equally responsible for the success of the exhibion. Kristof and Tim Hargreaves were responsible for installing the state-of-the-art stereo system, loaned by an Edinburgh hi-fi dealer, comprising the latest flat polystyrene wall speakers, two big speaker cabinets, a couple of amplifiers and three reel to reel ferrograph tape decks. This equipment was to play the music, created by Hargreaves in a London studio, in the Maze Room, as the petitioner wended their way through the exhibion to the Ancient Cell Wisdom Room.

Before the exhibion opened the I Ching was cast once more. Hexagram 11, 'Peace' was thrown again, the perfect hexagram. A Press Viewing was held on Saturday 29 January and the doors were opened to the public the next day, a date chosen because it was the combination of a full moon and a full lunar eclipse. The public were charged a £1.00 entrance fee, although no one is sure whether this was split between Demarco and Hollingshead or went straight into Hollingshead's pocket. Other than receiving free food and accommodation, Kristof and the Pure Land Ashram members were not financially rewarded for any of their efforts.

Faced with the problem of how to do the I Ching justice in a 20th
century contemporary art gallery, Kristof and Hollingshead devised a
flow chart of what they envisaged the public's experience of the exhibion
would be. Once they had paid the entrance fee, the customer entered the
'Secretary's Office', staffed by Morning Flower, where they were offered
the opportunity to ask the Oracle a question. If they declined, they went
back out of the building. If they decided to continue, the petitioner
was asked to complete a 'Formality', a document stamped 'Nirvana
Travel Agency', which asked their name, religious beliefs, zodiac sign,
what their question was, why they were asking it and what answer
they expected. Details from this form were input into the Systemshare
computer and by the time the petitioner entered the 'Control Room'
a computer-generated card displaying a Hexagram based on their
question was waiting for them. Brian Barritt continues:

> *Up the stairs now to the 'Maze' room, where we have arranged walls*
> *of mirrored paper into a labyrinth, so that the seeker must see him*
> *or herself from all angles before reaching the Central Region. In the*
> *middle of the maze is to be found a soft, black foam chair to sit in*
> *and contemplate the tiny dot of light suspended in mid-air. This was*
> *done by a hidden light bulb reflecting onto a parabolic mirror, resting*
> *on a transparent plinth filled with writing smoke from an incense*
> *stick. "Silence; as you sit in semi-darkness contemplating the point of*
> *light, Aleister and myself sort out the trigrams' eight pieces of music*
> *and play the appropriate hexagram. After the 'Maze' experience, you*
> *continue to the 'Ancient Cell Wisdom Room' where, decked in oriental*
> *finery, four of our troop decode the hexagrams into verbal form."*[18]

After the meaning of the I Ching hexagram had been explained,
the petitioner left the building and the images and sound in the
Maze would be reset to await the next person, making each visitor's
experience unique.

The advance media publicity for Changes 72 ensured it was a well-attended. For once, Hollingshead had undertaken a project, worked hard and brought it to a successful conclusion, and he was elated. As Barritt recalled, "All Edinburgh came running".[19] Most visitors were extremely impressed with the exhibion, and some even had life-changing experiences; Liz Elliot recalling one girl who became hysterical, rushing out of the gallery, shrieking, "I've never had such a wonderful time in my life. I can't believe this. Now I understand the cosmos...."[20] When Richard Demarco returned from America he discovered that Changes 72 was the best attended event to date at his gallery. He forgave Hollingshead for the extra expenses he'd incurred at the hotel and extended the exhibion's run for several days.

To maintain momentum and generate further publicity, Hollingshead organised a poetry reading at Demarco's gallery on 4 February. Movers and shakers from Scotland's counter culture were entertained with poetry from Hollingshead, Kristof, Liz Davies, Tom McGrath, Tom Buchan and Alan Bold. Buchan and Bold were well-known poets and McGrath was the editor of the counter culture newspaper *International Times*. The reading was described as a "spontaneous audio-visual-tactile poetry reading", attendees being advised there was "no admission charge but a bottle would be welcome."[21] Successful though it was, Demarco had other bookings at the RDMG and Changes 72 had to close in mid-February. Before he left Edinburgh for London, Hollingshead sent a self-aggrandising letter, typed in red ink, to Brian Barritt, which seemed to sneer at his colleagues in the Pure Land Ashram, implying he was playing the role of father figure.

STOP PRESS

Today Michael Hollingshead, celebrated Magician of the Machine age, split; leaving the Pure Land Ashram to fend for itself. The PLA immediately dissolved into a wriggling heap of hippies. Holing's Head was finally tracked down in the restaurant of the Remarkable Gallery.

What about Kristof, shrieked your friendly neighbourhood reporter while visions of morality danced in his head. Om said Michael and smiled at his travelling companion Mourning Flower. Asked about the fate of his erstwhile companions he replied by taking off his paternity suit. The movie is over he said.[22]

Sarcasms about the Pure Land Ashram notwithstanding, Hollingshead returned to Tremlett Grove and finally began to work in earnest on his autobiography. The original title of *The Great Brain Robbery*, chosen by Hollingshead when he was in prison, changed to the somewhat pompous *The Man Who Turned On The World*, which he felt was descriptive of his achievements with LSD. Hollingshead was hopeful his autobiography would finally bring him public acknowledgement as the man who turned Leary, and the world, onto LSD. However, embodying his comment to his daughter Vanessa that, "only fools and mules work",[23] Hollingshead wrote little of the book, striking a deal with Kristof to do most of the work for him. "A ghost-written book is a pretty accurate way of putting it"[24] as the poet recalled.

Hollingshead verbally agreed with Kristof a 50% split of any publisher's advance on future royalty payments. Hollingshead had accumulated several trunks full of letters, documents and other ephemera related to his involvement with psychedelics and Kristof's role was to organise this material, asking questions of Hollingshead as he did so. The conversations were taped and transcribed by Liz Davies and others at the Archway house, after which Kristof edited and distilled Hollingshead's words of wisdom into a chronological narrative which Hollingshead later finessed to produce the final manuscript for the publishers.

This method worked well and in the spring of 1972, when a few chapters had been completed, Hollingshead sent them to several publishers in the hope of securing a contract. There was a problem though, of which Hollingshead was either ignorant or so arrogant he believed it wouldn't matter. By 1972 the glory days of psychedelia were over; the subject no longer held the glamour it once did, and insufficient time had passed for psychedelic memoirs to be of interest or historical relevance. Consequently, Blond & Briggs were the only publishers to express serious interest in the manuscript, no doubt a happy consequence of Hollingshead's meeting with co-owner Anthony Blond at a party in late 1965. On 28 March, Hollingshead telephoned Blond's business partner, Desmond Briggs, to discuss the sample chapters, Briggs later confirming the conversation in writing adding the caveat that though B&B were eager to publish the book, they didn't yet have enough material to justify issuing a contract. This setback was tempered with the generous offer of an immediate advance of £150 on receipt of the chapter dealing with Hollingshead's experiences in Kathmandu, after which B&B would consider a further advance and a contract.

Hollingshead concealed from Kristof the details of his negotiations with the publishers, and of the imminent cash advance, so the die was cast for another deception. Though Hollingshead was based at the Tremlett Grove communal house he was often away, travelling around Britain, visiting friends and getting to grips with the final stages of his autobiography. From late March 1972 his letterheads bear the address of Hilton Hall in Huntingdonshire, the scene of the acid and DMT freak out when the Pure Land Ashram overnighted there en route from Cumbrae to London. One occupant, Jenny Fabian, described Hilton Hall as hosting "a commune of writers in a house previously occupied by members of the Bloomsbury Set. It was full of literary ghosts and disembodied spirits, as well as a never-ending supply of LSD, cocaine, pot and Mandrax."[25]

Jenny Fabian had achieved notoriety in 1969 by writing *Groupie*, a thinly-fictionalised account of her exploits as 'special friend' to various rock musicians, including Syd Barrett, Andy Summers, and members of Family. Fabian remembers Hollingshead, then with a square, bushy beard, hair thinning on top and tied back in a pony tail, as one of many, "savants who congregated at Hilton, all rather vying to be the 'head honcho' on the mental awareness plane, though of course [Steve] Abrams considered himself the headiest of them all." Fabian thought Hollingshead just another aspiring 'head honcho', "One of those bearded, sandaled types who used a kind of guru-speak to indicate his higher consciousness which I found rather tiresome." Hollingshead arrived at Hilton Hall with Morning Flower, described by Fabian as "a pigtailed 'shakti', who also wore sandals and dowdy clothes and genuflected to his every whim", but he contributed little to everyday life, avoiding housekeeping duties and boring the other residents with tedious 'meaningful' conversations.[26]

A great deal of dope smoking and LSD taking took place at Hilton Hall and the availability of high quality LSD, along with his friendship with Abrams and occasional visitor Ron Stark, might have been one of the reasons Hollingshead went to stay there. Hollingshead certainly had the psychedelic credentials and lysergic 'air miles' to be mixing with the acid elite, yet Jenny Fabian recalls a puzzling incident which cast doubt on his alleged mastery of the psychedelic experience. One evening, during the communal watching of the latest episode of *Star Trek* while tripping, the drawing room door slowly opened to reveal Hollingshead in a crouching position. He looked round the room, paused and said, "So this is acid"[27] before leaving. Was this one of Hollingshead's attention seeking mind games; pretending he was awed by the Brotherhood's acid when in fact he could easily handle it? Or had he been caught out by not treating the drug with the respect it deserved?

Hollingshead and Morning Flower were eventually asked to leave Hilton Hall, although no-one can remember why. Before he left he received a letter from Blond & Briggs, who were impressed with the additional material he'd sent and, accepting his suggestion of *The Man Who Turned On The World* as a title, offered him a contract. Hollingshead signed on 15 May, agreeing to deliver the final manuscript to the publishers by 30 August. The contract gave Hollingshead an advance on royalties of £500.00; £225.00 being paid on signature of the contract, the remainder payable on delivery of the manuscript. Not long after his return to Tremlett Avenue he received a letter from Jenny Fabian, asking if he could give the Hilton Hall acid heads details of the laboratory preparation of LSD. Even though he'd been asked to leave Hilton Hall Hollingshead responded helpfully, suggesting sources in pharmacological journals where this information could be found, but why he was asked the question is a mystery. The Hilton Hall people had a supply of LSD from sources including the Brotherhood of Eternal Love and Ron Stark, who had funded LSD laboratories in France and elsewhere and was helping fund the Operation Julie LSD network, was also a source.

While Hollingshead was in Nepal, Scotland and London, his daughter Vanessa had been going through some personal upheavals. Life with Sophie, her mother, in the Bed-Stuy suburb of New York, had become intolerable due to Sophie's behaviours and Vanessa being assaulted by local youths, so she moved in with Big Grace, a friend's mother, in Brooklyn, where she felt loved and safe. Vanessa had not seen her father for several years, though he had occasionally written and once sent her a package of gifts from Nepal, so it came as a surprise when she received a letter from him. He said that he'd heard Vanessa was no longer living with her mother and he was concerned for her welfare, unaware that her move to live with Big Grace had been at her request and was working out well.

Hollingshead had plans for Vanessa's future: Myra Coppersmith (aka Morning Flower), Hollingshead's girlfriend at the time of the Changes 72 event, had returned to America and was going to visit Vanessa and encourage her return to her father in Britain. Vanessa thought this was just another of her father's wild ideas until Coppersmith, "the craziest looking hippy girl I ever saw" turned up unannounced to see her. At first, Coppersmith was effusive about Hollingshead, telling Vanessa how much she adored him, how inspirational he was and how much he wanted to be reunited with Vanessa. A few weeks later Coppersmith visited Vanessa, now claiming Hollingshead had mistreated her, "I was supposed to convince you that being with your father would be the greatest thing you could do, but it wouldn't. He is not nice and does a lot of things that are not good, and you wouldn't understand."[28] This sudden change of heart suggests Hollingshead had ended their relationship, almost certainly because he was now in a new relationship with Auriol Roberts. Coppersmith decided she was going to move to a commune in upstate New York and placed Vanessa in a dilemma by asking her to go with her. It was an impossible decision for an already troubled and traumatised twelve-year-old to make; Vanessa knew her mother was incapable of caring for her, and though she loved Big Grace and vice versa, Vanessa felt guilty for imposing on her because she had two children of her own. Eventually and despite not wanting to leave the support and warmth of Big Grace's family, Vanessa convinced herself it would be a good move. Big Grace argued against her going, but Vanessa was headstrong.

There was little room in Coppersmith's car and Vanessa arrived at Dawes Hill commune in West Danby with only two bags of clothes and very little money. Dawes Hill was the archetypal hippie commune. Its members lived a frugal existence without electricity or running water and subsisted on home grown food and meat and dairy provided by their goats and chickens. A small crop of marijuana supplemented their income and provided the means to get high. Compared to the warmth of Big Grace's family and the bustle of New York, Vanessa found communal living cold and hard and very isolated, but she was decided to stick it out because she was with Coppersmith. This illusion of security was shattered a few weeks later, when Vanessa was told Coppersmith had left the commune for good. Why she left was never explained but it left Vanessa devastated at being abandoned by someone she believed genuinely cared for her.

Back in Britain, in the summer of 1972, Hollingshead was on the move again, looking for somewhere he could complete his autobiography where he would wouldn't be disturbed or subjected to negative temptations. Since his involvement with the Christian monks at the Cathedral of the Isles Hollingshead's interest in the philosophies of the contemplative orders had deepened, and in July he booked a short retreat at The Society of St. Francis at Glasshampton in Gloucestershire. The monastery was ideal for his purposes, offering basic accommodation in a secluded setting and an opportunity to learn more about the Franciscan tradition. In between finishing his autobiography, Hollingshead ate, prayed and socialised with the monks. A letter to Jasper Newsome suggests Hollingshead took LSD with him for inspiration; "It was Full Moon last night, so I tuned in to something on a walk to the local with three of the monks, who also felt something. What? Biogenetic vibrations?" The clues being the full moon was a favourite time for Hollingshead to take LSD, and "tuned in" was one of Leary's expressions to denote changing one's consciousness. Trips to the pub aside, completing the final manuscript of his autobiography was taking its toll, "Meanwhile, I'm working my balls off writing to complete the last two chapters, and a pretty exhausting business it all is", wryly adding, "I shall be a pop star in my next incarnation; that or stay in Heaven."[29]

Having completed his autobiography, Hollingshead returned to Tremlett Grove and delivered the manuscript to Blond & Briggs on time, receiving the remaining advance a few weeks later. In theory Hollingshead should have split this amount equally between him and Kristof, but it was not to be. Kristof remembers putting his head round Hollingshead's bedroom door in September to find him packing his possessions. Unaware Hollingshead had imminent travel plans, Kristof asked what was happening, to which Hollingshead responded, "Well, I got the advance from Blond & Briggs and I've got some business in New York to sort out." Kristof was shocked and upset by Hollingshead's actions, which came as a complete surprise and seemed out of character for a man he held in high esteem and thought he knew well. "I [Kristof] was pissed off...very hurt that Michael did this because it was my first rip off. I trusted someone and ended up with nothing."[30] Hollingshead's treachery had far-reaching consequences for Kristof and members of the Pure Land Ashram, many of whom would stop using LSD and turn instead to the natural psychedelia offered by psilocybin mushrooms.

Hollingshead collected his new girlfriend, Auriol Roberts, and caught a transatlantic flight from Heathrow. Kristof never had any contact with him again.

Notes

1   Changes 72 document (quoted in), 16/10/71
2   Barritt, B. *The Road of Excess*. PSI 1998 p.171
3   Elliot, L. Interview 10/10/2013
4   Ibid
5   Changes 72 document, (quoted in) 16/10/71
6   Richard de Marco Gallery Changes 72 file, 1971 (text by Kristof Glinka)
7   Glinka, K. Interview 8/10/2013
8   https://www.beatlesbible.com/songs/while-my-guitar-gently-weeps/
9   Changes 72 document, 16/10/71
10   Changes 72 document, 16/10/71
11   Ibid
12   Changes 72 Press Release, late 1971
13   *Flow*, Vol. 3, Privately published, London, early 1972
14   *Frendz*, Changes: 1972, late 1971, London
15   Changes 72 Press Release, late 1971
16   Elliot, L. Interview 10/10/2013
17   Ibid
18   Barritt, B. *The Road of Excess*. PSI 1998 p.172
19   Ibid p.173
20   Elliot, L. Interview 10/10/2013
21   Pure Land Ashram Press Release, January 1972

22   Letter to Brian Barritt, 9/2/1972

23   Hollingshead, V. Email 8/12/07

24   Glinka, K. Interview 8/10/2013

25   Fabian, J. *A Chemical Romance*, The Do Not Press, London 1988, p.8

26   Fabian, J. Email 12/11/2013

27   Ibid

28   Hollingshead, V. *LSD Mafia*, unpublished ms, June 2012, p.66

29   Letter to Jasper Newsome, 24/7/72

30   Glinka, K. Interview 8/10/2013

SM-21

friends of
san francis

THE MAN WHO
TURNED ON THE
WORLD

OB|3|75

sinus
music

Atlantic Crossings

Michael is a catalyst, he simply exists to make things happen.[1]

Flying to America for Michael Hollingshead wasn't as straightforward as it should have been. Auriol Roberts remembers that he decided not to fly direct to New York City. He didn't offer her an explanation for the decision, but the most likely reason is that he was concerned he might be on a wanted or excluded list. Hollingshead's solution was to fly to Montreal in Canada, hire a car and drive across the border into America.

Earlier in the year Vanessa, who was still living at the Dawes Hill commune, received a letter from her father in which he wrote, "I am with Auriol, and I want to be with you as well, how about I come and stay with you?"[2] After the disappointment she suffered when she'd visited him in London at his request and her expense, Vanessa thought this plea was her father's guilt speaking and didn't respond, so it came as a surprise when he and Auriol arrived at Dawes Hill in late September 1973. Vanessa was overjoyed and invited them to stay with her in her yurt. It wasn't long before Hollingshead's drinking began to frighten and intimidate the Dawes Hill communards. He boasted loudly, reminding them who he was, forcefully pointing out that their hippie way of life, the pot smoking, the draft dodging and the acid taking was a culture he had been instrumental in creating. Vanessa observed: "Because they were so young, the intimidation tactics always worked. And because he was so charming when sober, and downright frightening when drunk, they always put up with him. And they loved me."[3] One consequence of this intimidation was that Hollingshead was placated by being given his own yurt and allowed to stay.

Besides his regular use of marijuana and alcohol, Hollingshead was still taking psychedelics and on one occasion he, Vanessa and Auriol took mescaline together at Dawes Hill. Vanessa found the mescaline trip overwhelming; Hollingshead took her for a walk in the snow to help her through it but then left her alone and returned to Auriol in their yurt. Vanessa was tripping hard, seeing each snowflake turn purple and explode as it fell to earth, so for comfort and company sought shelter in the commune's communal cabin. In her psychedelic state Vanessa quietly and carefully observed the hippies, certain she could see deep into their psyches, aware of who was crazy, who was sleeping with who and other mescaline-induced insights. After some time, wishing the trip would end, she went to find her father who gave her three aspirins and some marijuana to help her get to sleep. When Vanessa woke the following morning she felt relieved, "I was so grateful I was not tripping anymore."[4]

In late November or early December, Hollingshead left Auriol and Vanessa at Dawes Hill and travelled to Cambridge, Massachusetts, to visit Gunther Weil, his friend from the Harvard days with Leary. Weil was running the Media Centre at the University of Massachusetts and was no longer using psychedelic drugs, now being a follower of Gurdjieff. Weil introduced Hollingshead to his colleague, Peter Beren, who invited Hollingshead and his unnamed woman companion, to stay at his flat for a few days. Beren, initially at least, found Hollingshead to be entertaining company, "He was a charming raconteur and recounted the famous odyssey of the Mayonnaise jar and the 5000 LSD trips contained within it. He was steeped in the lore of LSD and the lineage of who had turned on who and how the drug had coursed through society."[5]

Hollingshead told Beren he was now a member of the Third Order of The Society of Franciscans, a lay order, open to those still living secular lives, which he had become increasingly attracted to following his stay with the monks at Glasshampton and other monasteries. After hearing of this religious commitment, Beren was quite surprised to find Hollingshead's humble spiritual ambitions were contrasted by him being, "… the only person I knew who travelled with a theme song. He had a small cassette player and at the slightest provocation, he would play a tape of this theme song which had the refrain 'He was the man who turned on the world.'"[6]

This song, a catchy gospel number called 'The Man Who Turned On The World', had been written by Pat Ryan and J. Tayler, friends of Hollingshead from his prison days at HMP Leyhill. Using session musicians and the choir of St John's Church in Harrow, Ryan and Tayler recorded the song under the pseudonym The Friends of St. Francis and gave Hollingshead a pre-release copy. It's unclear how Hollingshead's interest in the Franciscan monastic order translated into his friends writing and recording the song with him in mind. The lyrics were ambiguous and could be interpreted either as being about Jesus turning the world on to Christianity or, for those in the know, about Hollingshead being the man who turned the world on to LSD. Either way, Hollingshead exploited the song to boost his ego and promote his autobiography.

The song was later released in Britain on the Charisma Label in 1974. Sales were poor, but the song enjoyed some radio play on Radio Luxembourg, ensuring its release in Belgium and the Netherlands. A year later, it appeared on *Beyond an Empty Dream*, a compilation LP of spiritual songs featuring famous musicians of the early seventies including Clifford T. Ward, John McLaughlin, The Charterhouse Choral Society (Mike Rutherford and Anthony Phillips from Genesis) and Anawim, a band led by Tom McGuinness of Manfred Mann. The enigmatic sleeve notes for 'The Man Who Turned On The World' seem to amplify Hollingshead's claim the song was about him, "The Friends of St Francis conceal a strange number of experiences and people." Hollingshead carried the song round with him for years, playing it to anyone who expressed an interest and, inevitably, to many who didn't.

Beren, a former journalist on the left-leaning *Boston Phoenix*, thought Hollingshead's story was worth retelling and suggested he interview him. Hollingshead agreed, knowing it would be useful free publicity for his memoir, which had recently been published in America. The interview appeared in a December 1973 issue of the *Phoenix* as, 'LSD Era: It All Started With a Mayonnaise Jar'. It stuck mainly to the narrative arc of *The Man Who Turned On The World* but included some new opinions and observations. Hollingshead was dismissive of the guru game, saying "There are many teachers in the world. But ultimately everyone is their own guru. If you need help on the way it will come to you"[7] and claimed people appeared to have lost the art of taking responsibility for themselves on acid, "LSD was always a tool or sacrament for standing on your own two feet...People, we thought, would no longer be content to have their lives dictated from without by career structures, political structures, or religious structures. In all aspects of their lives, people would attempt to make their external lives match the internal vision. We were wrong."[8] Beren perceptively summed up Hollingshead's writing style with the comment "the overblown tone reflects Hollingshead's Woody Allen whimsy."[9]

Shortly after the interview was published, Hollingshead announced that he was 'liberating' Beren's apartment; Beren could stay but Hollingshead had no intention of leaving as he now considered it his own. Perhaps Beren should have foreseen this from a comment in the interview, "The mystic of today", says Hollingshead with a twinkle, "must be a pragmatist"[10]. Despite Beren's numerous attempts to reason with him, Hollingshead was resolute, he was not going anywhere. In desperation, Beren appealed to Gunther Weil who intervened and eventually persuaded Hollingshead to leave. Back at Dawes Hill, Hollingshead's mood gradually worsened and he rarely left his yurt other than at communal meal times. His continued presence was causing tensions in the commune; while people were accustomed to his rages, his threats to blow the place up or to shoot anyone who came near him were unnerving and unconducive to the peace and love lifestyle Dawes Hill aspired to. The situation began to change when Hollingshead and Auriol visited Gunther Weil just before Christmas and again met with George Litwin, who promised the couple work at his company in the new year.

Having secured work and sensing he had outstayed his welcome, Hollingshead decided to leave Dawes Hill. The first Vanessa heard about this decision was at breakfast one morning when he gave her an ultimatum: either she moved to Boston with him and Auriol or she would never see him again. Vanessa didn't want to stay at Dawes Hill forever but wasn't sure if she wanted, or could, continue living with her father and his moods. But Vanessa loved Auriol and the feeling was mutual, so she agreed, soon finding herself in the Boston suburb of Dorchester sharing a house with a group of "hippies missing any ounce of humanity or brain cells."[11] Litwin gave Hollingshead and Auriol jobs at his management and training consultancy and Vanessa attended an expensive private prep school where she did well educationally and it wasn't long before they moved again, this time to a basement apartment in Hollingshead's old stomping ground of Cambridge.

In early February 1974, Hollingshead met up with Tim Leary's partner Joanna Harcourt-Smith in Boston, where she gave him a copy of Leary's latest book, *Terra II/The Starseed Transmissions*. Hollingshead was impressed and effused to Leary, "It is the most fantastic, beautiful, accurate and inspiring work I have read, a truly magnificent goal for the society of the present and the future; and one we must all get behind."[12] *Terra II* (aka *The Starseed Transmissions*) was written by Leary in Folsom prison and was a mixture of musings about the possibility that life in the universe might have been spread by comets, along with discussion about Comet Kohoutek and why its discovery in 1973 had not been more widely reported. This scientific speculation was blended with Leary's conspiracy tinged concerns the US government were covering up information about UFOs and contact with extraterrestrials, "If you start speculating about Higher Intelligence visiting planet earth, a galaxy of embarrassing issues gets raised. What would the celestial visitors think of how we are running the planet? Whose selfish securities and biased superiorities would be threatened?... Could there be a secret conspiracy to censor extra-planetary contact?"[13] Leary perceptively argued that if extraterrestrials did exist the notion of them travelling in 'flying saucers' was naïve, suggesting that contact with ET was more likely via human consciousness than by visiting spacecraft.

Hollingshead agreed with the thrust of Leary's ideas, hyperbolically lauding them as "the first truly original philosophy presented to the world since Aristotle"[14] and speculated whether alien craft had landed on Earth millions of years ago. Hollingshead's espousal of Leary's latest theory gives rise to the observation that whenever he met someone he respected as his intellectual equal, he tended to enthusiastically believe, adopt and promote their theories, almost as though they were his own. This happened with Leary's ideas in the early sixties, with Joe Mellen's brainbloodvolume and trepanning theories and latterly, Kristof's enthusiasm for the I Ching. Whether Hollingshead believed these ideas were innovative expressions of psychedelic culture and his fealty to them was sincere, or whether he adopted them as a cynical means to financial or social ends is debatable.

At this time Auriol believes Hollingshead was living as ordinary a life as he could. Whatever personal demons he was masking with alcohol and other drugs, a deep sense of personal frustration that he had not been as personally successful as he wished was certainly one of them. "My background has eaten up my foreground",[15] he often lamented to Auriol, implying he felt defined by how others perceived him. The irony that the perception of Hollingshead by others was a result of the behaviours he had displayed appeared not to have occurred to him. Vanessa, always observing her father's behaviour, wrote to her mother from her new home, listing what she saw as her father's good and bad points. "Well, Mr Hollingshead is (negative qualities) stubborn, likes to boss people around, thinks he's the top man, clumsy, can't face up to something bad he has done, talks and gives you a lecture before he tells you what he really wants to say, ruthless at times. Positive qualities – Good sense of humour, always saying how bright you (Sophie) are, likes helping people, says a lot of nice things about you, can convince you very easily, outgoing, impressive, thoughtful, nice to be with, that's if you get him in a good mood, which is usually easy."[16] For a fourteen-year-old, who had spent much of her life separated from her father, Vanessa's slightly tongue-in-cheek summary of her father's good and bad qualities was perceptive and accurate. Out of all the intelligent people in Hollingshead's life – academics, mystics, scientists, clergy and other intellectuals – it was his daughter who often had the clearest insight into, if not understanding of, her father's strengths and weaknesses.

Having now re-established himself in America, Hollingshead began to catch up with the latest psychedelic research. Controversial Mexican psychedelic therapist Salvador Roquet invited him to visit the Instituto de Psicosintesis (Institute of Psychosynthesis), which he did in March 1974. The three weeks he spent at the IDP was, he wrote to Leary, one of the most notable experiences of his life. Hollingshead's impression of Roquet's brand of psychedelic therapy was that it achieved in months what psychotherapists took several years to attain with a patient. Hollingshead advised Roquet how to persuade Mexican prison authorities to sanction psychedelic therapy with inmates, but had limited success with this, probably because the methods Roquet used were too extreme. He would run group sessions with up to twenty-five subjects who had taken a variety of psychedelic drugs at different dosages, planning the experience to overload the participants' senses and raise their anxiety levels, often to the point of panic. Then, by skilfully guiding their experiences and using the participants as co-therapists in the chemical chaos, Roquet brought them back to ordinary consciousness. Hollingshead took two 'treatments' while at the IDP. The first, with an unnamed but potent psychedelic, he described as a descent into hell. This prepared him for the second session, conducted using mushrooms supplied by the legendary Mexican curandera Maria Sabina, which Hollingshead described as being the richest of his psychedelic trips.

Back in Boston, Vanessa was doing well educationally but suffering personally, upset because her father was still drinking heavily and occasionally beating her and Auriol. Vanessa didn't understand alcoholism and the causes of domestic violence, or why her father seemed intent on hurting those who loved him, dealing with the intolerable situation herself by drinking in secret. Hollingshead did have periods of sobriety, but his alcoholism and mood swings eventually led to George Litwin sacking him, although this wasn't how Hollingshead explained the situation to Vanessa; "My dad informed me that he was going back to England. He said 'Americans just don't understand me. I need to go home.'"[17]

Hollingshead and Auriol returned to London without Vanessa in September 1974. Vanessa sensed life in England with her father wouldn't work out and decided to remain in Boston: "I couldn't get on that plane to England. I knew England with him was not going to be pleasant. And I knew as wonderful as he was sober, it was short lived. He would clean up at a Franciscan Monastery and be 'good' for a month or two, and then start with the pot, then the wine, then the vodka."[18] But with few friends and nowhere to stay in Boston, after a couple of weeks sleeping rough, Vanessa unhappily boarded a plane for London, thinking "I still loved my dad. But he was a bully."[19] Vanessa found her father and Auriol living with Auriol's parents in West Hampstead. Auriol's mother was a housewife, her father a clergyman, and living in that calm and structured family environment appeared to suit Hollingshead. Vanessa remembers that although he was still drinking he would carry out domestic chores and his moods and behaviours weren't as problematic as they had been. Hollingshead was unable to find, or chose not to, work and signed on weekly at the Lisson Grove Benefits Office in order to receive the 'dole', as weekly unemployment payments were called, and bought a moped so he could travel around the city.

Hollingshead's autobiography wasn't selling particularly well. The LSD era was petering out and many people were unwilling to devote twelve hours to the intense psychedelic experience; drugs such as cocaine, heroin and amphetamine which offered a shorter, more socially acceptable high, were gaining ground. *TMWTOTW* garnered a few reviews in newspapers as far afield as Australia, but none offered any penetrating insights. The more telling comments came from Hollingshead's contemporaries. Hollingshead's and Tim Leary's mutual friend Brian Barritt, now a drug dealer in Amsterdam, was scathing about the book, writing to Dave Ball: "Almost forgot to thank you for sending Michael Hollingshead's book, it's like some old Duchess's memoirs, totally terrible. He turned on everyone in the world but himself."[20] Barritt complained to Leary, "Michael Hollingshead wrote a book called *The Man Who Turned On The World*, but it hasn't got any sparkle."[21]

In 1975, Hollingshead, Auriol and Vanessa moved from Auriol's parents' house to a large squat on Huntley Street in Bloomsbury where Pat Ryan, co-writer of *The Man Who Turned On The World* song lived. Ryan became good friends with Vanessa, who credits him with helping her reach a better understanding of her father, balancing the negative aspects of his personality with the accurate observation: "Michael is a catalyst, he simply exists to make things happen".[22] Hollingshead occasionally visited his friend Jasper Newsome at a squat on Haverstock Hill in Hampstead, where Paul Sieveking, co-founder of *Fortean Times* magazine, remembers him as dull and self-obsessed, an impression shared by others who knew him during that time. Journalist Mary Finnigan recalled "Michael was pretty much a burnt-out case by then. Very hesitant and quite shy. Fancied himself as an acid guru but not many people took him seriously."[23] Auriol found a well-paid job as Publicity Manager for Batsford Books but though Hollingshead was brimming with ideas for writing and travel projects, mentally he was in the doldrums, lacking direction and focus.

High Times, the American drug culture magazine, was a significant factor in Hollingshead resuming his writing career in 1975. The American publication of *TMWTOTW* generated some interest in Hollingshead and he was interviewed for the magazine by Peter Stafford, a chronicler of American psychedelic history. The interview, featuring a photo of a bearded and pensive Hollingshead, appeared in the January 1975 issue. The piece stuck to the *TMWTOTW* narrative, adding little of relevance, but again noted his membership of the Third Order of the Society of St. Francis. Hollingshead had always dabbled with various religious and philosophical beliefs, intellectually if not practically, but as he aged it was the simple philosophy of the Franciscans that held his attention. He never wrote anything specific about his involvement with them but Auriol, who accompanied him to several Franciscan monasteries and retreats believed that "the Franciscan thing was genuine...he was seriously considering the degree to which he could relate to this lay Church of England group. He kept up a correspondence with Brother Jonathan. He wanted to engage with a religious tradition because, after acid – his particular experience – he felt he knew what it was all about."[24]

Hollingshead's *High Times* interview upset several people. The March 1975 issue included a terse letter from Robert Masters, partner of

Hollingshead's former colleague at the Agora Trust, Jean Houston, who complained that Hollingshead's statement that he'd given Houston and Masters their first LSD session was a lie, as both had used psychedelics before meeting him. This wasn't the first, or last, time Hollingshead would be accused of lying, about who he had guided through their first LSD experience. In the same issue, psychologist Bruce Eisner took Hollingshead to task over his claim that contemporary LSD was inferior due to it being made with synthetic, rather than organic, ergot. Eisner argued that this was a false perception, with any reduction in the potency of recreational LSD being due to impurities or incompetent synthesis rather than the source of its ingredients.

The publication of *TMWTOTW* and the *High Times* interview gave Hollingshead hope he could forge a career writing about LSD and psychedelic culture. This blossomed into reality in late 1976 when Heathcote Williams, poet and advocate for the squatting movement, introduced Hollingshead to Lee Harris, owner of Alchemy, one of Britain's oldest Head shops. Harris wanted Hollingshead to be involved in his new venture, Britain's first magazine devoted to recreational drug culture. Although *High Times* was available in Britain it focused on the American drug scene and Harris believed that, by attracting key writers from the domestic counter culture, a British drug culture magazine would be a success. Hollingshead was enthusiastic, seeing the opportunity to help cement his writing career and further raise his profile, and became involved with the project from the start: "Michael Hollingshead, who first turned Leary on, was on hand to guide me and came many times to my flat/office in Ladbroke Grove where I interviewed him."[25]

The first issue of *Home Grown*, the magazine that emerged from these meetings, was published in June 1977 with a full colour cover. It was a diverse mix of news, opinions and articles contributed by the leading lights of Britain's counter culture, heavily illustrated by British hippie artists like Bryan Talbot and Edward Barker. As one of the Contributing

Editors, Hollingshead persuaded Leary to contribute the previously unpublished *Declaration of Evolution* and introduced Harris to London socialite Mim Scala, who wrote a piece on his Moroccan adventures with the hash-fuelled Gnaoua trance musicians. Hollingshead was interviewed under the heading, 'LSD and The Mind Alchemyst' in which he discussed obtaining the 'magic gram' from Sandoz, his time with Leary at Harvard, the importance of set and setting and, once again, his doubts about the potency of the currently-available LSD. He answered the final question, "Should one take acid?", with the gnomic, "As the old alchemists said, 'You need a bit of light to find the light,' and that pretty well sums up *why* acid."[26]

Home Grown's first issue received a mixed reception. The hip crowd, who previously only had publications like *Oz, Frendz, Ink* and *I.T.* to rely on for drug information, thought it was great. But some in the prevailing counter cultural 'establishment' took a different view. *International Times* (IT), which had chosen not to review Hollingshead's autobiography, devoted a full page to contrasting reviews of *Home Grown*, both highlighting Hollingshead's input. The first complained: "Home Groan" (sic) is full of self-congratulatory codswallop. Hollingshead comes through with flying colours – such an asinine intro – I was there, all our yesterdays, LSD changed the lifestyle of a generation. Did it? So "Home Groan" asks Hollowhead some questions which he answers on page 15 in true Hollowhead form. Like his fucking book *(The Man Who Turned On The World)* compiled and written by Kristof Glinka (exiled in Bogota) and claimed by Hollowhead. Rip-off! Watch out Hollingshead, we are on to you."[27] The second review was more positive. While critical about Leary's contribution, 'E.M.' was complimentary about Hollingshead's, writing, "Hollingshead on the other hand, in a *Home Grown* exclusive, gives us some great insights into the dawning of the Acid Age."[28]

By the time the first issue had been published, Hollingshead was in Kathmandu where he spent the summer months guiding trekking groups of wealthy hippies. His relationship with Auriol Roberts was crumbling and she remained in London, but they kept in touch and Auriol flew out to join him in December, not with the intention of resuming or saving their relationship but to meet Hollingshead and end it in person. Following their separation Hollingshead went to Goa for a while, before returning to London in the spring of 1978. He hadn't been back from Goa long before he met Lee Harris in a London pub, in the company of his new partner, a "posh lady", as Harris remembered. The new woman in Hollingshead's life was Everilda, 'Ev', Dorothea Hesketh, 37-year-old daughter of Charles Hesketh, former architecture correspondent for the *Daily Telegraph*. The genesis of their relationship wasn't directly related to Hollingshead's psychedelic life, but there was a correlation. Hollingshead met Ev in March 1978 at a party given by her cousin, Anthony Blond, an old acquaintance of Hollingshead's and a partner at Blond & Briggs Ltd, publishers of *The Man Who Turned On The World*. Hollingshead and Hesketh were together for three years, but never married.

The summer of 1978 saw Hollingshead's fortunes on the rise as he began to submit writing to several drug culture magazines including *High Times*. He also received recognition for his contribution to American psychedelic culture when the tabloid drug newspaper *Blotter* ran *The Sayings of Michael Hollingshead*, a feature consisting of twenty-one paragraphs of quotes taken from his autobiography and other sources. His first submission to *High Times*, published in December 1978, was a lavishly illustrated history of The Brotherhood of Eternal Love, whose ranch Hollingshead had lived at in the late sixties. He followed this up in the January 1979 edition by revisiting his theory that LSD held enormous potential as a performance-enhancing sports drug. In *The New Secret Weapon: LSD*, he noted that LSD sessions had helped champion sky-diver Jim Arender, and shared reports of surfers and skateboarders using LSD to help perfect their skills. Hollingshead had continued to test the theory on himself, taking LSD when water skiing, high-jumping and bowling, among other sports, claiming that LSD had enhanced his skill in all of them. A frisbee enthusiast claimed that using LSD had improved his technique: "there is no question that a more direct link becomes established between thought and bodily action",[29] and the coach of a famous Ivy League football team believed his team's LSD use enabled them to break a long running losing streak. The article concluded with Hollingshead's *Seven Steps to Enhanced Athletic Awareness* which outlined the key elements of introducing LSD into sport training programmes. Hollingshead missed a chance by not developing this fascinating, if contentious, idea into a book proposal. A wave of books claiming that consciousness-altering techniques could boost sporting performance emerged in the late seventies and early eighties, and Hollingshead's theory would have fitted in well.

Hollingshead became a father, for the third time, on 16 January 1979, when Ev gave birth in London to a girl they named Esther Mary Hollingshead, following which Ev sold her house in Hammersmith and moved to America to be with Hollingshead in New York. Asked if Hollingshead used Ev's money to help sustain his lifestyle, she replied: "Yes, by the end the money I'd saved after selling my house in Hammersmith was disappearing fast, and like all addicts Michael could be a real bully when he wanted money."[30]

Hollingshead's published articles were often flawed, with factual errors or unevidenced personal claims, but he wrote well and had little problem in finding outlets for them. But the more he wrote, the more the pressure increased to find future subjects for articles, and not everyone wanted to be connected to him; psychiatrist Ronnie Laing, for instance, snubbed Hollingshead's request in a curt letter. Even an appeal to Laing's literary agent, guaranteeing Laing the final edit, was to no avail. This, and similar set-backs, didn't dismay Hollingshead too much, but he realised he was going to have to work hard to find future subject matter. For the March 1979 issue of *High Times*, Hollingshead reviewed John Marks' book on CIA mind control, *The Search for the Manchurian*

Candidate. There was an irony to this review, as Hollingshead has often been accused of working for the CIA or other intelligence agencies. In it he revealed that he had been dosed with LSD prior to delivering a talk to scientists at the home of the governor of Raleigh, North Carolina. Hollingshead claimed he only emerged unscathed from this attempt to chemically disrupt his talk because of his ability to easily navigate high dose LSD trips and keep his cool under pressure. But he failed to mention the event in his autobiography, or anywhere else, and it is highly possible that the story may be yet another of his self-aggrandising fictions. Another irony was Hollingshead's indignation at those in power sanctioning dosing people with LSD without their knowledge, something he had done himself on many occasions.

Ralph Metzner, Hollingshead's colleague from Harvard and Millbrook, was his next interview subject for *High Times.* Metzner had never been Hollingshead's greatest fan but seemed to have set his distrust aside for the interview, which drew out Metzner's thoughts on LSD and other psychedelics, along with astrology and the effects of diet on consciousness. Metzner, like many individuals from the early days of LSD research, felt the psychedelic revolution had failed to realise its potential, telling Hollingshead, "I think socially LSD was an experiment that failed", adding, "I think the residue in terms of how people are using it now is not that constructive", because fewer people were using it for spiritual purposes.[31] The contrast in philosophies of LSD use, between the Kesey school of psychedelic hedonism and the quasi-mystical school of Metzner, Leary and Alpert, was still very apparent.

Timothy, Hollingshead's first child, now aged 25 and living in his home country of Sweden where he was attended university, rarely saw or heard from his father, but in May 1979, in what he called "one of my periodic notes", he brought his son up to date with his latest activities. Hollingshead enthused about his writing commissions, claiming he was now writing for four magazines in New York City alone adding that *OMNI* magazine had commissioned him to interview the famous American behavioural psychologist, B.F. Skinner. He also mentioned that he'd started work on a new book, but failed to say what it was about, and that he was excited about going to Los Angeles to work on a film. The letter was upbeat, suggesting Hollingshead was content and he praised Vanessa, telling Timothy she was doing really well at theatre school and how "She is actually very, very, good; at least she always impresses me. Actually, her teachers say the same thing."[32]

Hollingshead interviewed Leary for the May 1979 edition of the short-lived American magazine *HiLife*. The promotional text for *The Once and Future Timothy Leary* featured a photograph of the perma-smiling, healthy-looking Leary with his arm round the almost bald and beardless Hollingshead who was billed as "A native of England, he now lives in New York where he interviews those who life the *HiLife* or help to create it."[33] The blurb named several musicians and celebrities who Hollingshead had introduced to LSD, although as usual this was full of errors. Leary gave Hollingshead a good interview, ranging across the ideas expressed in *Terra II* via Darwinism and speculation about who would play Leary in a biopic he hoped would be filmed soon. Hollingshead remained deferential to his old friend, concluding the interview with, "He may not always be right, as he would be the first to admit, but at least he has the courage to extend his thinking into new areas. In that sense, he is perhaps above all else an impresario in the manner of an Apollinaire, a Gurdjieff, or a Diaghilev – that is, someone who is rarer than a holy man."[34] The success of these articles showed Hollingshead to be an insightful commentator on psychedelic culture and the commissions continued to roll in, with further articles appearing in magazines throughout 1979 and into 1980, including the B.F. Skinner piece Hollingshead mentioned to Timothy.

1979 had been a good year for Hollingshead, possibly his best since the early seventies and the success of the Changes 72 installation and publication of his autobiography. Between 1973 and 1979, supported by Auriol Roberts, he had struggled with alcohol and drug issues, relationship and family problems and a lack of paid work. Yet despite those setbacks he seemed to have come through this long dark night of the soul, falling in love again and working hard to get to the stage where several publications were jostling to commission work from him. Hollingshead's relationship with his daughter Vanessa and son Timothy were now arguably better than ever before and there was little indication during 1979, on the surface at least, that his use of drugs and alcohol were causing significant problems. Furthermore, there was no indication that he had deceived or defrauded anyone, or that he'd failed to deliver on any of his promises. Few letters or personal writings from this period of Hollingshead's life exist, so it is not possible, with certainty, to know how he felt. But the evidence of his writing career and the tone of letters to his son Timothy and other correspondents suggest that everything was going well and the future for Michael Hollingshead looked bright.

Yet, over this apparent period of calm prosperity loomed the long shadows of his past exploits and the ever-present psychological demons which drove him to seek refuge in drink and drugs. Hollingshead had been through this cycle of failure and success many times before, driven by his propensity for wilful self-destruction, an aspect of his personality he acknowledged but seemed powerless to prevent. As the seventies gave way to the eighties Hollingshead must have fervently hoped those days were now behind him.

Notes

1   Hollingshead, Vanessa. *LSD Mafia*. Unpublished ms. 2013 p.99
2   Ibid p. 89
3   Ibid p. 90
4   Ibid p. 90
5   Beren, Peter. Email 8/12/13
6   Ibid
7   *Boston Phoenix*. 'LSD Era: It All Started With a Mayonnaise Jar'. December 1973
8   Ibid
9   Ibid
10   Ibid
11   Hollingshead, Vanessa. *LSD Mafia*. Unpublished ms. 2013 p.92
12   Letter from Hollingshead to Leary, 12/2/74
13   Leary, T. Starseed. Level Press. 1973
14   Letter from Hollingshead to Leary, 12/2/74
15   Roberts, Auriol. Email 24/4/14
16   Letter from Vanessa Hollingshead to Sophie Hollingshead, 1/3/74
17   Hollingshead, Vanessa. *LSD Mafia*. Unpublished ms. 2013 p.94
18   Ibid p.94
19   Ibid p.95
20   Letter from Brian Barritt to David Ball, undated, 1974
21   Letter from Brian Barritt to Tim Leary, undated, 1974
22   Hollingshead, Vanessa. *LSD Mafia*. Unpublished ms. 2013 p.99
23   Finnigan, Mary. Email 29/12/18
24   Roberts, Auriol. Email 28/1/15
25   Harris, Lee. Email 3/10/14
26   Hollingshead, Michael. 'LSD and the Mind Alchemyst'. *Home Grown* no. 1 June 1977
27   'Home Grown Controversy'. *International Times*, no date, 1976
28   Ibid
29   *High Times*. January 1979
30   Hesketh, Ev. Email, 30/12/18
31   *High Times*. March 1979
32   Letter from Michael Hollingshead to Timothy Shinkfield, 28/5/79
33   *Hi Life*. May 1979
34   Ibid

Bolivia, Oblivia, Oblivion

Too much of nothing makes a man feel ill at ease.[1]

After a successful year in 1979, Hollingshead's writing career began to flounder following his move to California. This was unfortunate as one of the main reasons for the move was his belief that California offered a wider range of source material for his writing projects; but as 1980 dawned he was finding it increasingly difficult to obtain commissions. Another reason for his move was the interest shown by a film director friend of Thom Keyes in making a biopic of Hollingshead's life, with speculation that Hollingshead would be played by John Hurt and Tim Leary by Jack Nicholson, but the project faltered at the discussion stage.

Hollingshead's last piece of published writing, a thoughtful interview with Robert Anton Wilson, appeared in the April 1980 issue of *High Times*. Wilson was well known as co-author (with Michael Shea) of the psychedelic *Illuminatus Trilogy*, and latterly the ground-breaking *Cosmic Trigger*, with an approving introduction by Tim Leary. *Cosmic Trigger*'s eclectic mix of psychedelics, occultism, philosophy and pranksterism became as important to the post sixties generation of psychonauts as Leary's books were to the original LSD users. The interview with Wilson was a strong finish to Hollingshead's writing career and, together with articles published in 1978 and '79, would prove to be useful leverage in his final, doomed, encounter with the publishing industry.

Hollingshead, Hesketh and their daughter rented a cottage in Laurel Canyon in the Hollywood Hills near Los Angeles, not far from Thom Keyes. Hollingshead and Keyes had been friends since the late sixties, but the friendship could be corrosive as both men were heavy drinkers individually, and more so when together. LSD barely featured during this period of Hollingshead's life, but he was drinking daily and supplementing the alcohol with hashish, marijuana, cocaine and other drugs. Hesketh commented, "I think Michael was taking anything he could lay his hands on then. I seem to remember the name Quaaludes."[2] Known in Britain as Mandrax, Quaalude was the brand name of a powerful sedative and hypnotic medication that became a popular recreational drug in the sixties and seventies. If Hollingshead was combining alcohol with Quaaludes, irrespective of any other drug he was using, he could have found it difficult to function with a clear head, which would hardly have helped his writing. Hollingshead had pressed his self-destruct button once again, but losing income from writing commissions was only the start of the problems he was to face.

Thom Keyes' house on Mulholland Drive was a "meeting place for all the rascals from the neighbourhood, including Timothy Leary"[3] and it was here that Hollingshead met businessman Michael Froehlich. Froehlich liked Hollingshead immediately, "He was so much fun to be with. There was always so much mischief happening, and he was ready at any time to get you into mischief. And, of course, he was a party man at that time."[4] Hollingshead liked Froehlich too and respected him for his intelligence. They enjoyed each other's company, liked getting high together and became good friends, "Our general outlook on life was that it was fun. If anyone ever fell into the trap of being too serious, we just took a load of drugs. Ha, ha!"[5]

While living in Laurel Canyon Keyes developed the idea for the University of Hollywood (UoH) which Hollingshead and Michael Froehlich were also part of; a venture described by Froehlich as "our other crazy event".[6] The seeds of the UoH were sown on 12 August 1980 when Keyes invited twelve friends, including Leary, John Lilly and Hollingshead, to a lecture. The event was a success, with everyone getting on so well that Keyes invited them to form the University's core, the 'Gang of 13'. The original idea was that each 'professor', as contributors to the UoH were known, would "do two events a year for the school calendar, which could be anything from giving a half hour lecture to taking 15 people a year to Kathmandu after wildflowers".[7]

The UoH held its Founder's Day event on 14 September 1980, at the Moon Fire Ranch in Topanga Canyon, a spectacular hilltop location owned by Lewis Beach Marvin III, heir to the Green Shield Stamp empire and one of the UoH's wealthy backers. Over 300 guests attended the lavish celebrations which featured hang gliders, parachutists and a stunt plane, all trailing rainbow coloured smoke, as well as a roaming menagerie of llamas, goats, peacocks and a zebu. There was a limitless supply of champagne and drugs of all kinds including MDMA, then little-known, handed out free by legendary chemist Sasha Shulgin. Hollingshead, who was named in the media as Vice President of the UoH, spent the day partying hard and giving interviews to perplexed journalists, naming Chuck Berry, who was present but didn't perform, as the UoH's professor of music, Rod Stewart the captain of the football team, Tim Leary's wife the professor of high-altitude sex and so on. The event was more of a sixties-style Happening, or something the Merry Pranksters might have staged, than it was a traditional university ceremony. The concept of the UoH was a heady blend of the surreal and the serious and it was difficult for journalists to discern the difference. It's easy to understand their confusion: Keyes claimed that the UoH would "undertake serious competition in that extremely vicious game, croquet"[8] and publish comic book versions of classic texts including *The Decline and Fall of the Roman Empire* and *Gravity's Rainbow*; elsewhere, John Lilly could be found speaking dolphin to the UoH's Professor of Heresy, Paul Kantner of Jefferson Airplane, who appeared to understand him.

Even the UoH's corporate-looking logo wasn't quite what it seemed. The pink, brown and green image depicting one of Christopher Columbus' ships, circled with the motto 'Navigare Necesse Est' (It Is Necessary to Navigate), was emblazoned on the sweat shirt worn by Keyes. Asked if the colour scheme had any meaning, Keyes answered, "Money– green, shit– brown, pussy– pink".[9] At the high point of the day the celebrants were encouraged to sing along with the UoH's theme song, a koan-like ditty which went, "We begin – at the beginning. Go on – until the very end. Then stop – until the next time. Which is NOW! NOW! NOW!"[10]

The key to understanding these celebrations was hidden in plain sight in the press release for the event, in which Keyes cited French symbolist writer Alfred Jarry's College of 'Pataphysics as a model for the UoH. The UoH's core ambitions mirrored the 'Pataphysical intention that "Its activities have an ambiguous character. The superficial observer is amused, even delighted: he imagines he has come across a group of cruel practical jokers, cynical or subtle irony, collections of pungent curiosities, merciless exposures of pretence."[11]

If the journalists present found it hard to understand the Alice-in-Wonderland-like party, they found it even harder to make sense of Keyes' and Hollingshead's plans for their University. Asked if he hoped to attract a large student body Keyes responded, "Not really. Students always ruin a university"[12] while Hollingshead trivialised the UoH's very existence: "I don't think we would have done it if we couldn't get the University of Hollywood name."[13] All of which still begged the question: what form the UoH would take when the drugs wore off and the publicity faded.

Founder member Michael Froehlich remembers the intention was "to make a University without members, just teachers, with the lectures going via satellite to all the schools in the world with free access."[14] One of the UoH's financial backers, the CEO of Texas Instruments, funded the equipment needed for this and some lectures were recorded and broadcast. But the UoH concept, though ahead of its time, was confusing and never caught on with the public. Within two years of its inception, when Texas Instruments appointed a new CEO and the money dried up, the UoH slowly faded away. Hollingshead had proclaimed himself as the UoH's Vice President and was named as such in numerous media reports, but he wasn't named in the Statement of Aims and Purpose, or in the list of original professors. Hollingshead was keen to be involved in the initial stages of the scheme, and gain from its publicity, but when the UoH failed to develop, or offer opportunities for income, he moved on.

With no regular income and an increasing drink and drug problem, something in Hollingshead's life had to change. Sobriety, which could have saved him even at that late stage, was not an option he appeared to want, or perhaps was incapable of taking. Ev Hesketh found the worsening situation intolerable and in late 1981 ended their relationship, returning to London with Esther. Hollingshead's drink problem had played a major part in the split, Ev remembering "This was the main reason that I left and came back to London. I gather he had been an extremely heavy drinker since he was young and was certainly a full-blown alcoholic by the end of his life".[15] Ev believed Hollingshead regretted his negative behaviours, and was sad the relationship ended but, "I had a small child and had to get out".[16] Hollingshead later commented ruefully to Ev, "I know what I do is stupid, but I genuinely can't help it."[17] Reflecting on the Michael Hollingshead she knew for several years, Ev summed him up as "A compelling, tricky and complex character",[18] adding, "His friend, Pat Ryan, who I knew in London, described him as a catalyst. I think that's quite apt!"[19]

With Ev Hesketh and her financial support gone, Hollingshead moved back to New York, which didn't surprise Ev, who reflected, "From what I can gather, Michael tended to move somewhere with big plans, then it never quite happened, and things would go awry, and he'd move on."[20] Hollingshead's letters to Ev, initially affectionate and pleading with her to come back soon changed to missives of a bitter and aggressive nature. The reason for this change was simple, Hollingshead had met and moved in with the woman who was to be his final partner, Eileen O'Connor. Vanessa had seen several women come and go in her father's life and did not see this new relationship as positive, though she was infatuated with Hollingshead. "She was not that heavy a drinker when she met him. She was a good deal younger. Not all that attractive, very typically Irish. She was in a car accident and it had damaged her ear canals, so her balance was very bad; pour alcohol on top of that and... they were a match made in heaven. I did not like her one bit."[21] Michael Froehlich, however, saw Eileen in a different light, "I liked her very much, she was a good person, a morally good person. She loved Michael, they loved each other very much. It was wonderful. It was a joy to see them together."[22] But Froehlich acknowledged "She was like a naughty street kid sometimes and, of course, provocative. When she was with Michael, they tried to beat each other and would get into the craziest ideas."[23]

Vanessa believes it was when her father became involved with O'Connor that his luck finally ran out. New York had acted like a magnet to him since he first arrived in 1959, but it had never served him well due to its alcohol culture, the availability of any drug he desired and people to indulge them with. But by the early 1980s drugs were the least of Hollingshead's problems – he was now a full-blown alcoholic. His drinking was spiralling out of control and he was running up unpaid bills at liquor stores in his neighbourhood. Vanessa watched as her father and Eileen's dysfunctional relationship sunk further into a co-dependency underpinned by alcohol. Vanessa sensed that while

Eileen and her father might have been in love, Eileen's compensation money was also a factor in the relationship. "I loved your father" Eileen later told her, "so I figured I might as well join him you know, so I had him move in with me, and I had some money from the car accident, so we were living off of that."[24]

The writing commissions had dried up, and there was nothing of substance on the horizon, despite Hollingshead having a pro-active literary agent. Perhaps remembering Keyes' idea of adapting classic texts into comic books, Hollingshead wrote a proposal for a series of comic books based on popular science. He knew that if he could find a publisher for the idea it would solve his financial problems and he would be on the road to success as a writer again. His literary agent sent Marvel Comics Bizarre Adventures editor Lynn Graeme an outline. She thought the idea had promise and invited Hollingshead to a meeting with her and well-known comics artist Steve Bissette. Bissette remembers Hollingshead as "a smooth-talking British gentleman who looked a bit like William Burroughs (and, I soon discovered, shared Burroughs' appetite for drugs) and charmed Marvel personnel with his Brit accent and manners."[25] Bissette thought Hollingshead's comics were exactly the kind of venture Marvel's Editor in Chief, Jim Shooter, was looking for. To demonstrate his credentials Hollingshead sent copies of his articles from *High Times*, *OMNI* and other magazines to Marvel; he also produced documentation from several popular science personalities including John Lilly, Carl Sagan and Robert Jastrow, showing that he had permission to adapt their work into scripts.

Reassured as to Hollingshead's sincerity, Bissette arranged for a contract to be drawn up between him and Marvel. It was now the task of Marvel's publicity department to ensure the comic buying public had advance notice of the project and the March 1982 edition of *The Comics Journal* featured a news item about the series, "Marvel's Titan Series Nearing Completion", which explained that Michael Hollingshead "... represents Marvel to scientists whose work he is interested in adapting, and then provides Marvel with abstracts of the material they're expert on. Marvel then works to dramatise this scientific information, converting it into a comic book format; then the completed material is given back to Hollingshead and the scientists, who edit and approve it."[26] Marvel had invested significant amounts of time and money in Hollingshead's project and Jim Shooter's plan was to market the series, "...every which way – newsstand, direct-sales, bookstores...you name it."[27]

Bissette and Hollingshead worked closely on the debut issue of the series, which was based on Robert Jastrow's 1977 non-fiction history of the universe, *Until the Sun Dies*. But when Hollingshead delivered the final script to accompany the artwork Bissette was dismayed, finding it rambling and chaotic. The discrepancy between Hollingshead's promises and what he delivered should have rung alarm bells, but Hollingshead had charmed Marvel's commissioning editors with his well-worn but effective smokescreen of upper-class British accent, humour and impeccable manners. In retrospect, Bissette believes he should have sensed something was wrong at their first story conference with Jim Shooter when Hollingshead arrived at Marvel Comics' Madison Avenue headquarters clearly stoned and slurring his words. As they went up in the lift, Hollingshead mumbled to Bissette, "Excellent hash oil".[28] Hollingshead became increasingly incoherent as the meeting progressed and when Shooter left the room to make a phone call, much to Bissette's disgust, Hollingshead slid from his chair onto the floor, only regaining his seat with Bissette's assistance. If that embarrassment wasn't bad enough, on the return drive to Hollingshead's apartment Bissette stopped at a bank where Hollingshead was almost handcuffed during an argument with a security guard. By way of an apology Hollingshead phoned Bissette a few days later saying, "I am sorry, Stephen, my boy, but I'd been bingeing on a particularly excellent strain of hash oil and other delights the evening before."[29]

During work on the first issue Hollingshead constantly and aggressively pestered Bissette to contact *OMNI* to arrange delivery of promotional artwork which *OMNI* had commissioned to feature in its news section. Hollingshead's insistence is a puzzle because after Bissette rushed the artwork to *OMNI*, an *OMNI* editor phoned him to say they had never commissioned the artwork from Marvel, and they regarded Hollingshead as a con man. Jim Shooter also spoke to an *OMNI* editor who told him that Hollingshead had previously scammed them into commissioning work which he was paid for but never delivered.

Worse still, Hollingshead did not have permission to adapt any of the books or authors he had claimed, and further investigation revealed that the letters and documents he had produced to prove his associations with Jastrow, Lilly, Sagan and others were all forgeries. When Robert Jastrow discovered the con, he threatened Marvel with legal action if they used any of his writing. In a panic, Shooter checked the material Hollingshead had submitted so far and found it riddled with factual errors. It was too late for Marvel to extricate themselves from their contract as Hollingshead's literary agent had cleverly locked them into an unbreakable deal; the only way to break the stalemate and salvage their reputation was for Marvel to pay Hollingshead an undisclosed sum of money, cancel the project and sever all their ties.

The Marvel debacle appeared not to have dented Hollingshead's bravado because in January 1983 in a letter to Leary he boasted that *The Cosmic Egg* would be out in mid-February, quickly followed by *Jumping Alive* and *Heavens Above*. This was a blatant lie, as he knew that the comic books would be never be published. In the same letter Hollingshead lied again, reeling off a list of over forty people he claimed to have guided through their first LSD session, claiming many of those he turned on had said "'It all happened naturally'" or "'It was so simple, we did it all ourselves.' But of course, they didn't, it required concentration on my part of the very deepest kind."[30] He had initiated *some* of those listed but many, including his former friends Joe Mellen and Kristof Glinka, had taken LSD before they had even heard of Hollingshead and Bart Huges, Donovan, John 'Hoppy' Hopkins and

Billy Bolitho had all used LSD prior to meeting him. It's doubtful these errors were ones of memory, as he repeated similar claims in his 1973 autobiography. It was simply Hollingshead's self-importance and self-belief as the man who turned on the world; he had come to believe his own myth.

The Marvel scam soon became public knowledge and any remaining shred of integrity and credibility Hollingshead had in the publishing world vanished. As an impoverished alcoholic with his professional and personal reputation in tatters, running out of friends and places to live, his future looked bleak. He was thrown a lifeline in early 1984 when Michael Froehlich invited him to move to Cochabamba in Bolivia to tutor his young son, Kephra, being under the impression Hollingshead had studied at Oxford University, which was another lie. Thom Keyes was also moving to Cochabamba, having previously spent a year there, and recommended the city to Hollingshead, telling him he would have no problem finding work teaching English at one of the schools or universities. Hollingshead announced his plans to Leary in February 1984 as, "Time to pack up and move to a new spot. That's the way gypsies relax. For some people, it's scary to set off into the unknown; for me, it's scary not to."[31] The reason he gave Leary for the move was his desire to get away from the "...oppressive, aggressive, dangerous, atmosphere of New York"[32] and from various failed projects. The Marvel scam was presumably one of those failed projects, yet at least eighteen months after that deception had been exposed Hollingshead was still clinging to the lie, telling Leary, "Book one of my *Titan Science Series* is at last ready for the printers...should be out in April."[33]

Hollingshead's Marvel scam was clearly cynical, pre-planned and dishonest. But was there something more than criminal intent at work? Bissette's claim that Hollingshead was often so high he could barely function in meetings suggests he was again losing his lifelong battle with addictions. Was the bungled Marvel con a hint that Hollingshead's mental state was finally deteriorating through his drug and alcohol use? For instance, had Hollingshead been in full control of his faculties, why would he have pestered Bissette to contact OMNI, "suicidal, as it turned out",[34] knowing just one phone call would reveal his deception? And why lie to Leary about the Marvel comics being published in early 1983, knowing that was untrue, compounding the lie again a year later, insisting they would be published in early 1984?

It was Hollingshead's plan to fly to Bolivia alone initially and establish himself there before Eileen O'Connor flew out to join him at the end of summer. He and Eileen had been inseparable and were still "hopelessly in love. Just knowing Eileen gives a whole new meaning to life. I am very, very lucky to have finally found someone who I can love most of all in the entire world."[35] Hollingshead might have seen the move to Cochabamba as the beginning of a new life but to his daughter Vanessa it was just his old pattern of behaviour repeating itself: "Long story short, he moved to Bolivia, just said he couldn't take New York. Like he couldn't take England, like he couldn't take anything. He was always running. He was always running away from himself."[36]

Hollingshead flew to Bolivia on 17 February 1984 and moved into Michael Froehlich's house in Cochabamba. In letters to Leary between March and June, Hollingshead seemed happy, talking about the writing he was doing, claiming Bolivia, or Oblivia as he often punningly but presciently called it, was the most beautiful place in the world. Bolivia in the 1980s was a violent and unstable country; there was a huge demand for cocaine from America and Europe, and Pablo Escobar and the cartels were fighting among themselves and with the government to gain control of the drug trade. Hollingshead described Froehlich's house as a kind of secure compound and explained how he kept a loaded revolver and shotgun in his room at night. A few days earlier, he told Leary, a right-wing government politician neighbour had his house raked by machine gun fire and armed guards with dogs were on patrol at night. Hollingshead also wrote at length about getting involved in what sounded like a madcap scheme to become a partner, with Michael

Froehlich, in a jojoba plantation with the intention of marketing the oil which was becoming very popular in shampoos and cosmetics.

The idea of Hollingshead being involved in a jojoba plantation sounds far-fetched, leading some to have suggest that it was a cover for growing Coca, from which cocaine could be extracted. Yet there is nothing to suggest from his letters that when he was talking about jojoba, he meant anything else. Michael Froehlich, who was developing the proposed jojoba plantation, brought in a large 'caterpillar' tractor to clear an airstrip allowing easy access to the site which was seven-hours away by Land Rover. Hollingshead sent Leary a photo showing a twin-engine plane which Froehlich had bought, and a Bolivian Airways pilot who was on a $500 a month retainer. Froehlich and Hollingshead were, he told Leary, "Jojoba Witnesses in this, the nuttiest scheme of them all – Perfect!"[37]

These lengthy, eloquent descriptions about his jojoba farming ambitions sounded impressive, but it turned out they were yet another of Hollingshead's grandiose fantasies. According to Froehlich, Hollingshead wasn't involved in his jojoba business at all: "Oh, no, Michael didn't like working! This was real work. We had 300 workers and Indians are not the most enthusiastic workers so we did not need Michael as an example because everyone would have just sat down and thought how wonderful it was having Michael as a boss. Michael didn't like working, he wasn't made for work!"[38]

Fantasies aside, Hollingshead had set up a small classroom in Froehlich's house in which he began to tutor his son Kephra on a regular basis. How successful this was educationally is debatable: Froehlich remembers going into the classroom one day to find he could barely see Hollingshead though clouds of marijuana smoke but could hear him teaching Kephra a smutty nursery rhyme with the lyrics "Little Miss Mitsy had big titties". Hollingshead and Kephra certainly liked each other very much; on the reverse of a photograph showing Hollingshead and Kephra together on a beach he had written, "Kephra, my ward and my worry, whose mythological roots may be Egyptian but can't tell me the square root of 2."[39]

While living in Bolivia with Froehlich and Keyes, Hollingshead enjoyed many wild drug-fuelled adventures. Once, on their way to a carnival, Froehlich, Hollingshead and several friends first travelled to Rio where they checked into a hotel and got so high they missed their onward flight. The ever resourceful Hollingshead immediately thought of a solution and, although it was 8 a.m. and he was still very stoned, he phoned the British Embassy telling them in his best upper-class British accent that he was filming for the BBC and demanded they provide him with a plane! The Embassy weren't fooled but did suggest a private airline as an alternate means of travel; so, as one of Hollingshead's party was carrying lots of cash, they chartered a plane. Once on board, instead of sitting back to enjoy the ride, Hollingshead began to deliberately annoy the pilot to such an extent that he landed at a military base to have him arrested, a situation only narrowly avoided by the pilot and crew being bribed with a large sum of cash.

Once at the carnival Hollingshead and friends were swept along in the crush of tens of thousands of people following the floats, which carried massive soundsystems and dancers in colourful costumes. One float, its occupants dressed as 'African Savages', noticed the distinctive tall, white Hollingshead in the crowd and lifted him onto the float, dressing him in 'native' garb and crowning him king of their tribe. The delighted Hollingshead enthusiastically joined in with the dancing and singing as they drove slowly through the crowds but was so stoned that he fell off the float and broke his leg.

Photographs of Hollingshead from the summer of 1984 show a very different man to those taken even a few years earlier. He was now almost totally bald and clean shaven with a thin, gaunt appearance, suggesting he was ill. This impression is given some credence by his sister Janette, who remembers her brother writing from Bolivia complaining that he was suffering from a stomach problem for which he needed an operation.

In the last letter that he wrote, Hollingshead told Leary how excited he was about the imminent arrival in Bolivia of his girlfriend, Eileen O'Connor. His plan was to fly to Santa Cruz in California on 1 July, meet Eileen and fly back to Bolivia with her. He never made that journey.

At some point between 30 June and 14 July he became seriously ill and was rushed into hospital. Around this same time period Vanessa remembers her annoyance when her father phoned and asked her to pay for the call, which she did, despite being short of money. She was further annoyed when she discovered her father wasn't interested in her, just what had happened to Eileen. Vanessa was furious, and they argued. She remembered the gist of the call being, "I need you to reach her. I haven't been able to reach her. I need her to get down here. I love her. You have to get a fucking hold of her. You fucking get a hold of her. I need her. I love her",[40] before she hung up on him. Despite being upset, Vanessa left a message for Eileen on her answer phone. She couldn't have known, but that argumentative phone call was the last time Vanessa would hear her father's voice.

Hollingshead went into a Cochabamba hospital for an operation, most likely for complications caused by a stomach ulcer, and died there on 14 July. There are conflicting accounts of the circumstances and location of his death. Thom Keyes' wife Regine believes he was discharged from hospital and was later found dead at home. "His stomach ulcer broke in the end and he was found in a puddle of his blood in his bedroom."[41] Michael Froehlich, on the other hand, has a far more detailed, if unusual memory. He was in Paris on business at the time of Hollingshead's death and before he was formally notified, he remembers, "I was walking in the hotel I was staying in and it came over me, boom, as I was walking into the garden, that he had died."[42] A telegram from Eileen, sent a few hours earlier, was waiting for him at the hotel reception desk, telling him Hollingshead was hours from death. Froehlich went to his room and focussed his mind on Hollingshead and concentrated on the advice to the dying given in the *Tibetan Book of the Dead.* "There was a completely intense blue light in my mind. It was quiet, he was completely at rest, we travelled together to a certain point and he said, 'now you can leave me alone'. That was the end of our story."[43]

It took Froehlich a couple of days to return to Bolivia and on arrival he met Eileen, who had flown to Cochabamba to be with Hollingshead before he died, telling him Hollingshead's stomach ulcer had burst and he was rushed into hospital. Hollingshead had allegedly asked Eileen to smuggle a bottle of vodka into hospital for him, which she did. He drank the entire bottle and died shortly after at the age of 52. Hollingshead's death didn't come as a complete surprise to Froehlich: "He killed himself. Since I knew him, he had this tiredness of life, he had talked about a death wish."[44]

Hollingshead's Bolivian Death Certificate was issued the day after he died, giving the time of death as 20:44 on 14 July 1984, cause by the haemorrhaging of a burst duodenal ulcer. His occupation was given as 'Professor', taken from details in his passport.

Vanessa first heard of her father's death in a phone call from Eileen's brother, Brian. She was shocked, but not surprised, as she had suspected from photographs that he was ill. She was surprised though when Brian O'Connor told her, "Michael loved you so much, all he could do was talk about you. He bragged on about you, on and on."[45] A few days later, a drunk Eileen phoned Vanessa, and rambled about a blue sweater Vanessa had sent her father at Christmas, telling her he had worn it for over a month, simply because it had come from her. These remarks meant a great deal to Vanessa, "I realised he could not say he loved me, nor even give me a Christmas present, but the one I gave him was treasured and worn day in and day out. That meant more to me than anything. That put to rest him screaming for Eileen, she had no idea the peace she gave me at that moment. I was just so happy he loved me. And at that moment I loved him too. I was just so sorry I couldn't have seen my father again, one last time, and that we had to argue yet again."[46] Ev Hesketh was told of Hollingshead's death in a telephone call from his mother who said, "At least I know he's safe",[47] a comment reflecting the decades of worry Hollingshead's exploits had caused his parents and grandparents.

Hollingshead's mother flew to Cochabamba but didn't register his death with the British consulate there. Nor did she register it on her return to Britain, which meant Hollingshead did not have a British death certificate and is not legally regarded as being dead. His family could not afford to repatriate his body to England and, unsurprisingly, Hollingshead had no savings or medical insurance. This presented a problem for the disposal of his body as there were no British cemeteries in Cochabamba and interment in Cochabamba's public cemetery would have put his remains at risk of being looted. To prevent this, he was interred in the 'Cementerio Alemán' (the German Cemetery), which offered security from grave robbers. His remains were later exhumed and placed, with 38 others, all German except him, in a larger grave.

Hollingshead does not have a separate grave marker but is listed on a simple marble plaque bearing the words 'Exhumaciones aqui descansan en paz' (Exhumations here rest in peace). Other than his date of death and name, which is spelt wrongly as 'Michael Hollengshead', no other information is given. Hollingshead's death was not reported in Cochabamba's newspapers nor to the British Embassy, and no obituaries appeared. The Bolivian death certificate obtained by his mother and sister was lost and, until a copy was obtained during research for this book, the official time and cause of his death remained unknown.

This dearth of information meant news of Hollingshead's demise spread slowly and created a vacuum which was quickly filled with rumour and speculation; the legend of Michael Hollingshead refused to die with him.

One story circulating in London claimed that Steve Abrams and Thom Keyes had been visiting Hollingshead, all three partying on cocaine, when he collapsed and died. Another rumour claimed he choked to death on a hamburger which had been smuggled into the hospital where he had been admitted with an unknown illness. Others suggested he was not dead but had just melted away into the jungle to live out his life peacefully under a different identity.

The stark truth of his death was simple. Decades of poor nutrition and alcoholism, coupled with intermittent addictions to methedrine, heroin and cocaine, and years of daily use of tobacco, marijuana and hashish, had caused his body to devour itself in the form of an ulcer. His odd behaviour during his final years; the Marvel scam, the increasing lies and contradictions suggest his mind was not anywhere near as sharp as it once had been. By the summer of 1984, if not before, he was aware he had serious stomach problems and, if Michael Froehlich's recollections of what he was told by Eileen O'Connor are correct, he made the decision to commit suicide by drinking a large quantity of spirits, exacerbating his stomach problems and leading to his death.

His last words to Tim Leary, a handwritten addendum to a typed letter, served as an apt but unwitting elegy, "Here, like big condors, we have room to fly!"[48]

Michael Hollingshead, veteran of thousands of psychedelic flights, flights from country to country, flights from justice, and flights of fancy, had taken his last flight.

Notes

1   Dylan, Bob. 'Too Much of Nothing'. *The Basement Tapes*. 1975
2   Hesketh, Ev. Email, 30/12/18
3   Froehlich, Michael. Skype interview 13/1/19
4   Ibid
5   Ibid
6   Ibid
7   *The Los Angeles Times*. 'A University Without Walls, Etc'. 16/9/80
8   Ibid
9   Froehlich, Michael. Skype interview 13/1/19
10   *The Los Angeles Times*. 'A University Without Walls, Etc'. 16/9/80
11   http://www.college-de-pataphysique.fr/presentation_en.html
12   *The Los Angeles Times*. 'A University Without Walls, Etc'. 16/9/80
13   Ibid
14   Froehlich, Michael. Skype interview 13/1/19
15   Hesketh, Ev. Email, 30/12/18
16   Ibid
17   Ibid
18   Hesketh, Ev. Email, 29/12/18
19   Ibid
20   Hesketh, Ev. Email, 2/1/19
21   Hollingshead, Vanessa. *LSD Mafia*. Unpublished ms. 2013 p.125
22   Froehlich, Michael. Skype interview 13/1/19
23   Ibid
24   Hollingshead, Vanessa. *LSD Mafia*. Unpublished ms. 2013 p.125
25   http://library.hsu.edu/Special/bissette/findingaid.html Folder 13
26   *Comics Journal*. No.71. March 1982, p.9
27   Brisbois, Mike (quoted in). Email, 25/7/18
28   http://library.hsu.edu/Special/bissette/findingaid.html Folder 13
29   Brisbois, Mike (quoted in). Email, 25/7/18
30   Letter to Leary from Hollingshead 6/1/83
31   Letter to Leary from Hollingshead 8/2/84
32   Ibid
33   Ibid
34   Brisbois, Mike (quoted in). Email, 25/7/18
35   Letter to Leary from Hollingshead 8/2/84
36   Hollingshead, Vanessa. *LSD Mafia*. Unpublished ms. 2013 p.125

37   Letter to Leary from Hollingshead 15/6/84
38   Froehlich, Michael. Skype interview 13/1/19
39   Note on reverse of photograph, May 1984
40   Hollingshead, Vanessa. *LSD Mafia*. Unpublished ms. 2013 p.126
41   Keyes, Regine. Email 29/12/18
42   Froehlich, Michael. Skype interview 13/1/19
43   Ibid
44   Ibid
45   Hollingshead, Vanessa. *LSD Mafia*. Unpublished ms. 2013 p.126
46   Ibid
47   Hesketh, Ev. Email 31/12/18
48   Letter to Leary from Hollingshead 29/6/84

Afterword: Sympathy for the Devil

I often saw Michael as quite an ordinary person who'd got himself into extraordinary circumstances.[1]

Michael Hollingshead died aged 52 over six thousand miles from his place of birth, abandoned and all but forgotten by the culture he had unintentionally helped to found. His life had been an enigmatic, multi-faceted chaotic adventure played out across three continents, a "nine-mile skid on a ten-mile ride" as Jerry Garcia sang of another wayward character. *Divine Rascal* could have concluded with Hollingshead's lonely death but, because he was such a complex and conflicted character, I didn't want his undignified end to be the final word. Instead, I want to draw the strands of his personality and experiences together and, linking those with his patterns of behaviour, attempt a synthesis of what I have discovered and suggest an explanation as to who Michael Hollingshead was and why he acted as he did.

When I set out on the trail of Michael Hollingshead I realised that no-one, except perhaps his daughter Vanessa, knew much beyond the superficial details of his life, unless it was what he wanted or allowed someone to know. I always knew Hollingshead had a dark and destructive aspect to his personality, but I was surprised just how pervasive my research discovered this to be. His many negative behaviours were not isolated, spontaneous reactions to events but a fundamental part of his personality and represented a clear and predictable pattern which repeated throughout his life. As my research progressed, I became concerned at the number of people who had experienced negative encounters with Hollingshead. Several people, ex partners, old acquaintances and family members, simply refused to discuss him. Others were prepared to, but insisted I refrain from publishing the darker details of their encounters with him. Even those interviewees and correspondents who were fond of Hollingshead often had caveats as to how much they would reveal about him. Typical of the messages I received was this from Regine Keyes, who knew him for many years: "Are you aware of his dark side, do you want it in the book? My stories are on the whole not so charming".[2]

These concerns almost led me to abandon the idea of writing Hollingshead's biography. He was dead and couldn't defend himself or offer justifications for his actions, and I was mindful that at least some of what I had discovered might taint his memory in the eyes of his family and ex-partners. But he was a significant and mysterious piece in the jigsaw puzzle of LSD's history and his story cried out to be written.

When his autobiography was published in the early 1970s, Hollingshead probably believed that his own, heavily airbrushed, account of his life would act as his memory and legacy, blissfully unaware that, thirty-five years after his death, the layers of his existence would be peeled back and exposed. It was obvious his biography, if it were to be written, would have to be 'warts and all' if it were to accurately reflect his life. My fears about misrepresenting Hollingshead were allayed by the lengthy email conversations and meeting I had with Vanessa, his daughter, who assured me she was well aware of her father's dark side but still wanted his story to be told, albeit with some caveats. Another boost came from Ev Hesketh, his partner between 1979–81, who commented, "You have great insight into Michael's character".[3]

Then there was the problem of the book's focus. Writing *Divine Rascal* would have been simpler and, possibly, superficially more interesting had I concentrated on the years between 1960 and the early 1970s when Hollingshead was at the height of his psychedelic notoriety. Yet, like the LSD experience, in which the induction and assimilation phases are as important as the peak, exactly how Michael Hollingshead became the man who turned on the world and what happened to him afterwards are of equal relevance. Running parallel to Hollingshead's more glamorous exploits is a very real trail of human sadness; permutations of alcoholism and drug addiction, crime, fraud, relationship breakdown, infidelity, domestic violence, child neglect, collusion with the police and FBI, and the betrayal of trust and friendships. That these behaviours were repeated by Hollingshead throughout his life suggested they must be a symptom of an underlying corrosive psychological and emotional issue. If that sounds presumptuous or even pretentious, the alternative, by default, is to dismiss Hollingshead as a 'bad seed', deviant or corrupted from birth. Some people believe he was just that, but I disagree. With the knowledge revealed by my research, we must go back to his early years in order to understand how his childhood experiences may have affected his life, culminating in his sad and lonely death in Bolivia.

By all accounts Hollingshead's childhood until he was fourteen appears to have been a happy one. He was an intelligent young boy, curious about the world and his place in it. His family weren't financially well off and, although his father was strict and a heavy drinker – which can have a destructive influence on a child's development – from what he told his daughter Vanessa, he felt secure, loved and wanted: the optimum conditions for the development of a healthy personality. Then, in his teens, he witnessed and was involved in events that would now be termed Adverse Childhood Experiences (ACE), the consequences of which affected his life more than any of his LSD experiences. Witnessing the domestic violence of his father beating his mother, and the total confusion he felt when she defended him when Hollingshead tried to intervene, was a game changer.

As Hollingshead said later to Vanessa, "When my mother did that, I locked the door and threw away the key".[4] His previously held beliefs about his parents and how they felt about him and each other were shattered by that experience and soon after he did the unknown 'something'. He was 'punished' for this mysterious and presumably serious transgression by being sent to the therapeutic environment of Red Hill School. This must have seemed like a further rejection from his family and suddenly he was isolated from his parents, his siblings and his friends; 300 miles away from everything he had come to accept as normal at a crucial stage in the development of his personality.

Stuck in this adolescent and geographical limbo, not knowing how long he would be at Red Hill, the highly-intelligent fourteen-year-old likely had no idea how to repair the past and perhaps didn't even want to. Hollingshead did realise that he now was on his own and, rather than wallow in self-pity or guilt, he began to take control of his life. From his arrival at Red Hill School right until his death, Hollingshead managed and curated his persona, creating the public identity he wanted people to believe was really him. Firstly, he masked his distinctive north English accent which betrayed his working class background, replacing it with a more refined southern English pronunciation. Then, in the 1950s, after his stint in the RAF, Hollingshead moved to Sweden and then America, where he was completely unknown. In New York he continued this process of reinvention by changing his surname from the plain-sounding Shinkfield to the more resonant and 'English' sounding Hollingshead and, though he had no vocational qualifications or university degree, began to claim he had been to Oxford.

Like his father, Hollingshead became a habitual, often heavy user of alcohol, to which he later added LSD and a series of addictions and habituations to methedrine, heroin, cocaine and other drugs, which often had a detrimental effect on those close to him. This life-long abuse of mood altering substances served several purposes for Hollingshead. At the basic level he very much enjoyed the physical and psychological pleasures alcohol and chemicals gave him; he liked getting high, very high, and as often as he could. As many people do, Hollingshead also used drugs and alcohol as social lubricants, to enable him to cope more easily with people in a variety of situations. In my opinion he used drugs and alcohol to self-medicate his underlying psychological and emotional turmoil, using combinations of drugs and alcohol as a crutch, or for motivation when he felt depressed, and as a scapegoat to justify or excuse negative behaviours in his relationships with people. Drugs and alcohol were also an easily-available self-destruction mechanism to facilitate or justify major life changes; for example losing his job at IBACE, the dissolution of the World Psychedelic Centre and the ending of his relationship with Ev Hesketh.

Hollingshead rarely accepted responsibility or apologised for his treatment of anyone, man or woman, and no-one was above being manipulated or deceived by him if he thought doing so would be of benefit. Yet Hollingshead liked people and wanted to be liked and loved in return. He was not conventionally attractive in appearance or fashionable in dress, and women were attracted to him initially because of his intelligence, wit and charm. He married twice and had several long and short-term relationships, yet with few exceptions each time he became close to a woman or fell in love he sabotaged the relationship with his behaviours. Hollingshead's relationships with women ended for a number of intertwined reasons, including relationship neglect, infidelity, physical or psychological domestic violence and the impact of his addictions. The emotional and psychological fall-out from some of his relationships was occasionally severe, with some ex-partners being unable to form permanent relationships with men and at least one woman suffered serious, albeit temporary, psychological damage. Although I saw no benefit in revealing her name in *Divine Rascal*, it is worth noting that one ex-partner was committed to a psychiatric ward where a visitor found her 'writhing like a snake' on the floor. Arguably even darker was Hollingshead's predilection for employing LSD, often in high doses, as a seduction tool without permission; an unconscionable act of manipulation and assault which reveals him to be an occasional opportunist sexual predator, perhaps a rapist. There is no doubt that Hollingshead was often extremely and calculatedly cruel to many of the women who loved him.

Conversely, there was another side to his female relationships. Although he abandoned her when his deceptions meant he had to leave Sweden in a hurry, Bodil Birke found him to be a loving partner, her comments to me and his letters to and about her showing how much they cared for each other. In his friendships with other women, including Liz Elliot, Kami Kanetsuka and Zina Rachevsky, Hollingshead was polite and respectful, which begs the question why he treated some women badly and others not. I believe that if he respected a woman's intelligence and believed it to be on a par with his own, or if he believed women were useful to him socially or financially, he treated them well until they had served his purpose or were replaced by another emotional or sexual interest. In an era when the Women's Liberation movement was emerging and many men were changing their attitudes to women and relationships, Hollingshead was still a male chauvinist, a radio man in a television world. It can be argued that to an extent these oppressive attitudes and behaviours were the legacy of the older generation; but what was LSD use about if it wasn't to change outmoded and repressive behaviours and break down barriers between the sexes? Chauvinism was a choice, perpetuated by some males in the counter culture simply because it made for an easier lifestyle.

Hollingshead's friendships with men were also often predicated on his estimation of the benefits to be gained from them. He abused his friendship with John Beresford in order to obtain the Magic Gram and meet Leary and further abused his relationship with Beresford by barging into the Agora Trust hierarchy and passing information to the police. This pattern of behaviour continued throughout his life. For instance, Desmond O'Brien, his wealthy Old Etonian friend who financed the World Psychedelic Centre, was forgotten as the WPC disintegrated; Hollingshead also betrayed the trust of Kristof Glinka who helped Hollingshead write *Flow* and was pivotal in the creation of Changes 72. He even deceived Tim Leary, the man he respected most of all, but quickly realised that this was a massive error and went to great time and trouble in justifying his actions and repairing that relationship because, to Hollingshead, Leary was the gift that kept on giving.

Although Hollingshead liked children he was not always a good parent to any of his own and frequently put his personal life and aspirations before nurturing and maintaining a consistent emotional relationship. He rarely saw his first child, Timothy, although his letters to him show a pride in his development and achievements, and he had minimal contact with his last child, Esther. His most consistent relationship was with Vanessa, but that was a turbulent one. Hollingshead flitted in and out of Vanessa's life, often not seeing her for years at a time and rarely providing her with any financial or emotional support, especially when it was most needed. He did love Vanessa and although he found it difficult to express his feelings to her personally, he often articulated them to others. Regardless of their often distant relationship, she understood who he was behind his façade and what he wanted: "When my dad was sober or sweet, there was nothing like it. He was so incredibly charming, and stripped bare of all his quirks and darkness, he just wanted to be loved, accepted, famous, but something in him stopped himself from doing better for himself."[5]

The 'something' to which Vanessa alludes is, I believe, Hollingshead's adverse childhood experiences and the separation from and perceived rejection by his family, which caused him to develop psychological conditions I will expand on in due course. As Vanessa noted, her father wanted acceptance and fame. He wanted success, financial security and to be known for his achievements, and many times during his life he had all those things, but each time he undermined and destroyed them. Before his fateful encounter with LSD Hollingshead was a successful broadcaster on Danish radio and his language skills and wide general knowledge subsequently led him to write travel guides for students in Copenhagen and Amsterdam. All those experiences, and the professional and social contacts he made, stood him in good stead when he moved to America, enabling him to secure a prestigious post with the Institute for British American Cultural Exchange (IBACE). Up to that point Hollingshead was an ordinary young man. He could be challenging at times and was troubled by his past but was driven to succeed and, crucially, as yet unknown and inconspicuous.

It was the personality-shattering effects of LSD that precipitated the breakdown of his marriage to Vanessa's mother and undermined his job with IBACE, setting his life on a course he could not possibly have imagined. Had he not abused and manipulated his friendship with John Beresford to acquire and spread the Magic Gram, Michael Hollingshead and his name would be lost to history. LSD was responsible for Michael Shinkfield becoming Michael Hollingshead and for the creation of Michael Hollingshead the Legend, a legend he came to believe in and identify with. At the same time, LSD was responsible for the gradual unravelling of Michael Hollingshead, plunging him headfirst into a search for identity and purpose and driving his desperation for the acknowledgement and status he believed he was entitled to. The tensions caused by this chemically-triggered dichotomy inexorably took Hollingshead further away from an understanding of who he actually was. To frame this paradox in terms LSD users might use: Michael Hollingshead never really left Chapel Perilous after his first LSD trip, although he firmly believed he had.

The series of lies and deceptions by which Hollingshead integrated himself into Leary's Harvard circle, his subsequent involvement with the Agora Scientific Trust and later at Millbrook were all successes though, despite the methods used to achieve them. But Hollingshead's behaviours undermined each success within months. Had he not been deceitful or impatient and worked conscientiously with Leary or Beresford, Hollingshead might have achieved the same long-lasting success and respect that those men earned and all that came with it.

When Millbrook was falling apart, Leary was kind enough to throw Hollingshead a lifeline by funding his move to London, which offered the ideal opportunity for him to redeem his past and forge a bright future. The financial support given to him by O'Brien to set up the World Psychedelic Centre should have guaranteed its success, but within months Hollingshead's behaviours caused it to fail. Had he not been consumed by methedrine-fuelled arrogance, playing the guru game in the belief he could be to Britain what Leary was to America, Hollingshead might have been remembered as an influential force in the development of psychedelic culture in Britain. His eighteen-month prison term enabled temporary respite from the addictions which plagued him, almost certainly saving his life, but the root cause remained untreated, and after his release the cycle of success and failure continued, repeating itself in Scandinavia, America, Nepal, Scotland, Tonga and America.

But how and why did an unknown Englishman with no prior connection to LSD and no scientific or academic qualifications, appear in Tim Leary's life bearing a large quantity of LSD? Introducing Leary to LSD caused a sudden and significant shift in his focus, from psilocybin to LSD, and resulted in his emergence as the spokesperson for widespread recreational LSD use, the so called 'psychedelic revolution'. In view of Leary's admitted links to the CIA and recent speculations that LSD was introduced into society by covert intelligence services, it's not surprising that Hollingshead has been suspected of a role in this conspiracy. His own careful airbrushing and compartmentalisation of his life have helped nourished these speculations. Many people have taken literally his references to the IBACE being a "semi-official British propaganda agency", as though those words alone constituted evidence of his complicity with covert intelligence services.

While there is no substantive evidence to support the theory, this should not lead to complacency, as there are many anomalies and inconsistencies scattered throughout Hollingshead's life which could hint at deeper, hidden connections and darker motivations. For instance, how and why he obtained the Magic Gram and introduced Leary to LSD and the mystery of whether he took Morning Glory seeds or SPOFA LSD to London in 1965 are all open to interpretation, but in lieu of quantifiable evidence they don't reflect anything other than the chaotic nature of Hollingshead's life and the mysteries of memory.

We are on firmer ground with John Beresford's claim that Hollingshead helped pass information to the FBI about the Agora Scientific Trust and facilitated the tapping of his phone. But even that is an anecdote based on a belief and not a proven fact. Even if Hollingshead was, at times, a police informer, or passing information to the secret intelligence agencies, it is unlikely definitive proof will ever emerge, although absence of evidence is not evidence of absence. Hollingshead never 'confessed' to being an informer or involved with the intelligence services, and nothing to suggest he was has been found in numerous Freedom of Information requests to police forces in Britain. However, MI5 and MI6 are not subject to the FOIA and, although an FBI file on Hollingshead is known to exist, I have been unable to access it; the American researcher who does claim to have a copy has not indicated that it contains anything of relevance. Speculation and wishful thinking aside, if Hollingshead *was* an asset of the intelligence services, or a police informer, then he was most likely operating at a very low level, receiving little or no payment and being allowed – encouraged even – to self-destruct when he was of no further use. And if he did occasionally pass information to the police or to the FBI, knowing what we do about his behaviours, it's far more likely that he was merely trying to save himself from arrest or prosecution than that he had a role in an over-arching conspiracy to subvert, or catalyse, the psychedelic revolution.

State infiltration of, and influence on, psychedelic culture is undoubtedly of historical significance, but to date no concrete evidence has appeared to suggest anything other than various national intelligence agencies' interest in LSD as an interrogation tool. It's my belief that these state agencies soon discovered, as MI6 did in the 1950s, that the behaviours LSD caused in individuals and groups were so chaotic and unmanageable that it was impossible to direct or predict its use with any certainty.

To return to the adverse childhood experience which led to Hollingshead being banished to Red Hill School; had Hollingshead allowed himself to become engaged in the psychoanalysis he was offered there he may have been able to understand and manage his psychological demons. That he chose to avoid or subvert the psychoanalytical process and other therapies on offer suggests a refusal to accept that he had any psychological or emotional issues, and this belief, coupled with his IQ of over 140, likely played a part in his subsequent behaviours.

Many people, including his daughter Vanessa and his former Harvard and Millbrook colleague Richard Alpert, have referred to Hollingshead as being a sociopath; others have called him narcissistic and selfish, comments which bear some examination. Whilst one must be cautious of assigning formal psychiatric diagnoses based only on second hand reports and without the benefit of a proper face-to-face examination, those descriptors of Hollingshead certainly bear some characteristics of the profile of someone with Narcissistic Personality Disorder (NPD) and an Anti-Social Personality Disorder (ASPD). Hollingshead's behaviours more than fulfil all nine personality traits psychologists linked to NPD, and eight of the nine linked to ASPD. For a diagnosis of either only five of the former and four of the latter are needed. If this sounds like pop-psychology, I recommend comparing each of Hollingshead's behaviours in this book with the descriptors of NPD and ASPD found on academic and medical sites on the internet. (A good starting point is the simple but comprehensive overview of *What's the Difference Between a Sociopath and a Narcissist.*[6])

Whether or not my analysis of who Michael Hollingshead was and why he behaved the way he did is correct, it provides a lens through which to understand his character, based on the evidence of his actions, one which, however harsh it might appear, is intended to illuminate and not demolish his character. It's also worth making clear that everything Hollingshead did was done, as many people commented, with his usual disarming humour and charm – albeit these are the acknowledged trademarks of the con man – and not with any obvious or overt maliciousness. In *Psychedelic Prayers*, Leary's book inspired by the *Tao Te Ching*, he lists the kind of people in whom the Tao or underlying principle of the universe is likely to be found, one being "Smiling men with bad reputations", a description which can certainly be applied to Hollingshead, although the Tao ultimately eluded him!

Hollingshead had a positive and creative side to his personality too, although this and his many achievements are sadly often overshadowed by, or embedded in, his negative side. Turning Leary onto LSD helped to trigger a psychedelic revolution which changed the lives of millions of people, mainly for the better, and had a lasting impact on western culture. This was a success of historical magnitude. Hollingshead's influence on Leary and Beresford at Harvard and Agora, and his involvement in the experiments in lysergic living and psychedelic art installations at Millbrook, were also successes. The crowning glory of Hollingshead's creative achievements, and one which people are least aware of, was the concept and creation of Changes 72, the art installation at the Richard Demarco Gallery in Edinburgh, which was years ahead of its time. Had it been held in London, New York or San

Francisco, Changes 72 would be legendary in psychedelic history and Hollingshead regarded as a forward-thinking innovator.

Another positive was Hollingshead's natural aptitude for navigating the LSD experience at high doses and his ability and willingness to guide people, particularly acid neophytes, through their trips. I have given several examples in the book but Tim Hargreaves, who lived with Hollingshead on Cumbrae during 1971, summed this up well: "He has a warm place in my heart for his unique form of alchemical anarchism. More than anyone I have met he knew the art of being a 'Guide', yes indeed a trickster, thus someone who will inevitably take the blame for others' incomprehension."[7]

Hollingshead brought a uniquely British surreality to the American psychedelic scene which was not lost on Leary: "That was the great contribution of the British acid people like Hollingshead. They brought humour. They brought a dignified, respectable, do-it-yourself, British arrogance to the situation..." Leary believed that beneath Hollingshead's persona and his addictions he was "one of the great heroes of our time. He's never had the recognition or social support for his brilliance. And that's his own fault, because he gets too freaked out. I think he's one of the funniest!."[8] Being adept at navigating the psychedelic experience and having an ability as a guide doesn't outweigh Hollingshead's many failings as a human being. But it was a skill few had and one he wasted, letting it slip through his fingers in the pursuit of something he could never quite identify or attain.

One justification I was offered to account for Hollingshead's more unconventional, even criminal, actions and methods is that at his level of psychedelic intensity it was necessary for him to seize the moment and do whatever he felt was necessary to achieve his goals, irrespective of risk or consequences. It is said there is often a fine line between the actions and results of the revered eastern holy man and those of the despised western hustler. Commenting on Hollingshead and Leary in this regard, Michael Froehlich wrote, "Most of them used sex, drugs,

& booze to catapult themselves out of the prevailing social conventions and mind frames. In order to 'survive out there', or even be successful, they had to be flexible, ingenious, immoral, deceptive and whatever else it needs not to get killed, jailed or wind up in some nuthouse or ditch",[9] a sentiment echoed in Jefferson Airplane's lyrics in 'We Can Be Together', "In order to survive we steal, cheat, lie, forge, fuck, hide, and deal." But these behaviours can't possibly justify the collateral damage not only to himself but also to his partners, family and friends, and ultimately don't excuse his sociopathic and narcissistic personality traits.

Ultimately, adverse childhood experiences, personality traits, behaviours and motivations aside, Michael Hollingshead was a catalyst who had a significant effect, whether positive or negative, on almost everyone he encountered. For all his faults, Hollingshead can be considered a major figure in the history of LSD, one of the few British people of the time, along with Gerald Heard, Aldous Huxley and Alan Watts, who believed that LSD could be a force for individual and collective good. Unfortunately however, in trying to change himself, and the world, with LSD, Michael Hollingshead, the divine rascal, became a victim of his own game.

Researching and writing *Divine Rascal*, more than any book I have written, has had a personal impact on me. I grew up in the hippie counter culture of the 1970s and have written two other books on aspects of LSD and psychedelic culture. I spent thousands of hours interviewing and talking to people about Hollingshead, reading what he wrote and what others wrote about him. I thought about him constantly, trying to inhabit his world, at times believing I was even thinking like him and mentally assessing situations with "What would Hollingshead do?" I wanted Hollingshead's story to be a story of psychedelic daring, of a flamboyant cosmic courier outwitting the authorities and helping people break free of their personal and societal conditioning. There was a degree of that, but those achievements were offset and outweighed by the sadness of Hollingshead's life. Instead his story came to represent the dark side of the hippie dream, illuminating the cracks TV documentaries, social histories and memoirs often ignore or gloss over in favour of more celebratory narratives. Hollingshead's experiences demonstrate that LSD isn't the personal or universal panacea some believe it to be although, used with intelligence and intent, it has many proven benefits both recreationally and as a medicine. But LSD didn't solve any of Hollingshead's problems, in fact it just added to them. For all Hollingshead's talk of LSD's use to change the world or for purposes of spiritual and personal growth, his story reveals that unless you face your psychological demons and can love and accept love unconditionally, the joys and sorrows implicit in being human are meaningless.

Notes

1   Letter from A. Roberts to A. Roberts 28/1/15
2   Keyes, R. Email 29/12/18
3   Hesketh, E. Email 30/12/18
4   Hollingshead, V. Email 3/12/06
5   Hollingshead, V. Email 3/12/06
6   https://www.psychologytoday.com/gb/blog/toxic-relationships/201801/
     whats-the-difference-between-sociopath-and-narcissist
7   Hargreaves, T. Email 10/9/13
8   Stafford, P. (ed) *Magic Grams*, Privately Published 1985
9   Froehlich, M. Email 26/1/19

Bibliography

Alpert, R. *Be Here Now*, Hanuman Foundation, San Cristobel, 1978

Barritt, B. *The Road of Excess*, PSI, 1998

Dass, R. & Metzner, R. *Birth of a Psychedelic Culture*, Synergetic Press, Santa Fe, 2010

Fabian, J. *A Chemical Romance*, The Do Not Press, London 1988

Forte, R. (Ed) *Timothy Leary: Outside Looking In*. Park Street Press, Rochester, 1999

Hofmann, A. *LSD – My Problem Child*, McGraw-Hill, New York, 1980

Hollingshead, M. *The Man Who Turned On The World*, Blond & Briggs, London, 1973

Hollingshead, V. *LSD Mafia*, Unpublished ms. 2013

Horowitz, M. & Palmer, C. *Sisters of the Extreme*, Park St. Press, Rochester, 2000

Hunter, R. *The Storming of the Mind*, McClelland and Stewart, Toronto, 1971

Kleps, A. Millbrook, *The Original Kleptonian Neo-American Church*, Austin, 2005

Leary, T. *Psychedelic Prayers*, University Books, New York, 1966

Leary, T., Metzner, R, Alpert, R. *The Psychedelic Experience*, University Books, New York, 1964

Leary, T. *High Priest*, Ronin, Oakland, 1995

Leary, T. *Flashbacks*, Tarcher/Putnam, New York, 1990

Leary, T. *Starseed*, Level Press, San Francisco, 1979

Leary, T. *Re/search:Pranks*, Re/search Publications, San Francisco, 1988

MacLean, R. *Magic Bus*, Viking, New York, 2006

Mellen, J. *Bore Hole*, Strange Attractor Press, London, 2015

Miles, B. *London Calling*, Atlantic Books, London, 2010

Miles, B. *In the Sixties*, Jonathan Cape, London, 2002

Michel, J. *Eccentric Lives and Peculiar Notions*, Adventures Unlimited, Kempton, 2002

Miller, J. *A Simple Life*, Saint Andrews Press, Wells, 2013

Neihardt, J.G, *Black Elk Speaks*, University of Nebraska Press, Lincoln, 2014

Savage, J. *1966: The Year the Decade Exploded*, Faber & Faber, London, 2015

Shaw, O. *Maladjusted Boys*, Allen & Unwin, London, 1965

Stafford, P. (ed) *Magic Grams: Inquiries into Psychedelic Consciousness*. Privately published. 1985

Stevens, J. *Storming Heaven: LSD and the American Dream*, Heinmann, London, 1988
Tirella, J. *Tomorrow Land*, Lyons Press, Lanham, 2015
Tomory, D. *A Season in Heaven*, Thorsons, London, 1996
Various *The Book of Cumbrae*, unpublished ms, 1971
Watts, J. & Watts, A. *Collected Letters of Alan Watts*, New World Library, Novato, 2017
Wilson, R. A. *Cosmic Trigger*, New Falcon, Pheonix, 2013

Recommended Further Reading

Black, D. *Acid: A New Secret History of LSD*, Vision, London, 2001
Douglas, A. *The Oracle of Change*, Penguin, Harmondsworth, 1983
Green, J. *Days in the Life*, Heinemann, London, 1988
Greenfield, R. *Timothy Leary*, Silberman, Orlando, 2006
Hagenbach, D. & Werthmuller, L. *Mystic Chemist*, Synergetic Press, Santa Fe, 2013
Jarnow, J. *Heads*, Da Capo, Boston, 2016
Lachman, G. *Turn off Your Mind*, Sidgwick & Jackson, London, 2001
Leary, T. *The Politics of Ecstasy*, MacGibbon & Kee, London, 1970
Lee, M. & Shlain, B. *Acid Dreams*, Grove Weidenfeld, New York, 1985
Lundborg, P. *Psychedelia*, Lysergia, Stockholm, 2012
Maclean, I. *Behind Open Doors*, lulu, London, 2019
Masters R. & Houston, J. *The Varieties of Psychedelic Experience*, Dell, New York, 1966
Partridge, C. *High Culture*, OUP, New York, 2018
Penner, J. *Timothy Leary: The Harvard Years*, Rochester, 2014
Roberts, A. *Albion Dreaming*, Marshal Cavendish, London, 2012
Scott, A. M. *Alexander Trocchi: The Making of the Monster*, K&B, Edinburgh, 2012
Shaw, O. *Prisons of the Mind*, George Allen & Unwin Ltd, 1969

Index

A leaf, a flower, a fruit or water,

Whatever devotee Offers for me with love,

That I accept and eat with love:

(The Bhagavad — Gita, 9.26).

Kathmandu, January 1978